ASWB Masters Study Guide 2024-2025

Complete Review + 680 Questions and Detailed Answer Explanations for the LMSW Exam (4 Full-Length Exams)

Printed in the United States of America

Table of Contents

Chapter 1: Introduction 7

About the ASWB Master of Social Work Exam 7

How to Prepare for the ASWB Master of Social Work Exam 8

Chapter 2: Human Development, Diversity, and Behavior in the Environment 9

Human Growth and Development Throughout the Lifespan 9

Theories of Human Development 9

Development Norms Throughout the Lifespan 18

Health and Wellness Throughout the Lifespan 21

Concepts of Abuse and Neglect 31

Alcohol and Substance Abuse with Regard to Neglect and Abuse in Families 34

Diversity, Social and Economic Justice, and Oppression 38

Additional Topics Related to Growth and Development 41

Chapter 3: Assessment and Intervention Planning 42

Basic Terminology to Know in Social Work 42

Determining Program Effectiveness 46

Assessments as a Social Worker 46

Biopsychosocial Assessment/History and Collateral Data 48

Assessment Method Outlines and Key Factors 49

Conducting Assessments Involving Parents and Children 50

Client Involvement with Client Assessments 51

Intervention Planning 52

Psychotherapies 53

Immigration, Refugee, or Undocumented Status with Regard to Service Delivery.....62

Chapter 4: Interventions with Client Systems 63

Intervention Processes and Techniques for Use Across Systems...............................63

Client Engagement and Motivation in the Intervention Process 75

The Role of Feedback, Active Listening, and Nonverbal Communication in Interventions 76

Placement Options Based on the Level of Care Required..78

Discharge, Aftercare, and Follow-Up Planning 79

Case Management in Social Work.. 80

Chapter 5: Professional Relationships, Values, and Ethics 82

Professional Values and Ethical Issues 82

Social Workers and Ethics Codes 83

Models of Supervision and the Ethical Responsibility of Supervisors and Managers .85

Client/Social Worker Legal and Ethical Professional Boundaries 87

Social Workers, Professional Development, Risks, and Developing Protocols.......... 90

Confidentiality in Social Work..92

Professional Development and Use of Self in Social Work..93

Development and Organization in Social Work..94

Test 1: Questions.. 97

Test 1: Answers and Explanations 145

Test 2: Questions 172

Test 2: Answers & Explanations 229

Test 3: Questions 253

Test 3: Answers and Explanations... 301

Test 4: Questions 332

Test 4: Answers and Explanations.. 379

Chapter 1: Introduction

As you well know, social work is a career dedicated to public support and service. The Association of Social Work Boards is a nonprofit organization whose purpose is to ensure that individuals seeking to be social workers possess the necessary skills and abilities to pursue this career.

The ASWB was organized in order to develop, update, and maintain a uniform examination for social workers. Local boards and the ASWB work hand-in-hand to set requirements for candidates, approve those candidates who meet the requirements to register, direct those candidates to schedule and take the exams, and allow scores to be issued to states and provinces in order for licenses to be administered through the social work board to those who pass.

The ASWB is made of a comprehensive system of Social Work Boards and other organizations from 10 provinces in Canada, the District of Columbia, Guam, the Northern Mariana Islands, the Virgin Islands, and the entire United States in order to create and uphold a standard of education, support, and services.

This network's sole focus is public protection through sound, safe, and ethically based education, support, and services. They ensure candidates wishing to pursue this line of career are eligible through adequate testing and issuing a license to document and certify their credentials. Additionally, they also require licensees to continue their education and update their knowledge, skills, and practical abilities in order to renew their licenses and continue to work in the field.

About the ASWB Master of Social Work Exam

The ASWB Masters Exam is for candidates who have successfully completed their master's degree in social work. This exam is not for entry-level social workers but rather for those who have continued their education and honed their skills to specialize further in the field.

The ASWB Masters Exam is comprised of 170 questions, all of which are multiple-choice. All of the questions you will encounter are intended to be diverse in regard to ethics, gender, geography, practical settings, and race that may be encountered in the field as a social worker.

With that goal in mind, the Association of Social Work Boards utilizes guidelines from the American Education Research Association, the American Psychological Association, and the National Council on Measurement in Education to ensure that exams are created in an unbiased manner while also ensuring that they cover the real-world situations that may be encountered and experienced as a social worker.

The 170-question exam is given electronically on a computer. The ASWB, like many others that use testing for licensing and certification, utilize testing services through Pearson VUE testing facilities. Pearson VUE is a globally recognized testing proctor that offers testing for academic, government, IT, and professional programs and companies.

How to Prepare for the ASWB Master of Social Work Exam

In the following chapters, you will find the five key topics that are covered on the ASWB Master of Social Work Exam. Additionally, you will find the percentage that each of those topics make up in the exam, the subtopics that are covered under each of those key topics, and detailed information on how those topics apply in the world of social work.

This study guide will focus on the master's exam, which requires applicants to have a master's degree in social work. College graduates most often take this exam. However, it is also taken by those continuing their education and advancing their careers. The exam is therefore designed for those with more focused knowledge and practical skills training.

Chapter 2: Human Development, Diversity, and Behavior in the Environment

This chapter will cover three key topics and several subtopics.

The three key topics that will be covered in this chapter are human growth and development, concepts of abuse and neglect, diversity, social justice, economic justice, and oppression.

The items that will be discussed in this topic will make up 27% of the overall Master of Social Work Exam.

Human Growth and Development Throughout the Lifespan

The complex topic of Human Growth and Development covers one's entire lifespan from conception to geriatrics. In its most basic definition, growth and development starts when the egg of a human female is fertilized, through to the full maturity of that egg into a grown adult, and finally to its eventual demise.

Growth and development are broken down by age range and the anticipated growth and development that will occur during that time. The first stage is typically conception to 3 years, which is known as the infant and toddler stage. Age 4–6 is known as the young child stage, age 7–12 is the older child stage, age 13–17 are the adolescent years, age 18–35 is the young adult stage, age 36–64 is the middle-aged adult stage, age 65–79 is the older adult stage, and age 80 and older is known as the elders stage.

Theories of human growth and development all focus on how physical, cognitive, social, emotional, and personality skills and traits expand and grow over time and how stages of life impact that growth and development.

Theories of Human Development

When it comes to the growth and development of humans, there are five widely accepted theories of human development. These five theories are based on behavioral, cognitive, emotional, physical, and social development. These five theories are:

- Bandura's social learning theory.
- Bowlby's attachment theory.
- Erikson's psychosocial development theory.
- Freud's psychosexual development theory.
- Piaget's cognitive development theory.

Below you will find a description and further explanation of each of these five theories and how they apply to human growth and development.

Albert Bandura's Social Learning Theory

Bandura's social learning theory was developed by Albert Bandura and is now a widely accepted theory throughout the world. Bandura theorized that children learn and develop in multiple ways. Those developments can be learned through an experience that a child has or witnesses. While people commonly learn from the experiences they encounter throughout their lifetime, Bandura also theorized that children learn by observation of those around them and tend to model themselves and their behaviors based on what they observe.

These observations can be made in one of two ways. First, they can be something a child sees, hears, or feels; or second, they can be something a child witnesses another person experience or react to. Children often mimic the behavior of their parents, caregivers, teachers, siblings, friends, peers at school, TV or movie characters, or other influences in their environment, such as pets.

Typically, children seek approval. With that in mind, it is easy to understand that a child would want to copy the behaviors that gain them approval and praise. For instance, if your child sees someone bring you a soda from the cooler at a family party and you smile, the child might then repeat the behavior and bring you a soda themselves to get you to smile at them. If the desired reaction is gained, the child might then repeat the behavior, regardless of your need for a drink, simply to achieve the desired response again.

The key takeaways from Albert Bandura's social learning theory are that children best and most commonly learn their behaviors, actions, and reactions through observation of their environments. A child's responses are learned when a stimulus is introduced to the child, the child watches the reaction to that stimulus by others, and then the child mimics that behavior in the hope of evoking the same response.

John Bowlby's Attachment Theory

John Bowlby developed the Bowlby attachment theory that we use today. His theory advocates that children need to bond and form attachments. These attachments are not only for people but also for things and places. This theory emphasizes the importance of these attachments for the child's overall health and development.

Bowlby's theory has been proven and enforced over the years through the observation of supporting evidence in mother and newborn bonding after delivery or adoption. We also see children attach to people in their lives, comfort items like stuffed animals or blankets, and comfortable places like their home or schools where they feel safe and nurtured. These attachments help children to be comfortable and feel safe in their surroundings, nurture healthy relationships with others, cope with change, and grow in life in a way that helps them to flourish.

Bowlby breaks his attachment theory down into five key points, which are explained below:

I. First, Bowlby theorized that children are born with the innate instinct to bond with their primary caregiver. Most often, this is the child's mother. However, in the absence of a mother, the primary individual who provides an infant's basic human needs is the one that they will attach to. This attachment is biologically derived through instinct, rather than a behavior that needs to be learned.

II. Second, Bowlby theorized that the child's attachment to their primary caregiver was important enough to the child's overall growth, health, and wellness that it should be nurtured and maintained for, at a bare minimum, the first two years of the child's life. He stated that it was of the utmost importance to establish this kind of bonding relationship before the child reached a year old. Failure to do so could cause the child to be irreparably damaged and suffer lifelong effects. He further theorized that while the first two years were most important for attachment, children were still at risk of damage from a lack of attachment until they reached at least 5 years of age. His second key point can therefore best be summarized by saying that the attachment and bonding of an infant are most critical from birth to age 5.

III. Third, Bowlby theorized, based on his conclusions from the second point of his theory, that if a child suffered what he called "maternal deprivation" during the first five years of life, there could be lifelong effects. These effects are permanent and irreparable. Such effects could be standalone or multilayered and may include but are not limited to:

- Affectionless psychopathy (i.e., A person who is not able to show affection for others or to have any form of concern for others, which can make them highly impulsive, reckless, and even dangerous).
- Depression.
- Delinquency.
- Overly aggressive.
- Less intelligent.

These and more could be related to attachment deprivation. Such effects could be cognitive, emotional, or social and would last through childhood and reach into the expanse of that individual's adult life.

IV. Fourth, Bowlby theorized that a child's short-term or temporary separation from their mother or attachment person could cause a great deal of distress. Bowlby breaks that distress down into three specific stages:

- The first stage of distress is the protest stage. During this stage, Bowlby suggested that the infant or child will cry, scream, or otherwise express outrage or anger to protest the absence of the source of their attachment.

- The second stage of distress is the despair stage. During this stage, Bowlby suggested that the protestation from the first stage would begin to subside. The infant or child would become calmer and less outwardly upset while still being upset at the absence of their attachment source. During this stage, the infant or child may appear calm. However, they are withdrawn. They will most often be uninterested in engagement in the activities around them and will refuse or avoid any sort of comfort from others.

- The third stage of distress is the detachment stage. During this stage, Bowlby suggested that if the infant or child continued to be separated from their primary attachment source, the child would eventually reengage with those around them. However, if and when their primary caregiver returns, it is often likely that the child will show their feelings of anger or resentment toward their caregiver for their absence. The infant or child may even choose not to engage with the caregiver upon their return or flat out reject their affections, attention, or presence altogether.

While this point of Bowlby's theory is widely acknowledged, it should also be noted that some other studies have shown that a child's attachment, especially to their mother or primary caregiver, is underrated, and that a child will recover from short absences, infrequent absences, or regular limited separations from that individual without suffering long-term harm.

V. Fifth, Bowlby theorized that the attachment a child forms with their mother or primary caregiver is the foundation on which infants and children develop internal cognitive correlations to self, to others, and to the world around them, which Bowlby referred to as an internal working model. He cited three key points to support his internal working model idea, which were that the infant or child's attachment to their mother or primary caregiver resulted in the child making mental correlations between:

- Their own self-value.
- The trustworthiness of others.
- The interaction of themselves with others.

In summary, John Bowlby's attachment theory stresses the vital importance of a mother or primary caregiver and their child. In the theory, the child's first five years of life are deemed the most essential and critical years to their bonding and attachment. Failure to make that bond or sustain it would be detrimental to the child's overall development and would pose lifelong harm.

Erik Erikson's Psychosocial Developmental Theory

Erik Erikson developed the Erikson psychosocial development theory. His theory proposes that there is an organized outline of the growth and development of humans. This outline breaks down the lifespan into eight separate stages. He proposed that people, from infants through to adulthood, are shaped by their experiences throughout these stages, and that this shapes their core principles on social interactions and their psychosocial health.

Each of these stages takes place at different points as we age, and they each play into aspects of our overall psychosocial development and health throughout our lives. Erickson's theory is explained best by these key points:

Stage 1: Trust vs. Mistrust – This stage occurs between birth and 18 months of age and was considered by Erikson to be the most fundamental of all the stages. This is because the first stage is the cornerstone on which all the other stages are built. This is when a child has the potential to develop and grow a sense of hope. A baby is entirely dependent on their mother or primary caregiver for absolutely everything. This bond provides an infant's basic needs, fosters trust, and instills confidence in their caregiver to keep them fed, safe, warm, nurtured, and cared for.

- In his theory, Erikson states that if the caregiver provides for the child and ensures they feel protected and well cared for, the child will, in turn, apply those feelings of safety and security to the outside world.
- On the other hand, Erikson notes that children who do not receive consistent love, care, and security, or who do not have consistent and responsible caregivers during their first 18 months of life, develop feelings of mistrust. While they will not necessarily fear the whole world and everything in it, they will be skeptical, distrustful, and unwilling to put their faith in others.
- Erikson further explains that in neither scenario will a child develop absolute trust or absolute mistrust from a psychosocial perspective.

Stage 2: Autonomy vs. Shame – This stage occurs between 18 months and 3 years of age. During this stage, the child has the potential to develop and grow their will. According to Erikson, this is because it is the period when children most often start to learn and begin to achieve aspects of personal control and independence.

- Erikson cites that when a child in this age group is given the opportunity to make a choice, such as when they are allowed to choose a snack from two options, pick their own outfit, or select the next activity to engage in, it helps the child to develop their sense of independence and autonomy.

- One of the developmental milestones achieved by children in this stage is becoming potty trained. This is a skill that allows them to gain control of their own bodies; it also enables them to be more independent.
- Erikson's theory notes that success during this stage leaves children with a lasting sense of confidence, security, and achievement. This is especially true when their caregivers offer encouragement and support. Children who are shamed for having accidents, have choices made for them, and are made to only do as others influence them. Moreover, they can develop a lack of self-esteem and self-confidence, as well as a lack of personal control that could prove detrimental.

Stage 3: Initiative vs. Guilt – This stage occurs between 3–5 years of age. This is when children have the potential to develop and grow their sense of purpose. This is because most children are able to interact with the outside world in settings like preschool, where they have the ability to explore and exercise their self-control through social interaction with their peers and learning through play.

- The ability to learn and grow through play and peer interaction allows children to feel confident, develop more control, and feel more capable in what they can do and what they can accomplish.
- Children who are not granted these experiences or who are not allowed to explore and expand their choices and control during this stage, or those who are given more control and freedom than they can actually manage, often develop lasting issues in regard to their initiative and drive and their ability to interact and work well with peers. They also may experience a deep sense of guilt when they become overwhelmed by too much.

Stage 4: Industry vs. Inferiority – This stage occurs between 5–12 years of age. This is when children have the potential to develop and grow their sense of competence. These are the early years of elementary and middle school, where children are pushed to work hard and achieve more demanding goals.

- Children learn to socialize and interact with peers as well as how to deal with the pressures of added school assignments.
- Erikson found that the children who succeeded and adjusted to the new environment and added challenges of this new level of education and social interaction were those who had supportive parents or primary caregivers who praised their accomplishments. Such support allowed them to develop a sense of competence through their achievements.
- Children who did not have that type of support, however, often showed signs of self-doubt and insecurity rather than growth.

Stage 5: Identity vs. Role Confusion – This stage occurs between 12–18 years of age. This is when children have the potential to develop and grow their sense of fidelity. Erikson felt these teenage years were a critical period in a child's growth and development. This is the point when personal identities are formed, along with a sense of self, which will be carried through the rest of the individual's life.

- These qualities are best developed through healthy encouragement and positive reinforcement. This support helps individuals to grow their feelings of independence, feelings of control in their own lives, and their sense of self.
- A lack of support and encouragement during these years can cost children dearly and result in insecurity, lack of self-identity, and confusion in one's beliefs and ideas.

Stage 6: Intimacy vs. Isolation – This stage occurs between 18–40 years of age. In this stage, individuals have the potential to develop and grow the virtue of love. During this stage, an individual can flourish through connections of intimacy and form healthy loving relationships with others.

- This is when people are able to make connections in healthy ways with others. They most often find that they have the ability to build strong relationships, which they can grow and nurture throughout their life.
- Erikson theorized that those who can build and grow healthy personal relationships during this time are best equipped to hold onto those relationships and to build lasting relationships in the future as well.
- Those who fail to make those connections most often suffer from long-term feelings of isolation, unhealthy close personal relationships, and lifelong struggles with loneliness.

Stage 7: Generativity vs. Stagnation – This stage occurs between 40–65 years of age. During this stage, adults potentially develop a sense of care for themselves and others, the idea being that as adults, we create, nurture, and grow things that withstand time.

- Accomplishment of such healthy development most often leads to sustained personal relationships, having children, or public contribution to one's own home or community. These contributions are made in such a way that the relationship lasts and flourishes.
- The virtue of care is reached when this period of growth and development is accomplished in a healthy and meaningful way.
- On the other hand, when individuals are not able to establish these relationships or achievements, it is often difficult to feel anything

other than failure, a lack of productivity, or a lack of meaning in their lives.

Stage 8: Ego Integrity vs. Despair – This final stage in Erikson's theory occurs in those who are 65 or older. This is when he considered wisdom to be gained. Here, wisdom is defined as something that can be gained from reflection on one's life.

- Erikson surmised that if one could reflect on their life and feel happy and fulfilled by the life they led, then they had gained wisdom.
- On the other hand, Erikson felt that those who could not reflect on the life they led and find those feelings of fulfillment would instead be plagued by feelings of despair and regret.

Sigmund Freud's Psychosexual Development Theory

Sigmund Freud is one of the most well-known theorists of our time. His psychosexual development theory focused on and outlined what he considered to be the five psychosexual stages. He theorized that children developed their personalities through pleasure-seeking behaviors, which included oral, anal, phallic, latency, and genital.

Before Sigmund Freud published his psychosexual development theory, it had previously been thought that sexual stages did not develop until a child hit puberty. Freud's theory, however, proposed that such stages began at birth and developed over time as the child grew. The idea behind it was that we seek out, focus on, and put energy into the behaviors that bring us the most pleasure.

The five stages of Freud's psychosexual theory are explained as follows:

Stage 1: Oral – The oral stage, which occurs from birth to the first year of life, revolves around the infant's mouth. Infants associate their mouths with feelings and tastes that make them feel secure and are therefore pleasurable. This feeling of security develops when their basic and essential needs are met. Freud hypothesized that the pleasure an infant received orally as an infant could result in oral fixations later in life. He used people's habits as adults, such as smoking or nail-biting, as supporting evidence.

Stage 2: Anal – The anal stage occurs between 1–3 years of age. Freud noted that at this time in life, young children develop and learn to express themselves as individuals with ever-increasing control of their own selves. Freud concluded that during this stage of life, it was expected that children would find pleasure from being able to have control of their own bodily waste, as well as when and how they chose to expel that waste.

Stage 3: Phallic – The phallic stage occurs between 3–6 years of age. Freud felt that it was at this point that a child develops an awareness of genitals and the differences between males and females. This revelation kicked off a child's awareness of bodily differences and started to drive their curiosity to the differences of the opposite sex.

To support this stage, Freud noted that children in this age range, and sometimes younger, had been known to experience physical and sexual reactions. Male children develop erections or manually explore their genitals once they develop the realization that it is part of their body. Female children have been documented to develop vaginal discharge and to explore their vaginas.

Stage 4: Latency – The latency stage occurs between age 6 and the time the child starts puberty. Freud surmised that during this time, sexual drives and curiosities are dismissed. Instead, the child's attention is diverted to new things, and play becomes an important focus during this time.

Stage 5: Genital – The genital stage occurs from the time that puberty starts through adulthood. Freud believed that it was at this point that sexual experimentation developed. The individual would shift from the self-pleasure that they had been drawn to in the past to mutual pleasure with a partner.

Jean Piaget's Cognitive Development Theory

Jean Piaget developed his cognitive development theory in which he theorized that a child's intelligence changes as they grow. More specifically, Piaget outlined four stages of cognitive development.

1. The sensorimotor stage occurs from birth to 2 years old.
   Object permanence is the focus of this stage. This means children begin to understand that objects still exist even when they cannot directly sense them. During this stage, infants and children learn through sight, sounds, smell, touch, and taste.

2. The preoperational stage occurs between 2–7 years of age.
   Symbolic thought is the focus of this stage. Children of this stage learn to understand symbolism, where one thing can represent a separate thing. They enjoy playing pretend and learn to represent objects with words or pictures.

3. The concrete operational stage occurs between 7–11 years of age.
   Logical thought is the focus of this stage. This means that children begin to rely more on logical, concrete thinking. This allows the child to start putting events in sequence and organize their thoughts and feelings.

4. The formal operational stage occurs from age 12 and continues throughout adulthood.
   Abstract thought is the focus of this stage. Individuals can think about abstract concepts and use logic and reason to solve problems. Large character and developmental changes occur during this stage.

Jean Piaget's stages of cognitive development focus on how children of varied ages require both structured environments and the use of their five senses in order to learn and grow mentally.

Rational Choice Theory

Another important theory in social work is rational choice theory, which states that individuals will use rational thought to make choices that benefit their own self-interests. Adam Smith developed this theory in the mid-1700s.

Person-in-Environment or PIE Theory

The concept of person-in-environment is also known as PIE theory. This is prevalently used in the field of social work. The PIE theory suggests that a person is influenced heavily by their environment. In this case, the environment includes the home, community, economic environment, and cultural environment in which the person is raised. The theory further surmises that any issues that an individual develops can most often be associated with environmental influences that they have been exposed to.

Development Norms Throughout the Lifespan

There are four core types of typical development. These core developments are cognitive, emotional, physical, and sexual development. It is vital that social workers know the indicators of normal and abnormal development so they can observe this in others.

Infants and Toddlers – Birth to 3 years

Infants and toddlers grow rapidly in their first three years and experience several growth spurts during this time. This is the time when their brains develop the most. This age group is like a sponge. They learn by using their sense of taste, touch, and smell, and especially through play.

In the beginning, infants cry as their primary source of communication. Many mothers describe their babies having unique cries for different needs. So even if we do not speak their "language," we still find ways to understand their language and their needs. Later, they develop "baby talk" to further their communication abilities until they are finally able to make simple sentences and clearly communicate their wants and needs.

In the first three years of life, infants and toddlers attach and bond with their mothers or primary caregivers. Their dependence on their mother allows them to first develop a healthy and trusting relationship with her before moving on to trust others. As infants and toddlers develop trusting relationships with others, they develop and grow their own sense of self as well.

During this age range, it is especially important that a child's health and development are followed closely. Parents or primary caregivers need to nurture the physical bond that babies need. They should also ensure that well-child checkups and immunizations are scheduled and conducted as their pediatrician recommends. Caregivers should also make sure their child gets the nutrition, skin care, hair/scalp care, and sleep that they need to be healthy.

Young Children – 4 to 6 years

Children grow at a slower rate during this age range. This is the age when young children learn to improve their gross motor skills and self-help skills, and become potty trained, if they have not already. At this age, young children develop their memories, expand and develop their imaginations, and find a greater interest in stories and books.

This is also a time when children grow more independent and develop compassion and sensitivity to the feelings of others. This is especially true with friends in playgroups and school.

Young children best respond to praise, reward systems, and clear rules and boundaries. Safety protocols should be taught and reinforced. Safety protocols include things such as car seat and seat belt safety, caution when crossing streets or parking lots, and use of safety pads during participation in certain activities.

To support their child's growing independence, parents should encourage independence, answer their questions and curiosities, teach and encourage healthy hygiene, and promote good eating habits.

Older Children – 7 to 12 years

Children at this age continue to grow at a slow and steady pace, usually having a growth spurt when they reach puberty. Children in this age category learn to correlate cause and effect, improve their reading, writing, and math skills, and are eager to learn. They also expand their independence.

Kids at this age like to be engaged, feel useful, and feel like they are capable of making useful contributions. Encourage children of this age to be safe, know their surroundings, and work on resolving conflicts in a peaceful and non-aggressive manner. Commonly, this is when children start discussing the topics of alcohol, tobacco, illicit drugs, and sex.

Caution is given in regard to the use of such substances and how dangerous they can be, and sex as a concept is typically discussed to bring understanding to the topic.

Adolescents – 13 to 17 years

In adolescence, teens go through growth spurts, experience puberty-based changes in their bodies, and develop the ability to begin reproduction. Adolescent minds have grown and developed to the point where they can think abstractly and choose the values that they will most likely carry into adulthood and expand on through life.

Teens develop their own identities and personalities. They develop relationships, explore interests of their own, and form peer groups. Adolescents also start to pay closer attention to their looks and clothing styles.

At this time in a child's life, they may challenge authority, want or even expect certain levels of privacy, and develop respect. With that in mind, it is important that driver's safety, violence prevention, and safety when out with friends are all raised by parents as topics for discussion.

Young Adults – 18 to 35 years

In young adults, physical and sexual maturity has been achieved and it is important to maintain a healthy diet. Problem-solving skills are well-developed, and new skills are learned often. Furthermore, a drive to seek relationships, achieve career pathways, and start a family are all critical components during this time in most individuals' lives.

During this age range, it is essential that individuals learn to communicate effectively, be honest, and respect others' personal values as well as their own. Young adults should be sure to have annual health checkups, take time to exercise, and live a healthy lifestyle. While it is important they realize and honor their commitments to themselves, their family, and their community, young adults should also be careful not to overextend themselves.

Middle Aged Adults – 36 to 64 years

In middle age, people begin to see the physical effects of age on the body. Women experience menopause during this time, and both men and women may develop health issues, some of which will be chronic throughout the rest of their lives. At this point in life, experiences have taught individuals to effectively and creatively problem solve.

It is vital that middle-aged adults continue to find hope and purpose in life through a balance of overall health and wellness. They should continue to get regular checkups with health professionals, deal with how their bodies are aging, and pay attention to any health risks they may have or develop.

Many people in this stage of life also begin to plan for their futures. This planning may include making retirement arrangements, preparation for future mental or physical health decisions, or development of the groundwork to balance their life, work, and dreams.

Older Adults – 65 to 79 years

At this stage in life, people are still gradually aging. There are natural declines that occur in regard to physical abilities and memory skills. This is a time when many individuals need to access and balance their own independence along with any assistance they may need.

It is essential that there is a focus on health and safety during this age range. This might mean people add memory skill building to their routine, install safety features to reduce fall risks or call for help, and ensure that they have a support system if they need help. It is also necessary for people to manage health care, see doctors regularly, and pay attention to any physical or mental health concerns.

At this stage, many individuals have retired. It is important during this time that individuals Find ways to connect with friends or make new ones, develop interests and activities that keep them active and engaged, and seek out support to cope with the loss of friends.

Elders – 80 years and older

At this stage in life, people continue to decline in health and experience health issues that are more significant. They are more prone to chronic health issues than in earlier years. Memory also declines, and new information takes longer to absorb and learn. Individuals and their families should also pay close attention to any signs of confusion or memory loss because it can be a significant sign of an infection or illness.

A difficult thing to face in this stage is the acceptance that one's life is nearing its end. Independence should be maintained as much as possible and engagement in social activities can be key. During this stage, it is essential to the individual's health and wellness that they attend regular health checks, ensure proper nutrition, lower stress, and stay active. It is also important to have friends or family who check in regularly to ensure they have safe living arrangements. Making end-of-life decisions at this time may be difficult, but it can ensure more quality of life and independence.

Health and Wellness Throughout the Lifespan

The effectiveness of overall growth and development in the human lifespan is contingent on proper health and wellness. Health and wellness are comprised of biological, physical, mental, cognitive, social, emotional, and spiritual health.

Humans have six basic needs that must be met as a minimum necessity. These needs include:

- **Food:** Adequate caloric intake is key for the body to grow, function, and heal. Typically, adults need to consume a minimum of 1,200 calories on a daily basis, while children need between 1,000 and 3,400 calories, depending on their age and pediatrician recommendations.
- **Water:** A large percentage of the human body is water. In order for the human body to remove waste, flush out toxins, and properly function, an adequate amount of water needs to be taken in each day. On average, it is recommended that people drink between 2.7 and 3.8 liters of water a day to maintain their health.
- **Shelter:** Humans need adequate shelter. The human body is not designed to withstand harsh conditions on its own. It needs shelter to protect it from things such as extremely high or low temperatures, high winds, and rain. Lack of protection can be detrimental and can also lead to life-threatening damage to the skin and internal organs.
- **Sleep:** Humans need between 6 and 9 hours of sleep, at minimum, in a 24-hour period. This ensures that the human brain can process information, absorb new information, and properly regulate the body. Lack of sleep or sleep deprivation can cause brain fog, an imbalance in the body's hormones and temperature regulation, and emotional mood swings, among other things.
- **Human Interaction:** Humans need physical touch and emotional connection. Human contact and emotional connection both release hormones in the body that support good mental and emotional health, physical and psychological development (especially during the first five years of life), and help to maintain an individual's healthy sense of well-being.
- **Novelty:** Novelty is the experience of something new. This experience provides the opportunity to learn, grow, succeed, or fail. Novelty is vital because it is how humans healthily maintain a sense of well-being. A lack of novelty results in a loss of that sense and leads to low self-worth, lack of purpose, and depression.

In order to maintain healthy growth and development throughout the lifespan, we must satisfy these six needs. The most basic and obvious thing to ensure is that we get an adequate amount of food, water, and sleep. We need these to survive. Having these needs met also promotes good mental and physical health overall. Having sufficient shelter is also a priority.

The development and maintenance of human relationships is essential in the long term. These include personal friendships, professional social groups at work, romantic connections with others, and involvement in your community.

Overall Physical and Emotional Health

The term "health and wellness" generally refers to physical, mental, social, emotional, and spiritual health.

- Physical health and wellness refers to proper care for the body, which includes a balanced plan of maintenance of both physical activity and nutrition.
- Mental health and wellness refers to a healthy state of mind and a person's ability to cope with life stressors. Life stressors refer to things such as stress in a person's home, personal life, work life, and social life.
- Emotional health and wellness is focused on personal control of behaviors, feelings, and thoughts. If an individual isn't emotionally healthy, it seeps into the other aspects of their health and wellness.
- Social health and wellness refers to the interpersonal relationships an individual has with others. It also relates to the ability to adapt and act in a comfortable manner when in a wide range of settings and situations.
- Spiritual health and wellness refers to an individual's emotions and feelings toward having a purpose in life. It also has a major impact on how an individual shapes their ethical principles and moral values. This kind of health is concerned with a person's ethics, morals, principles, and values. It can also be a system of spirituality, faith, or belief in a higher power.

Another aspect of overall health and wellness is a healthy self-image. Self-image is an individual's personal view of themself. This is learned and developed over time and influenced, in part, by parents and caregivers during childhood. Other people that can have an influence on self-image are those with whom an individual has close relationships, such as romantic partners, friends, family, and superiors.

A person's self-image can be positively or negatively influenced, depending on how others view them. It has been highly studied and observed that those who encounter a significant amount of negativity in their lives tend to develop poor self-images and low self-esteem. At the same time, the opposite is true for those who experience positive feedback about themselves and therefore tend to have more confidence and well-developed self-images.

There are many activities and actions that can help promote a positive self-image. For example, a person might create a self-image inventory, list their positive qualities, ask romantic or intimate partners to list their positive attributes, set reasonable personal goals, refrain from comparison of self to others, develop personal strengths, practice self-love and positive affirmations, and reflect on their growth and achievements over time.

The same things can be applied to positive body image. A person's body image governs the thoughts, feelings, and beliefs they have in regard to their own body, and the actions they take in regard to the way they look. While problems with body image are most often associated with women, it is vital for both men and women to overcome these. An individual's love and acceptance of their body, its strength, and its limitations and maintaining relationships with others who see them the same way can help the individual be more comfortable in their body.

Having a positive self-image and a positive body image are both concepts that influence and develop overall self-esteem. Child psychologists believe that self-esteem is developed through recognition of personal strengths, interactions with family, and social environment interactions.

How Parenting Skills Affect Health and Wellness

Being a parent isn't an easy job. How a parent does that job significantly impacts their child's overall health and wellness, as well as their development of self-identity, independence, confidence, and more.

From the moment a child is born, they begin to learn from their parents or primary caregivers. One of the most widely recognized principles for meeting overall health and development needs is the principle of attachment and bonding.

At birth and through at least the first year of life, it is crucial for babies to bond with their mothers or primary caregivers. That bond is essential to the child's brain development, helps them balance and regulate their hormones and body temperature until their bodies can sufficiently regulate themselves, creates a healthy sense of security, and builds feelings of love.

These bonds and attachments are essential because as the infant grows, the bonds they create in infancy will ultimately be applied to the world. As toddlers and young children, that attachment gives them a sense of security and trust that is needed to explore the world around them. As older children, it helps them to have the self-confidence to try new things, be self-assured enough to fail, and have the courage to try again. As adolescents, that bond continues to support the individual to develop a sense of self, grow independence, and create their own belief systems. Finally, in adulthood, that bond created in infancy helps to foster healthy relationships.

Building a child's self-esteem, encouragement and praise of good behaviors, set limits and consistency with methods of discipline, provision of quality time, being a good role model, good communication, and the expression of unconditional love are all key to being a good parent and fostering an environment that supports and empowers a child. Every child is different, so parents must have the flexibility to change their parenting style if necessary. It is also important that the parent knows and understands their own limitations.

Family Life Cycle Theory

The family life cycle theory explains how family development revolves around the patterns of change that occur in a family over time. These stages typically occur as follows:

Stage 1: Young single adults leave their parents' home and move out on their own. Young adults develop their own sense of self and become their own person while ties with family are still maintained at a distance.

Stage 2: Young adults develop interpersonal and romantic relationships of their own. Dynamics change as the partners are accommodated in one another's lives, friend groups, peer groups, and family dynamics.

Stage 3: Young families have children of their own. They introduce children into their lives, which requires them to make adjustments and realign their family dynamics.

Stage 4: The family now has adolescent children. Boundaries are tested as their children seek independence. Grandparents experience more of the aging process. Parents begin to refocus on their careers and care for their own aging parents.

Stage 5: Children move out and on with their lives as they become adults. Parents accept having an "empty nest" and shift their focus to renegotiate partnerships, realign their relationship, and deal with the failing health and death of parents.

Stage 6: Parents shift to noticeable aging in the middle stage of their life. Their children take on the role of assistance with their care as they age, and they are faced with loss as some of their friends and associates pass away.

Disabilities and the Effects on the Individual, Family, and Community

Being disabled or having a disabled parent or child can take a significant toll on the individual and family. The effects can be in relation to the cost of care, health care needs, and home health needs. It may limit an individual or family's ability to socialize, go out in public, and so on. Disabilities can affect health and well-being, cause undue stress, affect the family financially, or affect performance at school or at work. Regardless of what the disability is, it will affect and touch every part of an individual's life and their family life.

Addiction, Mental Health Issues, Family Caregivers, and Their Effects on the Family Dynamic

Substance Abuse:

Substance abuse can play a costly role and cause short- and long-term damage in the lives of individuals and families. Some of the ways addiction affects individuals and families are a lack of productivity, loss of employment, impaired physical and mental health, and lowered quality of life. It can also drive criminal actions and increase the chances of violence, lead to abuse and neglect of children and family members, and create a need for outside non-family support. The cost of care if the individual requires a hospital stay or inpatient treatment can cause stress for both the individual and their family.

Substance abuse and addiction can have many catalysts, and there are many theories as to why these abuses and addictions occur. There are five key catalysts for substance abuse, which are:

- Negative reinforcement, or pain avoidance.

- Positive reinforcement, or pleasure seeking.
- Incentive salience, or craving.
- Stimulus-response learning, or habits.
- Inhibitory control dysfunction, or impulsivity.

Mental Health Issues:

Mental health issues can also greatly impact individuals and families. Assured provision of proper care, treatment, or medical services as needed is key to the overall health and well-being of an individual with mental health issues. Their illness can affect those around them as well. The impact of a child or adult with a mental health issue can be stressful. Stress and emotional issues most often emerge in the children or caregivers of those with mental illnesses. This can create a cycle of issues for a family, since helping others with their mental and physical well-being should not be done without first ensuring your own personal mental and physical health.

To support loved ones who struggle with addiction or mental illness, family members should share their concerns and seek support from other family members. They may also seek professional support for themselves to help them cope with the stress of the situation in order to promote their own self-care. Family members should also try to inform themselves about the affliction and the crisis resources that are available.

Family Caregivers:

Whether it is caring for a parent, caring for a spouse, or caring for children, being a caregiver requires a lot of work. This is especially true in households where alcoholism, disabilities, or mental health issues are present. While typical caregiving such as being a parent to typically developed children is a job on its own, the provision of care for individuals with disabilities or mental health issues takes an even more significant amount of time and energy, and plays a more significant role in an individual's life.

Challenges that caregivers commonly face include:

- Time management.
- Emotional and physical stress.
- Lack of privacy.
- Financial strain.
- Sleep deprivation.
- Depression.
- Isolation.
- Fear of asking for help.

It is important that regardless of the type of caregiver an individual may be, they exercise self-care and access assistive resources and help when needed. Caregivers who do not take care of themselves are more likely to struggle not only as a caregiver, but also as an individual. It is important for caregivers to get sufficient sleep, have the ability to take short breaks and days off, eat healthily, have the chance to exercise, and have a support system. It is difficult to take care of others if you don't take care of yourself. Illness, mental health issues, and burnout are among the most common outcomes for caregivers who do not take care of themselves and lack a support system.

The Impact of Out-of-Home Placement

Out-of-home placement refers to a time when a child is placed in the care of another. This can occur for a variety of reasons, and it could be temporary or indefinite. Depending on the state or province, out-of-home placement can include but is not limited to foster care, group homes, residential care, or kinship care. Typically, the state or province a family resides in will help determine placement. In most instances, it is common to seek out close relatives to assume kinship care as a first option before state placement is sought.

Out-of-home placement has been scientifically proven to cause an array of behavioral, emotional, and mental health issues. Where the child is placed and the reasons placement was necessary both play a large part in the child's overall health and wellness.

Family Dynamics and Functions

Today, family structures are comprised in a variety of ways. Family dynamics are commonly classified as nuclear family, single parent family, extended family, childless family, stepfamily, and grandparent family. Studies have shown that no one family structure has been proven to be better than another. Love, bonding, affection, and support are considered to be the key factors in a successful and thriving family. That is regardless of whether the child is raised by their grandparents, in a blended family with stepparents and biological parents, an extended family comprised of relatives aside from a child's mother and father, a single parent family (where the child is only raised by one parent), or a nuclear family, which is the traditional family structure of two parents. As long as a child is loved and cared for, the structure is essentially irrelevant.

Couples without children form their own family dynamic. Childless couples are just as much a family as any other. Having a healthy relationship with your partner is key to having a happy and healthy family dynamic.

There are typically five stressful situations which families may find themselves in. These can strongly impact the family's members and their overall growth, development, health, and well-being. Those situations include:

- Financial difficulties.
- Moving to a new home or school.
- Separation or divorce.

- A new baby or child.
- Illness.

These situations can cause a varying amount of stress. Sometimes, they only require a short adjustment period or only last until someone in the home has recovered from an illness or injury. Others, like divorce, can have much longer-lasting effects.

Psychological Defense Mechanisms and Their Effects on Relationships

Typically, there are ten core psychological defense mechanisms that individuals utilize. These defense mechanisms are denial, repression, projection, displacement, regression, rationalization, sublimation, reaction formation, compartmentalization, and intellectualization.

Psychological defense mechanisms are not typically something that an individual thinks about or uses intentionally. Rather, these are responses that the body triggers on its own to protect an individual mentally, emotionally, or otherwise.

- Denial is the most common defense mechanism. When denial is used, an individual pushes events or circumstances to the side in order to avoid the need to deal with the emotional impact that those events or circumstances will have.
- Repression deals with painful memories or traumatic situations. The body essentially makes these memories disappear into the deepest parts of the mind in order to avoid the need to deal with them.
- Projection is when an individual has thoughts or emotions in regard to one individual (this may be themselves) but distributes those thoughts and feelings onto someone else.
- Displacement refers to an individual who takes out their emotions and frustrations on a person or thing that does not make them feel threatened or scared, as a way of getting those feelings or frustrations out in a way that will have the lowest risk.
- Regression refers to the unconscious action of mentally going to a time earlier in their development in order to cope.
- Rationalization refers to when rational explanations are used as an attempt to explain away unacceptable behaviors.
- Sublimation refers to taking negative emotions, thoughts, or experiences and channeling them into a safe and constructive activity or object. This is considered a positive and safe defense mechanism and may include activities such as boxing, baking, or art.

The Impact of Stress, Trauma, and Violence

Stress, trauma, and violence all cause strain on the human body. This strain can present itself in the form of physical, mental, or emotional issues.

Stress:

Stress is typically something that we deal with on a daily basis. Some stresses are things that our bodies can easily manage and can be dealt with through healthy eating, relaxation, decompression, and sleep. Other stresses may be harder to cope with; at times, they may even seem impossible to handle. When our bodies are under stress, the toll it takes on our body can manifest itself in the form of headaches, heart issues, high blood pressure, anxiety, depression, and other health concerns. Stress can also exacerbate existing health issues.

According to the American Psychological Association, stress can be broken down into three categories, which are acute stress, episodic stress, and chronic stress. Acute stress is the most common. It is a form of stress that we experience for a short time. Stress like this can be caused by isolation, being in large crowds, danger, hearing an unexpected noise, being startled, or other similar situations. Acute stress is often referred to as the "fight or flight" response. Episodic stress is mostly found in cases where individuals live or work in a high demand or chaotic environment. This form of stress occurs when individuals juggle several things at the same time or are always running around to get things done. Chronic stress is long lasting. This form of stress occurs as a result of internal or external stressors that last over long periods of time. Such stressors can include relationship trouble in a marriage or long-term relationship, having a significantly demanding job or schedule at work, and financial issues.

Trauma:

Trauma can be caused by a single event such as a car accident, an occurrence that happens multiple times such as having a chronic illness, or long-lasting suffering such as repeated abuse. The individual who experiences and has to deal with trauma can suffer a variety of health and wellness related issues. When trauma first occurs, it is common for individuals to experience agitation, anxiety, confusion, dissociation, and numbness, among other things. Typically, the feelings, thoughts, and behaviors that occur following a trauma are normal responses. However, mental and emotional issues that do not resolve can cause lasting effects.

Trauma falls into three key categories: acute trauma, chronic trauma, and complex trauma. Acute trauma is caused by an isolated stressor or dangerous encounter. Chronic trauma is caused by repeated incidences of similar or different traumas that happen over extended periods of time. A few examples of chronic trauma include bullying, child abuse, and spousal abuse. Complex trauma is similar to chronic trauma as it is trauma that happens repeatedly over a long period of time, however this is usually within a specific relationship and in childhood.

Violence:

Violence encompasses multiple areas and can be included in trauma. Being a victim of violence is associated with a wide array of health issues. Individuals who have experienced violence most often have to cope with anxiety or depression, though other mental health issues can also appear. In addition to the mental health issues, there are more serious risks that can occur. Science has proven that victims of violence commonly turn to risky behavior as a coping mechanism. Such behaviors can include unsafe sex as well as drug and alcohol use. Individuals may repeat behaviors that they experienced themselves, which causes the cycles of substance abuse or violence to continue.

The environments in which we are raised, exposed to, and spend significant portions of our time in impact our development and growth in the long run. The families in which we are raised, the social groups we interact with, the communities that we grow up in, and the organizations we choose to belong to, as well as those that we live in as an adult all have a significant impact on our worldviews, social lives, cultural exposure and experiences, our political beliefs, and our economic group.

The events, crises, and trauma we may experience and the stressors we are exposed to also have a significant impact on our lives. They help shape us, and in some cases they may break us. Every person handles stress differently. Part of what makes a difference is how we choose to cope. Research has shown that individuals who cope with life events, crises, trauma, and loss in a healthy way most often become well-adjusted and typically developed. In contrast, individuals who do not cope with these experiences in a healthy way more often end up with long-term physical and psychological detriments.

It has been found that individuals who have no past history of physical abuse and no family history of substance abuse or mental health disorders can often correlate their own relationship to these issues to a trauma, crisis, or some form of violence that they have experienced. In addition to these experiences, economic factors such as the loss of a job, the loss of a home, or other significant losses can be enough of a stressor to perpetuate alcohol use, substance abuse, or violence. This is especially true when individuals become incredibly stressed or depressed and do not find healthy ways to cope with those life stressors or find an outlet for them.

Theory of Trauma-Informed Care

According to the CDC, OPHPR, and NCTIC, trauma-informed care cannot be approached using any single technique. Rather, it should be handled with sensitivity and awareness. Their stance is that those who respond to public health emergencies or incidences of suspected or known trauma, should respond in a way that is open and expectant that the individual(s) involved have experienced a trauma. To do this, social workers use a six-step approach to trauma-informed care:

1. Safety.

2. Trustworthiness and transparency.
3. Peer support.
4. Collaboration and mutuality.
5. Empowerment and choice.
6. Cultural, historical, and gender issues.

The primary goal of trauma-informed care is to ensure that the individual is safe in regard to their physical and emotional health. The next step is to address the effects of the trauma they have experienced. By coping with their trauma in a healthy way, it helps to reduce, if not eliminate, long-term damage from trauma. This ultimately allows the individual to return to a normal or close to normal life that they can handle and cope with on their own.

Concepts of Abuse and Neglect

When it comes to the definition of abuse and neglect of children, there are a wide array of parental actions and behaviors that can be involved, and these can be multileveled.

Neglect refers to a failure to provide or adequately provide for the basic needs of a child. There are many ways to fail to provide for a child, which include:

- Failure to take a child to a doctor or dentist for regular checkups.
- Failure to seek medical, dental, or any other form of treatment that your child needs.
- Failure to provide adequately for a child's basic needs, which include food, clothing, shelter, etc.
- Failure to provide adequate supervision for your child.

Abuse refers to either actions against a child or failure to act in their interest in a way that causes harm or puts them at risk. Such things can include but are not limited to:

- Physical abuse.
- Sexual abuse.
- Emotional abuse.
- Mental abuse.
- Sexual exploitation.
- Exposure of a child to dangerous or risky situations.
- Parental substance abuse.

Psychological neglect and abuse is defined as suffering repetitive behavior that threatens, isolates, humiliates, bullies, confuses, or ignores an individual. This kind of negative behavior may include excessive criticism or belittlement, withheld affection, and setting unreasonable demands. Children and adults who are the victims of such neglect or abuse tend to avoid making eye contact, suffer from anxiety or depression, may be fearful or withdrawn, act out by bullying others, cause self-harm, or commit self-destructive behavior.

Physical neglect encompasses the neglect of a child's basic needs, such as good hygiene, shelter, and food. A child that is physically neglected might be unwashed, look malnourished, or have delayed development. Physical abuse is defined as physical injuries or trauma that occurs intentionally, such as when a child is hit, punched, kicked, or burned. Unlike mental abuse, physical abuse commonly leaves a physical mark, even when it is left somewhere covered by clothing where it may not be seen by others. Physical abuse is most often indicated by bruises, cuts, or unexplained broken bones. Bodily injuries most often occur on the face, mouth, torso, back, butt, or thighs. Broken bones tend to occur on the skull, nose, cheekbones, orbital socket, or arm.

Sexual abuse is defined as injuries that are sustained to the genital area or rectal area. Sexual abuse doesn't always show outwardly visible signs and can therefore go unnoticed. The impacts of sexual abuse depend on the victim's age, the extent of the abuse, whether the incident occurs once or happens repeatedly over a period of time, and the victim's relationship to the abuser. Those who experience sexual abuse may develop negative feelings toward sex, become highly sexual, have intense feelings of shame or guilt, blame themselves for the abuse, become self-destructive, cause self-harm, or become suicidal. Sexual abuse victims have a lower rate of reporting abuse than others because of the fear they will not be believed, fear they may be blamed for causing the abuse, or because they feel that reporting the abuse will make their situation worse.

Characteristics of Perpetrators of Neglect, Abuse, and Exploitation

Perpetrators of neglect, abuse, and exploitation can be anyone. There is no specific look that sets them apart from any other person on the street. In fact, many people report that the perpetrator of such acts:

- "Seemed like such a nice person."
- "Doted on their children."
- "Adored their spouse."
- "Was a pillar of the community."
- "Was such a confident and self-assured person."

In reality, perpetrators of abuse most often share characteristics. These include the following:

- Low self-esteem.
- Strong tendencies for jealousy.
- Highly controlling
- Unreasonable.
- Impulsive.

- Inflexible.
- Overly critical.
- Explosive tempers.
- Easily annoyed.
- Manipulative.
- Moody.
- Inconsiderate or belittling of individuals such as waiters or maids.
- Fascination with guns or knives.
- Strict stereotypical gender viewpoints.
- Display cruelty towards animals.

Additionally, they may show these signs as well:

- Place blame on others for their problems.
- Blame others for causing their anger.
- Threaten violence.
- Have issues with alcohol or drug abuse.
- Become angry or violent when under the influence of drugs or alcohol.
- Humiliate or belittle the victim publicly
- Demand unrealistic things from the victim for their own needs or wants.
- Have a past history of abuse, where they themselves were the target of that abuse.

Signs of Risky Parenting

Being a parent is one of the most significant undertakings some individuals will experience in their life. Being responsible and present is an important part of that role. Parenting requires an individual to give a lot of themself, their time, and their energy to the children they have brought into the world or to the children they were chosen to love. Ensuring that the child's needs are met over their own is a sacrifice that most parents experience. However, that is not always the case.

The first signs that parents are putting their child at risk include:

- Neglect of basic needs.
- Prioritization of the adult's own needs and wants over that of the child.
- Lack of routine in the home and allowing a chaotic atmosphere to persist.
- Unwillingness of the adult to accept services to support themselves or their child.

When a social worker assesses a home, these four key points are the most apparent signs a child is being neglected or abused.

Abusive Relationships and Their Development

Abusive relationships typically have a cycle in which the abuse occurs. The target of abuse in a household typically involves a parent, spouse, child, or combination of people. The cycle of abuse commonly has four steps that repeat. Those stages are:

Stage 1: The tension-building or catalyst stage. In this stage, stressors or strains build prior to the abusive incident. The abusive individual sometimes acts out in a passive-aggressive manner and chooses not to communicate. In the event that this cycle of abuse has happened previously or is repetitive, the person or people who are exposed to the abuse may notice the changes, feel the tension building, or even try to defuse the situation.

Stage 2: The act of violence occurs. This can mean physical abuse, sexual abuse, psychological abuse, or emotional abuse. Other extreme behaviors may include intimidation, controlling behavior, or stalking.

Stage 3: After the abuse comes what is known as the reconciliation or honeymoon stage. Abusers will commonly apologize and act in ways that are overly affectionate or doting. Or they may intentionally act as though nothing happened or blame the victim. During this stage, it is also common for abusers to use manipulation such as threats of suicide or self-harm in order to ensure they coerce the victim into staying in spite of the abuse.

Stage 4: Finally, things calm down, the tension that had been built has evaporated, and the relationship appears stable and peaceful again. This stage lasts for various periods of time before things erupt once again.

The cycle of violence is not restrictive and can grow over time. For example, it is not uncommon for an abusive spouse to later abuse their own children as their family grows. In many cases violence becomes perpetual. At times, children may be the focus of that abuse, or in cases where the spouse is the main focus of the abuse, once children come into the picture they may try to defend their abused parent and in doing so bring themselves into focus as an additional target.

Alcohol and Substance Abuse with Regard to Neglect and Abuse in Families

Research has shown that alcoholism and drug addiction can become chronic and result in long-lasting issues. Long-term effects include the deterioration of an individual's physical health and mental functions, and detriment to their overall physical, emotional, mental, and spiritual well-being. The users are not the only ones affected by their addiction. Alcohol abuse and substance abuse both have harsh impacts on families as well.

Science and psychology support the idea that addiction is a family disease, as it touches everyone in an addict's life in one way or another. The impacts can be financial, physical, or psychological.

In a family, every member plays a role, or in some cases several roles, in order to keep the unit functional and well-balanced. When substance abuse becomes an issue within a family, members will usually make adjustments in order to maintain their household around the addict and the strains that they place upon it.

Psychologists and experts considered there to be six family roles related to addiction, which are:

- The enabler.
- The hero.
- The scapegoat.
- The mascot.
- The lost child.
- The addict.

The enabler refers to a person who steps in and takes care of the things that the addict no longer does because of their addiction. Over time, this can involve increased responsibilities within the household. Normally, the enabler is a spouse or significant other in two-parent households or an older child in single-parent homes. The tasks that they take on include but are not limited to management of the household's finances, child care, and household duties. Additionally, it is not uncommon for the enabler to justify the addict's situation, deny how serious the problem is or has become, and make excuses to friends and family regarding the addict.

The hero refers to the individual in the household who stays confident, takes on a more serious nature, and steps up their responsibilities. This role is usually assumed by an older child in the home. They attempt to take on more and more responsibility as the substance abuser's addiction gets increasingly worse. They usually seek perfection and assume more responsibilities to cope as things progress.

The scapegoat refers to a child in the home who handles the stressors of having an addict present and the effects of that addiction on their family by acting out in negative ways. Misbehaviors occur both at home and in school and can eventually lead to legal issues as the child gets older and moves towards adulthood. All these behaviors are associated with the chaos that occurs when there is an addict in the household.

The mascot refers to an individual in the home who chooses to use humor as a coping mechanism for the chaos that occurs from having an addict present. The child typically uses humor in order to bring moments of comfort and relief into their home as a means of trying to balance the stressors.

The lost child refers to a family member who copes with the substance abuser's addiction through isolation. Children who cope this way usually have a hard time in social situations, attempt to lose themselves through video games or other such fantasy play, and use that play as a means of physical and emotional distraction from the chaos in their home.

The addict is a clear title for the substance abuser. Addicts typically come in two forms. First, there are those who are hurt by the fact that their addiction causes harm to their family. Second, there are addicts who have no remorse and have no desire to stop their use of drugs or alcohol. Addicts who chronically abuse drugs or alcohol often have feelings of incredible guilt, shame, and remorse about what they're doing to their families. Those who feel badly about the damage that they inflict are the most likely to accept help and attempt to recover from their addiction. In contrast, those who enjoy their substance abuse and do not care about the effects it has on their family or loved ones normally do not accept support and are often only helped through force such as a court order. These individuals are far more likely to relapse than those who want help, accept it, and enter recovery.

In many cases, children of alcoholics and drug addicts suffer the effects of their parents' addiction long into adulthood. Children of these addicts often develop a poor self-image and suffer from loneliness, guilt, and feelings of helplessness along with more serious issues such as anxiety, fear of abandonment, and chronic depression. Children who are born to addicted mothers suffer even more issues.

Due to the damage that having an alcoholic or drug addict parent can have on a child, children of addicts are more likely to become alcoholics or drug users themselves. Addiction often leads to continued toxic cycles of addiction. They are also more likely to end up with a spouse who is an addict as well.

The financial toll on an addict's family can be significant. This is especially true for families who are already at a low income. The financial hardships can lead to children that are malnourished, inadequately clothed, inadequately housed, or undereducated. In some cases, breakfast and lunch at school may be the only meals a child of an addict is able to get. Additionally, children who have parents who abuse drugs often end up in very unsafe conditions or involved in illegal activities through no fault of their own.

Alcoholism and substance abuse often lead to other types of abuse in the home. Research shows a strong correlation between addiction and other forms of abuse. Such abuse can be physical, emotional, or psychological. Studies have shown a significant amount of child abuse and domestic violence cases have a direct link to drugs and alcohol. The target of such abuse can depend on the family's dynamic and structure. Regardless of who the target is, when there is abuse in the home, it usually touches every member of the family.

When someone experiences addiction in a family, it quickly becomes evident that addiction and relationships do not go hand in hand. Being the significant other or spouse of an addict can be incredibly difficult. Such addictions can end long-term relationships and result in divorce for married couples. This is often because the sober parent becomes unfairly responsible for the household, finances, and children. Sometimes they may also be the only person with a job and income. Such responsibilities can be incredibly difficult and straining on a relationship, even for a short period of time, and cause devastation in the long term.

In relationships and families where the spouses or partners are both addicts, things can be even worse. In these instances, the addicted family members feed off one another and usually accelerate one another's addictions. It is not uncommon for the eldest child to step up and take care of any younger siblings. In many cases, neither parent will hold down a job, food and shelter become incredibly scarce, and the situation can deteriorate rapidly.

Signs of Addiction

There are three categories of addiction symptoms: behavioral, physical, and psychological. For each of these categories there is a set of signs that are associated with addiction.

Behavioral signs refer to the outward actions and behaviors people exhibit due to their substance abuse. Behavioral signs include but are not limited to:

- Obsessive thoughts or actions.
- Disregard of risky or dangerous behaviors.
- A loss of control.
- Denial of or attempts to hide the addiction.

Physical signs refer to the physical side effects of substance use, overdose, and withdrawal that result from that substance. Physical signs of addiction include but are not limited to:

- Enlarged or pinpoint pupils.
- Insomnia.
- Sudden weight loss or weight gain.
- Unusual body odors.
- Bloodshot eyes.
- Deterioration of the physical condition.
- Unkempt, haphazard, or unclean appearance.
- Slurred speech.

Signs of an overdose may include:

- Drowsiness.
- Trouble walking.
- Violent behavior.
- Difficulty breathing.
- Agitation.
- Hallucinations.

- Delusions.
- Nausea.
- Vomiting.
- Loss of consciousness.

Signs of alcohol or drug withdrawal may include:

- Shaking.
- Confusion.
- Hallucinations.
- Jumpiness.
- Nausea.
- Loss of appetite.
- Vomiting.
- Depression.
- Fatigue.
- Insomnia.
- Headaches.
- Fever.
- Seizures.

Prolonged alcohol abuse may cause:

- Unexplained paranoia.
- Significant mood swings.
- Emotional withdrawal from others.
- Mental withdrawal.
- Changes in personality.
- Irritability.
- Inattentiveness.
- Lack of motivation.
- Angry outbursts.
- Anxiousness.

Different signs apply to different substances, but the above listed items are fairly typical.

Diversity, Social and Economic Justice, and Oppression

When it comes to growth and development, diversity, socioeconomic justices, and oppression all play a role. The diversity in the community, social environments, economic environments, and family environments in which we're raised shape not only ourselves and our families, but also how we see the world.

Socioeconomic differences can play a large role in an individual's growth and development. Research has shown that individuals who grow up and are raised in environments that are socioeconomically disadvantaged have less access to adequate education, adequate healthcare, advancement and growth opportunities, and unemployment options.

In addition to the individual's socioeconomic and cultural environments, ethnicity, race, sexual orientation, and gender all play a part in growth and development. These characteristics, along with the stereotypes associated with these characteristics, influence behaviors, attitudes, and identity. Discrimination also has a dramatic impact.

As a social worker, it is essential to have a strong understanding of the effects of disabilities, discrimination, and stereotypes on growth and development. It is also key to have a robust understanding of the concepts and influence of gender, sexual orientation, gender identity, and the impact of transgenderism.

Social and economic justice also play a role in overall development. Social justice is defined as the way in which opportunities, privileges, and wealth are distributed in society, and the fairness that allows access to these opportunities. Economic justice refers to an individual's opportunity to build themselves up financially to have a fruitful and productive foundation.

Poverty and the Effects on Individuals, Families, Groups, and Communities

Poverty is defined as the inability to sufficiently provide for basic needs. Those in absolute poverty do not have any means whatsoever to meet their basic needs. Many individuals and families live below what is known as the "poverty line." The effects of this include homelessness or substandard housing, inadequate food for yourself or your family, inadequate childcare, no access to healthcare, residence in unsafe neighborhoods or communities, and children attendance in schools that are underfunded and lack resources.

Poverty in a community most often results in fewer to no employment opportunities, subpar schools, a lack of community support, and a lack of social programs and involvement. In turn, this generally creates a higher rate of crime, malnutrition, undereducation, domestic abuse, crime, and in some cases disease.

Effects of Culture, Race, and Ethnicity on Behaviors, Attitudes, and Identities

Culture is defined as achievements, customs, and institutions related to specific people. Race is defined as the characteristics that are physically expressed and are considered culturally significant in societies. Ethnicity is defined as the ancestry, beliefs, culture, and languages shared by a group.

Based on the definitions above, consider how culture, race, and ethnicity affect attitudes, behaviors, and identity. Culture has been proven to increase confidence as it allows individuals to express themselves outwardly by way of style, behavior, and values. Cultural identity has been proven to influence an individual's values on freedom, pleasure, social recognition, and self-sacrifice. Ethnicity is about the shared ancestry, biology, and connection to others through cultures and traditions. In many cases, ethnicity is something that is shared, instilled, and carried on intergenerationally.

The Principal Standards of Culturally Competent Social Work Practices

There are 10 standards of culturally competent social work practices. The reason for these standards is to bring awareness to social workers. This includes the development of their self-awareness in terms of their own background and identity in order to see any biases, stereotypes, or other facets that may affect their relationships with clients.

The 10 principal standards of culturally competent social work practices are:

1. Ethics and values.
2. Self-awareness.
3. Cross-cultural knowledge.
4. Cross-cultural skills.
5. Service delivery.
6. Empowerment and advocacy.
7. Diverse workforce.
8. Professional education.
9. Language and communication.
10. Leadership to advance cultural competence.

Gender, Sexual Orientation, Gender Identity, and Gender Expression

Gender, sexual orientation, gender identity, and gender expression all play key roles in the growth and development of individuals. This also affects their values and belief systems, self-expression, and self-esteem.

Gender refers to socially constructed roles and characteristics based on biological sex. Gender identity is an individual person's internal sense in regard to being male, female, both, or neither. Gender identities include but are not limited to:

- Male.
- Female.
- Transgender.
- Gender neutral.
- Non-binary.
- Agender.
- Pangender.
- Genderqueer.

Sexual orientation pertains to an individual's romantic or sexual attraction to another person.

Sexual orientations include but may not be limited to:

- Heterosexual.
- Bisexual.
- Homosexual.
- Pansexual.
- Asexual.

Finally, gender expression refers to how individuals express their gender in public. This outward expression refers to behavior, outward appearance, body language, and voice. It can also include an individual's chosen pronoun or preferred name.

Additional Topics Related to Growth and Development

Additional topics that social workers need to grasp with regard to human growth and development include:

- Feminist theory.
- Principles of human genetics.
- Family life cycle.
- Addiction theories and concepts.
- Systems and ecological perspectives and theories.
- Models of family life education in social work.
- Intrapersonal dynamics.
- Communication theories and styles.
- Systemic discrimination.
- Globalization impacts.

Chapter 3: Assessment and Intervention Planning

Assessments and interventions account for a large portion of the professional responsibilities of a social worker. In order to carry these out, you will need to be comfortable with many common terms related to social work. Once you know this terminology, it will help you to learn about assessment and planning an intervention.

Basic Terminology to Know in Social Work

As a social worker, you may choose any number of agencies or companies to work for, so it's important that you know some key terms found across the board in the field of social work. Consider these key terms and their use in the social work profession and among professional peers:

- Accessibility.
  - The ability to get and receive available services.
- Accreditation.
  - Recognition and certification from a school that is approved and accepted by the social work board in your state or province.
- Advocacy.
  - Intervention on behalf of another individual, group, or community in order to defend, represent, or support them.
- Best practice.
  - A technique that is deemed to be the best way to address, cope, or deal with a given situation.
- Caseload.
  - The number of individuals or groups that a social worker is responsible for at a given time. This includes but is not limited to management of assessments, implementation of intervention plans, arrangement of necessary services, follow-up of progress through those services, assessment of further needs (if any), and discharge for those who have completed treatments or services and no longer need any further attention from professional intervention services.
- Case management.
  - The review of available processes and services, the review of what a client, family, group, or community needs, and then the coordination process of the client's needs with the systems of service that are available to them to ensure that their needs are met.
- Code of ethics.
  - A set of rules that social workers are ethically bound to follow when practicing in the field. It outlines the proper way in which social workers are to conduct themselves, behaviors that will not be tolerated, and the procedures to be followed should an ethical dilemma occur.
- Co-dependency.

- An unhealthy relationship development between individuals in which one individual prioritizes the other individual's needs over their own.

- Community development.
    - When social workers interact with community members to assess community needs, develop resources, and promote networking within the community. This is all done to aid the community's overall growth and development.
- Confidentiality.
    - This is the ethical principle of protecting a client's private information. Confidentiality can be waived by the person in question if they wish to share their information. It can further be released without consent if it is being done for the safety of that person or others (such as in cases of suicidal individuals or those who plan to harm others), or for professional disclosure when it specifically applies to arrangement for services or treatment to be provided.
- Conflict of interest.
    - A conflict between a professional's work and their private interests that can affect how that professional responds to, cares for, or seeks services for another party.
- Continued education.
    - Refers to the education pursued after a social work degree has been obtained and practical and professional social work has begun.
- Core social work values.
    - This is the professional framework for the field of social work. These core values include a commitment to:
        - Service.
        - Social justice.
        - The dignity and worth of the person.
        - Integrity.
        - Importance of human relationships.
        - Competence.
- Critical thinking.
    - The process that includes challenge of underlying assumptions, consideration of all viewpoints, and use of reason, judgment, and knowledge in order to make informed, objective, and intellectually based decisions.
- Cultural competence.
    - One of many core responsibilities of social work. Cultural competence focuses on a social worker's responsibility to study and understand the diversity of cultures and ethnicities as well as understand how a person's culture affects their personal identity.
- Diagnosis.
    - The professional identification of a condition based on an individual or group's symptoms or assessment.

- Direct practice.
  - When social workers interact in a face-to-face capacity with clients.
- Eligibility criteria.
  - The criteria an individual, couple, family, group, or community is required to meet in order to receive or use services or benefits that may be available to them.
- Ethical practice dilemmas.
  - Refers to issues that arise in the field of social work where decisions must be made, but where there is a conflict in core values at the heart of that decision.
- Evidence-based practice.
  - Using empirical evidence to devise intervention and treatment methods helps ensure their effectiveness.
- Field of practice.
  - The different settings in which social work is practiced and needed. Such settings include but are not limited to professional, mental health, healthcare, school, gerontology, global social work, child and family service social work, and criminal justice social work settings.
- Functional assessments.
  - Conducted to assess an individual's ability to take care of themselves.
- Generalist practice.
  - Use of the problem-solving approach during assessment and intervention to engage, assess, plan, implement, evaluate, and terminate treatment and services.
- Global assessment of functioning.
  - A scale of zero to 100 that is used to assess an individual's likeliness to:
    - Inflict self-harm.
    - Cause harm to others.
    - Be able to care for one's self.
    - Be able to function and care for one's self while suffering from one or more issues.
- Indirect practice.
  - Social work practices that are non-face-to-face. Such practices include but are not limited to administrative, supervisory, research, policy development, community development, and consultation roles.
- Implied consent.
  - Consent or the appearance of consent that is given nonverbally or verbally that gives the impression that the individual agrees (consents) to the treatment.
- Informed consent.
  - Clearly informing individuals or clients of all necessary information they need in order to make a decision based on the complete knowledge available to them.

- Just cause.
  - An action or decision regarding an individual that is made on behalf of the individual when there is legal justification for this.
- Malfeasance.
  - Behaviors committed by a professional or a publicly appointed person that are wrong or illegal.
- Malpractice.
  - Actions that are wrong, negligent, or harmful, which violate the professional standards of care or professional ethics, or cause harm.
- Mentorship.
  - The relationship in which a more experienced or knowledgeable individual guides a new or less experienced individual through their professional position as they share their own knowledge and experience.
- Needs assessment.
  - An assessment carried out to determine the needs of a group or community, the system's faults and failures, and the available resources. This indicates needs that aren't being met, challenges being faced, and the required resources. A plan to help is then built around those findings.
- Networking.
  - The process of making contacts within a community and establishing relationships with those contacts to foster and grow a community network of resources.
- Parens patriae.
  - A legal term that is applied when the welfare or care needs of an individual are put into the hands of the state in order to provide a legal guardian for that individual. This ensures that their needs and their welfare are considered and taken care of when there is no one else or no safe alternative.
- Privileged communication.
  - That communication between social workers and clients is protected, both by ethics and law, unless a client is suspected of intent to commit self-harm, harm to others, or the client gives consent to share such information.
- Social justice.
  - The equal distribution of social rights and resources to all members of a community.
- Vulnerable populations.
  - Those groups of individuals who are at an increased risk for health, social, or environmental harm because of life circumstances or life conditions that ultimately leave them open to a lower quality of life.

Determining Program Effectiveness

It is important that the programs and treatment options considered and ultimately recommended by social workers be effective to help clients access the services they need and meet the goals they have set. Clients should eventually graduate out of these services or treatment options to grow and function in a normal and healthy life.

To that end, programs should be based on goals, processes, and outcomes. Objectives should be set, the process should help individuals meet that goal, and the outcome should be the successful completion of that goal.

To assess the effectiveness of a certain program, a social worker will need to do the following:

- Assess and review the skills developed by the program.
- Compare the progress made over time in the program.
- Decide if new resources need to be allotted for that service.
- Document success levels based on objectives met and accomplishments achieved.
- Ensure that there are accountability requirements and that such requirements are being met.

To better determine the above points, consider looking at:

- Service quality from past reviews.
- Mystery shoppers go in and evaluate the process firsthand.
- Post-service rating.
- Follow-up surveys.
- In-app surveys.
- Customer effort score.
- Monitored social media and things found there regarding the service.
- Documentation of the analysis conducted.

Assessments as a Social Worker

Social work assessments are an important phase in the social work process. The point of the assessment is to gather and assess an individual, family, group, or community situation from a variety of different angles. Assessments look at as much information as possible that is relevant and available. That information is then fact-checked for confirmation and credibility and later used to determine what assistance or services are needed. This is then used to form an intervention plan. Such items that are taken into consideration include:

- Employment status.
- Living situation.
- Physical health.
- Mental health.

- Financial status.
- Education.

Assessments are carried out to see whether there is validity in intervention. In the event that there is a valid need for intervention, a social worker will move forward with intervention planning.

The key principles to remember when conducting interviews with clients include the following:

- Ensure that those involved feel supported.
- Clarify why you are there and exactly what it is that you need to know.
- Focus on what the individual is telling you but also stay alert for any indicators, signs, or statements that raise a red flag.
- Comfort the individual or individuals as you work through the steps of the interview and assessment process.
- Validate the thoughts, feelings, and opinions of those involved.
- Ensure you are listening to their feedback and giving constructive feedback in return.
- Listen carefully to the language individuals use to talk about or refer to things, including any expletives they use. The way someone speaks can sometimes tell you more than what they are actually saying.
- Ensure that there are no language barriers. Have an interpreter available if necessary.
- Redirect the conversation if they get off point or if you need to go deeper into a topic that the individual seems keen to avoid.

Interviewing or Counseling Techniques

The following list includes techniques used to conduct interviews or counseling. They are an assortment of methods designed to help individuals, couples, families, groups, or communities better understand themselves and others. These methods include:

- Active listening.
- Confrontation.
- Empathy.
- Engagement.
- Interpretation.
- Open-ended questions.
- Paraphrasing.
- Prompts.
- Rapport building.

- Reflecting.
- Reframing.
- Summarizing.

Biopsychosocial Assessment/History and Collateral Data

A biopsychosocial assessment, or history, examines the biological, psychological, and social aspects of an individual's life in order to collect the levels of data needed for a thorough assessment.

The biological aspect of this assessment refers to an individual's genetics, mental health, physical health, age, and development. Questions that may be associated with the biological assessment seek to find out whether the client:

- Uses drugs or alcohol.
- Has a history of drug or alcohol abuse themselves or in their family.
- Has a history of mental illness or suicide themselves or in their family.
- Has any health issues that impact their life in a significant way.
- Is taking any medication, and if so, what medications.

The psychological aspect of this assessment refers to an individual's mental state, feelings, thoughts, and emotions and whether there is a history of abuse or trauma. Questions associated with the psychological assessment may relate to the following:

- Self-image questions.
- Strengths and weaknesses.
- Whether the individual has been to a therapist or counselor.
- Whether the individual has now or in the past thought about suicide or homicide.

The social aspect of this assessment refers to an individual's past and present relationships with family, friends, and romantic partners as well as their social support, work-related stressors, religious and spiritual affiliations, and financials. Some of the details you will seek to find out in the social assessment include:

- What, if any, community organizations the individual is involved with.
- Whether the individual has family support and, if so, how much.
- The amount of stress involved in the individual's employment and work environment.

The information that is collected in this assessment is known as collateral data. In other words, it is the information about the individual's situation, which then goes through the process of confirmation.

At times, targeted perspectives are used to best assess individuals to focus on core needs or specific criteria. Those perspectives include:

- Diversity.
- Ecological.
- Feminist.
- Generalist.
- Person-in-environment.
- Strength.

Assessment Method Outlines and Key Factors

The information that is gathered in the assessment is put into a written report. That information includes:

- Basic information.
    - Identifying information such as client name, gender, date of birth, age, marital status, race, ethnicity, nationality, spoken language, income, living arrangements, and community profile.
- Referral.
    - The source who referred the client and why the request was made.
- Presenting problem.
    - A description of the issue for which the client needs help, the client's description of the issue, a short history of the issue, how long the issue has been going on, any previous ways they attempted to fix the issue, whether a social worker has been involved before, and whether the client is considered high risk (such as a danger to themselves or others).
- Sources of data.
    - Interviews that have been conducted, observations that have been made, agency records, consults, records from the agency the social worker belongs to or other agencies that have also been involved, client involvement, who was there for interviews (such as colleagues, supervisors, or outside consultants), and the length of time in which the information was gathered.
- General description.
    - A description of the client, including appearance, attitude, behavior and reactions during the interview. Be sure that you note signs of anxiety, depression, mood, etc., or if the client talks about these issues.
- Background and current functioning.
    - Family composition and background.
    - Educational background.
    - Employment and vocational skills.
    - Religious and spiritual involvement.

    - Military service or history.
    - Physical disabilities, health conditions, and medical background.
    - Substance abuse.
    - Psychological and psychiatric functioning and background.
    - Social, community, and recreational activities.
    - Basic necessities.
    - Current legal issues and history of incarceration.
    - Other environmental or psychosocial factors.
    - Client strengths, capacities, and resources.
- Impressions, assessment, and recommendations.
    - Clinical summary, impressions, and assessment.
- Diagnosis.
- Final goals and recommendations to work with the client.

Conducting Assessments Involving Parents and Children

In your role as a social worker, assessment of a person's capability as a parent will sometimes be necessary. To do so, you will need to make observations and ask essential questions. When conducting assessments or interventions that involve parents and children, it's important to proceed with compassion, empathy, and understanding as well as thoroughly and effectively do your part as a social worker.

Social work organizations typically have a standard assessment that is used to evaluate parenting capacities adequately. This is used to identify weaknesses and strengths as a parent.

These assessments are designed to ensure that a child's health and development needs are met. The first thing often observed is that the child's basic needs are met. This includes an assessment that the child has food, water, sleep, and shelter, their health and development needs are met, their needs are prioritized first over the parents' needs, that consistent care and routines are established in the household, and that parents are willing to admit problems and accept help if necessary.

On top of basic care needs, parenting assessments also check whether the environment is safe, the parents are warm and caring towards the child, the parents are giving healthy guidance and setting reasonable boundaries, and ultimately whether there is a sense of overall stability in the home.

Parenting assessments also consider outside factors such as extended families, housing accommodations, parent employment, parent income, and social and community interactions and resources.

During family observation, it's important to check how parents or primary caregivers speak to their children, how affectionate and warm they are towards their children, and if and how they set boundaries and provide guidance to their children. These three key aspects will generally give you a good foundation to judge the parent–child relationship. Here are some things to consider within these:

- Does the parent or caregiver talk to the child on their level?
- Does the parent or caregiver listen when the child is speaking to them?
- Does the child stop and listen to the parent or caregiver when they're being spoken to?
- Does the parent or caregiver seem to give the child any affection at all?
- When receiving affection, does the child accept the affection, return the affection, or reject the affection?
- Is the parent or caregiver setting boundaries, and if so, are they being enforced and are they realistic?
- If boundaries are set and the child pushes those boundaries, what types of guidance if any does the parent or caregiver provide?
- Is the guidance negative, harsh, or far too critical?
- Is the guidance positive, encouraging, and age appropriate?

Client Involvement with Client Assessments

It is helpful for both the assessment process and the success of the intervention to have the client actively involved in the process. A client system is designed around not only the client but also their support network.

One important factor that should be considered in the assessment and intervention process is whether the client is ready to accept help and make a change. Social workers will carry out a readiness to change assessment as part of their overall assessment to better gauge the client.

Client intervention or treatment planning should include:

- Client's personal information.
- Psychological history.
- Demographics.
- A detailed list or diagnosis of current issues or problems.
- The most important treatment goals that the client and social worker want addressed.
- Measurable objectives to meet those goals.
- A timeline as to how that treatment or those services will be utilized to reach the goal(s).

Clients can help their social worker to shape their treatment or intervention plan so that all parties are comfortable. Treatment or intervention plans are a good way to:

- Set goals and achieve more when possible.
- Motivate and engage clients.
- Track progress and show clients how far they have come through their tracked progress.
- Help boost self-confidence.
- Help the social worker and client concentrate on the current goal.
- Avoid or eliminate confusion.
- Help alleviate the feeling of being overwhelmed, as goals are set one or two at a time to keep things manageable.
- Prioritize the most important things first and work from there.

Clients and social workers can come together to set goals by asking simple questions such as:

- What unhealthy behaviors does the client have?
- What can the client do differently to change these unhealthy behaviors?
- How can the social worker help the client to develop new, healthier behaviors?
- What does the client need to do to reach the goals they have set?
- What can social workers do to help clients accomplish their set goals?

To realize the issues that need to be addressed, accept help for those issues, and ultimately reach their goals of a healthier and happier living, clients must be able to:

- Admit they have an issue that they need help with.
- Understand the issue and how it is affecting them in an unhealthy way.
- Be willing to learn new skills to cope with their issues in a new and healthier way.

If clients show willingness to be involved with their intervention planning, set goals they would like to reach, and enter treatment or services, then they can successfully meet their goals and ultimately change their life for the better.

Intervention Planning

Intervention planning is a cornerstone of social work. A social care plan for an adult client should be specific to that person. Once an assessment has been carried out and it is concluded that intervention is necessary, an intervention plan is then developed. It is important that adult clients are as involved as possible in the planning process and how things will be done. It is a key component to keep them as active participants in the treatment or services being utilized.

There are generally six steps to an intervention plan, as follows:

Step 1. Choose a problem behavior that is earmarked for change.
Step 2. Collect data to measure the behavior.

Step 3. Determine the function (purpose) of the behavioral problem.
Step 4. Create a functional behavioral assessment.
Step 5. Create a behavioral plan.
Step 6. Teach the new, alternative behavior.

The first step starts out with the identification of a problem you want to fix. One behavior or issue should be addressed at a time. In the second step, you will then decide on a way to monitor that behavior on a daily basis. You will observe that behavior over a set period to figure out how bad the problem is. Step three will assess the function of that behavior using CASE (communication, acknowledgment, sensory, escape). That information will then be used in step four to conduct a functional behavioral assessment. The assessment should identify factors in the environment that affect the problem behavior. These are known as setting events (occurrences that make the problem behavior more likely to occur) and antecedents (factors that occur directly before the problem behavior). During step five, the intervention is then created from the targeted behavior and its function. Antecedents are changed so that they no longer trigger problem behavior, newly taught behaviors replace the old ones, and consequences are maintained.

Cultural Considerations in Creating Intervention Plans

Cultural considerations involve awareness of culture, cross-culture, and cultural dynamics. It's important to ensure that organizations, their staff, and their affiliates are culturally competent and aware. This allows them to understand, empathize with, and aid culturally diverse communities and their citizens. There are three key areas that need to be fulfilled for a social worker to be culturally competent:

- Awareness and knowledge – this refers to knowing yourself, the knowledge you have as an individual, and the biases you may have regarding a culturally diverse community.
- Skills development – this is developing your ability to effectively communicate to foster trust with those from varying and diverse backgrounds.
- Organizational support – this refers to an organization's policies, practices, and systems in place to respond and adequately meet the needs of individuals and families and their diverse backgrounds.

Psychotherapies

Psychotherapy is a general term for a variety of mental health treatments. There is a valid difference between counseling and psychotherapy. Counseling is designed for current issues that are resolved more easily. Psychotherapy is designed to deal with more comprehensive issues, some of which are from childhood. These most often require long-term treatment that is far more extensive than counseling.

Treatment modalities are an outline for how therapists and clients should meet. Environments should be confidential, safe, and supportive.

There are five key stages to the practice of therapy:

Stage 1: Initial disclosure.
Stage 2: In-depth exploration.
Stage 3: Commitment to action.
Stage 4: Counseling intervention.
Stage 5: Evaluation/termination/referral.

Therapy Types and Their Focus

Therapy types include:

- Cognitive behavioral therapy.
    - This form of therapy is generally designed to take place for a short period of time. It is a goal-oriented therapy that focuses on cognitive and behavioral links.
- Psychodynamic therapy.
    - This form of therapy focuses on specific life events that have occurred and past or present relationships. It explores how those things affect our feelings, thoughts, actions, and relationships now. This form of therapy takes upwards of a year or more to complete.
- Dialectical behavior therapy.
    - This is a form of cognitive behavioral therapy. It helps to build skills and change behavior patterns to help the individual handle their emotional health, cope with stress in a healthy way, improve their relationships with other people, and live a life of healthy mindfulness.
- Humanistic/experiential/holistic therapy.
    - This therapy, in contrast to behavioral therapies, highlights nature and not behavior. It revolves around the focus of the person as a whole. This form of therapy can be a good choice for those with anxiety, depression, and low self-esteem, among other things.

Different forms of therapy are practiced in different types of settings. The most common and prevalent treatment settings include outpatient services, residential or inpatient services, mutual help groups, 12-step programs, and faith-based counseling or faith-based rehab programs. Five treatment modalities include detoxification, group therapy, single-gender group therapies, couples therapy, and family therapy.

These therapies and programs often focus on activities that promote self-care, lower domestic violence risks, evaluate environmental factors that can promote alcoholism or drug use, improve communication, support effective daily functioning, discourage alcohol and drug use, promote motivation, and raise awareness.

When seeing a psychotherapist, they may recommend a combination of both therapy and medication to treat a client. Usually, the client's doctor will choose medications from one of these categories:

- Anti-anxiety medication.
- Antidepressant.
- Antipsychotic.
- Mood stabilizer.
- Stimulant.

Every medication has its own set of side effects, monitoring requirements, and instructions on how it should be properly taken. Normally, these medications are used to treat conditions such as:

- Anxiety.
- Depression.
- Bipolar disorder.
- A variety of sleep disorders.

Indicators of Mental or Emotional Health Issues

Mental and emotional health issues do not always have external signs. There can be many causes for mental illness, including reactions to environmental stressors, genetic factors, biochemical imbalances, or a combination of factors. Emotional issues are usually psychological and deal more with how someone copes in situations and processes their emotions.

Psychosocial stress occurs when the demands placed on us and our ability to manage them are not balanced. Psychosocial stress can cause both behavioral and emotional responses. Emotional responses include feelings of tension, irritation, anxiety, and depression. Behaviorally, individuals can experience avoidance, insomnia, tremors, restlessness, teeth clenching, and other signs associated with stress.

There are usually five key warning signs that illuminate the possible presence of a mental illness in adults, which include:

- The presence of excessive paranoia, extreme worry, or high anxiety.
- Sadness or irritability that lasts an excessively long time.
- Extreme mood swings.
- Social withdrawal.
- Significant changes to an individual's sleeping patterns or eating habits.

When children develop a mental illness, signs and symptoms can differ from that of adults. In contrast to adults, children may experience delays or disruptions regarding their age-appropriate behaviors, social skills, ability to relate to others, and ability to function well at home or in school. For those who are old enough to show early signs of a mental health issue, signs to look for include:

- Sadness that lasts more than two weeks.
- Avoiding or withdrawing from social interaction.
- Talking about or actually causing self-harm.
- Extreme irritability.
- Talking about death or suicide.
- Risky, out-of-control behaviors.
- Drastic mood swings.
- Drastic changes in behavior.
- Drastic changes in personality.
- Excessive changes in eating habits.
- Significant weight loss.
- Excessive trouble sleeping.
- Frequent headaches.
- Frequent stomach aches.
- Significant trouble concentrating.
- Significant changes in academic performance.
- Avoiding school or missing it altogether.

The problem in treating children with mental disorders is that it can be exceedingly difficult to see the signs, for the child to be old enough to communicate their thoughts or feelings, and for the child to be able to actively participate in their treatment. Additionally, since children present differently compared to adults, it can be exceedingly difficult to distinguish one mental disorder from another and properly treat it.

For a child to be diagnosed with a mental health disorder, they will need to see a doctor. Generally, after the initial consultation there will be an evaluation.

Explained below are the common mental and emotional health issues that present in adults and children:

- Anxiety disorders.
  For children, anxiety disorders often affect their ability to participate in play, school, and age-appropriate social encounters. The most common anxiety-related disorders that children are diagnosed with include social anxiety, generalized anxiety, and obsessive compulsive disorder.

- Attention deficit disorder or attention-deficit/hyperactivity disorder.

Children who suffer from ADD or ADHD often have a difficult time paying attention, are affected by impulsive behaviors, have difficulty coping with hyperactivity, or any combination of these issues along with others.

- Autism spectrum disorders.
  Autism spectrum disorder is a neurological condition. It is usually diagnosed before age 3. There are different levels of an autism spectrum disorder, but in general, it creates difficulties in interacting or communicating with others.

- Eating disorders.
  Eating disorders are defined as being overly occupied with achievement of a specific body type. Those who suffer from such disorders focus a great deal on their weight, weight loss, unsafe eating habits, and dieting habits. The most common eating disorders include anorexia nervosa, bulimia nervosa, and binge eating disorder. Such disorders can cause life threatening complications if not treated.

- Depression and mood disorders.
  Depression and other mood disorders usually cause persistent emotions and feelings related to sadness and a loss of interest. These are significant enough to interrupt the child's ability to interact with their peers or family and cause difficulty functioning in school.

- Dysthymic disorder.
  This is a persistent depressive disorder. It can be less intense than some forms of depression but occurs more chronically than others.

- Generalized anxiety disorder (GAD).
  This is characterized by uncontrollable nervousness that causes persistent worry and fear.

- Obsessive compulsive disorder (OCD).
  Those with this disorder experience impulses that occur repeatedly and are compulsory. This causes greater issues in teens and children.

- Panic disorder.
  Panic attacks that have multiple occurrences and are ongoing over time without implementation of coping skills or treatment constitute a panic disorder.

- Post-traumatic stress disorder (PTSD).
  This is a disorder with long-lasting effects that can include emotional distress, anxiety, memories and flashbacks, and nightmares that cause physical responses

due to their severity. Such behavior can include violent, abusive, or injurious actions toward others.

- Schizophrenia.
  This mental disorder is characterized by psychosis that causes an individual to lose touch with reality. Normally, children who develop this do not show signs until their late teens or early 20s. The disorder is characterized by hallucinations, delusions, and disorders regarding an individual's thinking or behavior.

Trauma – Warning Signs, Assessments, and Effects

Trauma usually shows itself in one of two ways. Trauma will either present with physical signs, emotional signs, or both. The initial signs of trauma can include but are not limited to an individual's pale appearance, lethargy, elevated heart rate, inability to concentrate, and fatigue.

When a history of trauma is reported or trauma is suspected, the first step is to conduct a screening or assessment. Screenings and assessments normally record:

- Symptoms related to trauma.
- Interruptions to sleep.
- Depressive or dissociative symptoms.
- Past mental health disorders.
- Present mental health disorders.
- Characteristics related to any specific traumas.
- Substance abuse.
- Individual's coping style.
- Risk of self-harm or suicide.
- Risk of harming others.
- Social support.
- Resources available.
- Health screening.

Once screenings or assessments have been conducted, it can then be determined whether there is an issue with trauma and what may have caused it. A plan is developed to cope with the trauma and treat any mental, social, or psychological effects.

Commonly Used Medications to Treat Mental Health Issues

There are a variety of prescription drugs that are used to treat various mental health issues. The chart below includes the name of the commonly used drug and its drug classification.

Drug Classification	Drug Name(s)
Typical antipsychotics	Thorazine Prolixin Haldol Trilafon Mellaril
Atypical antipsychotics	Abilify Clozaril Fanapt Zyprexa Invega Seroquel Risperdal Geodon
Anti-anxiety agents	Xanax Klonopin Valium Ativan
Stimulants	Adderall Adderall XR Focalin Focalin XR Dexedrine Vyvanse

	Ritalin, Metadate ER Methylin Concerta
Selective serotonin reuptake inhibitor (SSRI) A class of antidepressants	Celexa Lexapro Luvox Paxil Prozac Zoloft
Serotonin-norepinephrine reuptake inhibitor (SNRI) A class of antidepressants	Strattera Cymbalta Effexor XR Pristiq
Monoamine oxidase inhibitor (MAOI) A class of antidepressants	Marplan Nardil Emsam Parnate
Tricyclic antidepressants	Norpramin Tofranil Pamelor
Mood stabilizers	Carbatrol Epitol Equetro

	Tegretol Depakote Lamictal Lithium
Norepinephrine-dopamine reuptake inhibitor (NDRI)	Wellbutrin Ritalin Focalin

Common Medical Terms to Know

Here are some key medical terms social workers should understand and be familiar with:

- Abrasion – A scrape or cut.
- Abscess – A fluid-filled pocket that forms in the tissue of the body, often tender and the result of an infection.
- Acute – Something that starts suddenly.
- Benign – Non-cancerous.
- Biopsy – A small tissue sample is taken to perform a test.
- Chronic – A recurring health condition or one that persists for longer than three months.
- Contusion – A bruise.
- Edema – Fluid that gathers in the body and causes swelling.
- Epidermis – The outermost layer of skin.
- Fracture – A broken bone or cartilage. It is more often a crack in a bone or cartilage rather than a complete break.
- Hypertension – High blood pressure.
- Inpatient – A patient who is required to stay in hospital.
- Intravenous – Administration of a medication or fluid directly to a person through their vein.
- Malignant – Cancerous.
- Mortality rate – The rate of death relating to a specific time period and group.
- Outpatient – A patient receiving care who does not require a hospital stay.

Mental Status Exams (MSEs) in Psychological Analysis

The mental status exam is a component of the assessment process. These assessments are carried out to gauge an individual's mental health, substance use, and disorders. This information is used to create a treatment plan.

Mental status exams assess the client's:

- Appearance.
- Behavior.
- Speech.
- Mood.
- Affect (their expressions, tone, and movement).
- Thought process.
- Thought content.
- Cognition.
- Insight (degree of recognition of their problems).
- Judgment.

Immigration, Refugee, or Undocumented Status with Regard to Service Delivery

For immigrants, refugees, or undocumented individuals to receive services, it can be an overly complicated matter. There are various federal, state, and local laws that apply here. There are some states that take far more liberty with their distribution of resources than others.

There are many states that make services to immigrants more readily available. However, even with these resources, it has been reported by many U.S. states that immigrants commonly either turn in their assistance applications or never apply. This is due to the following five key reasons:

1. The difficulties of the application and eligibility process.
2. Administrative burdens.
3. Cultural boundaries, language boundaries, and literacy capabilities.
4. Transportation.
5. Fear and mistrust of what will happen if they apply.

Another factor is the lack of awareness of the services available in the first place.

Chapter 4: Interventions with Client Systems

Intervention is an important part of social work. Social workers are a community resource that investigate possible situations that may need intervention or support services. They are then expected to put action plans into place, supervise compliance of action plans, and graduate individuals who meet their action plan goals and can be released from the services or support.

Intervention Processes and Techniques for Use Across Systems

There are six phases of intervention and treatment. Those stages include:

Stage 1: Engagement.
Stage 2: Assessment.
Stage 3: Planning.
Stage 4: Intervention.
Stage 5: Evaluation.
Stage 6: Termination.

In the first phase of the intervention and treatment process, the social worker will engage with the client. There are certain principles to follow to conduct an effective interview. Social workers should be as prepared as possible for the interview, develop a rapport with those being interviewed, be thorough with their interview, stay in control of the process, and actively listen to the interviewee (what they are saying, and how they are responding to questions).

Techniques, Models, and Methods in Intervention Processes

In the intervention and treatment process, the information gathered in the first two stages is then used to create an intervention plan in stage three. Once the plan has been composed, stage four is the execution.

There are a variety of techniques that are used in intervention processes. These techniques include limit setting techniques, roleplay, role modeling, harm reduction, self-care and coping methods, self-monitoring, conflict resolution, crisis intervention and treatment approaches, trauma-informed care, anger management, contract and goal setting techniques, partializing techniques, task-centered approaches, psychoeducation methods, and stress management.

The common techniques and methods used for intervention processing are further explained here:

Limit Setting Techniques:

The limit setting technique provides individuals with an array of personal choices and consequences. Limit setting is designed to be a truly clear and simple technique that can be used at almost any age. The principle is that the client and social worker decide a set of limits and a set of consequences. It is important that these limits and expectations be noticeably clear. Ensure that you state exactly what the choices are and what the consequences for noncompliance will be. Ensure that you follow through. If the client does not follow through with the agreed upon limits, be sure that the consequences are clearly enforced and ensure that you are consistent every time they occur. Remind individuals that these are the consequences of their choice and avoid lectures and over-explaining. Ensure that you avoid power struggles when clients push back against the limits that have been set. In a power struggle, both parties will lose, so avoiding such instances is necessary.

Roleplay:

Role-play techniques can be an effective tool, as they provide opportunities to express strong emotions, can reduce the intensity of destructive emotions and behavior, and can improve self-perception and awareness. The benefits of roleplay include allowing the individual to adopt a decision-making persona separate from normal self-imposed limitations. This allows the individual to think beyond the confines of their environment, and develop a correlation between the act that is occurring and the real-life situation. It is important to set a parameter for the role which you play and the context in which it should be expressed. You should also ensure that there is a discussion and decompression at the end of the roleplay.

Role Modeling Technique:

The role modeling technique teaches clients learned behaviors by modeling those behaviors after another individual without the consequences of trial and error. The role modeling technique is a tool that uses imitation as its core and not verbal directions or specifically instructions. The role model framework outlines three functions of the role model. The first is to actually model the behavior, the second is to show the client what is possible, and the third is to inspire the client. This technique highlights the individual's aspirations. It supports and encourages them to accept these goals as possible and in turn reach for them.

Harm Reduction Techniques:

Harm reduction is an approach that uses a variety of techniques and strategies to tackle substance abuse in a public health format. These techniques meet an individual at their level of substance abuse and then help them work towards sobriety. This is opposed to making them reach a specific point alone before allowing access support on their journey.

These techniques center on judgment-free support, respect for the individual, and connections that foster healthy relationship building. Furthermore, these techniques spread awareness in the community to make it easier to learn about and access the help available to them.

Examples of harm reduction programs introduced to communities include safe ride programs, outreach, support, informational resources regarding safe substance use, therapies like methadone, programs for mental wellness, support from recovered substance abusers, and programs that provide clean substance paraphernalia and a safe place to stay when under the influence. Programs and support like this can increase the use of health and social services, reduce negative ideals surrounding substance abuse, reduce unsafe sharing habits related to substance abuse paraphernalia, reduce the spread of HIV and other diseases, increase the information available regarding the safe use of certain substances like opioids, and spread awareness regarding sexual health, safe sex, and the use of protection.

Self-Care and Coping Methods:

Self-care and coping are considered key survival skills. Self-care and coping methods help individuals engage in activities that reduce stress and maintain health in both a short-term and lifelong capacity. This fosters a healthy sense of well-being. When it comes to self-care, there are six key components which include physical, emotional, psychological, spiritual, relational, and professional components. To balance these components is important for both mental, physical, and overall health.

Some of the things that constitute self-care include friendships, regular exercise, healthy diet, ability to ask for help and accept that help when it's provided, prioritize yourself and your needs over those of other people, implementation of goals or other achievements as a means to move forward and work towards something of purpose.

Self-care is something that is not only important for clients but also for the social workers who help them. It is essential as a way of coping with the stressors that come with the job. Social workers may be exposed to an array of situations that others wouldn't normally see or be involved in.

Part of self-care is also the knowledge of how to cope with the stressors in your life in a healthy and meaningful way. Coping most often focuses on your emotional health and well-being. Some of the best ways to ensure your emotional health include an outlet for or release of emotions that build up, distractions or activities that take you away from those stressors for a time, expression and management of hostile or resentful feelings in a healthy way, meditation, and practice of mindfulness. All these things can help you to express your feelings, decompress, and let go of things to which you were previously holding on. This ultimately lightens your emotional load to take on the next set of challenges.

Self-Monitoring Techniques:

Self-monitoring techniques are used to help individuals learn and develop skills that increase their use of positive and appropriate behaviors, reduce behavioral issues, increase independence, and promote socialization. Self-monitoring works through the use of effective strategies to increase behaviors that are wanted and decrease behaviors that are considered negative and unwanted.

Social workers and individuals work together to identify a behavior that the individual would like to change. Once the behavior has been chosen, the social worker and individual will set a timeline to eliminate or reduce the undesired behavior and to achieve the new behavior. This means a plan for how long it should take to reach certain mile markers within your goal as well as the ultimate goal itself. Goals like these should be set with the understanding that they can be modified along the way if an individual needs more or less time.

Once those goals have been set and the timeline is established, the monitoring begins. Self-monitoring works in a way that reinforces the desired behavior. Individuals will monitor their progress and social workers will allow for time to review the individual's progress. The review should ensure that the self-monitoring technique is working to the individual's benefit and that the individual is reaching their set goals. Once a client reaches a goal, the social worker and client can determine whether that is the end of the client's work or whether there are additional goals they would like to achieve.

Ultimately, the self-monitoring technique generally achieves its success by increasing the client's awareness of their behavior.

Conflict Resolution Methods:

Social workers are often required to manage conflict in their line of work. Methods that may be utilized for conflict resolution can include negotiation, mediation, advocacy, evaluations, facilitation for a group, and family counseling. There are five key strategies for conflict resolution when involved in a direct conflict. These have varying degrees of success.

The first strategy is avoidance. This strategy allows an individual to remove themself from the conflict to eliminate the confrontation and dissolve the tension. Avoidance does not resolve conflict. It only delays the discussion and neutralizes the conflict at that moment. Avoidance is a short-term solution to a problem that will need a more elaborate solution in the end.

The second strategy of conflict resolution competing. This strategy is used when an individual goes into a conflict with the idea that they will win. This type of conflict resolution decreases cooperation and usually results in the loss of a solution. Competing ultimately creates more conflict and generally results in a worsening situation.

The third strategy in conflict resolution is known as accommodating. This strategy typically involves one individual or group that concedes to the demands of the other. There is a lack of assertiveness on the giving party's side. Though it may seem like this would solve the conflict, it most often results in feelings of being wronged and further conflict. This is because one individual or party feels like they have given too much and that another individual or party has achieved everything they want.

The fourth strategy in conflict resolution is known as collaborating. Collaborating works because both parties actively participate in the creation of a solution that works for everyone involved.

The fifth and final strategy for conflict resolution is compromising. This simply involves individuals or parties that come together to establish what they each want. The difference is split or middle ground is found in which everyone gains something. In these instances, neither party walks away with everything they wanted. Compromise is a fair way to resolve a conflict.

Collaborating and compromising are two of the most effective ways to resolve a conflict. In both instances, the parties involved are achieving at least part of what they set out to get when entering the conflict.

Trauma-Informed Care Method:

There are five key principles to trauma-informed care. Those principles are safety, choice, collaboration, trustworthiness, and empowerment. When it comes to trauma, the first thing the individual needs to know is that they are safe. The second thing the individual needs to know is that from that point forward, everything that they experience and do is their choice. If they feel unsafe or overwhelmed, they have the choice to stop until they are ready to proceed again. The third principle is that the individual collaborates and is actively involved in steps to move forward. The fourth principle seeks to ensure that those whom the individual works with make the individual feel comfortable and as though they can trust the people in that situation. The fifth principle is to empower the individual to take back control they feel was lost during the trauma.

Anger Management Techniques:

When it comes to strategies and techniques related to anger management, there are some key components. Individuals with anger management issues usually need to work on impulse control, self-awareness, involvement in meditation, breathing techniques, strategies for relaxation, time for personal reflection, and awareness of their emotions.

This can be achieved using 10 key strategies:

- The first strategy is to think before you speak, meaning to simply take a beat, take a breath, consider your emotions, and consider if the reaction is a rational one or driven by strong feelings.
- The second strategy is to relax and calm down first to express your frustrations or anger in a calm and healthy way.
- The third strategy is to exercise, since physical activity reduces stress, releases hormones that increase good feelings, and can be an outlet for anger.
- The fourth strategy is to take a timeout. This simply means to remove yourself for a short period to reduce your stress, deal with the feelings, come back to the situation with your anger in check.
- The fifth strategy is to focus, identify the cause, and explore solutions. Considering what made you angry in the first place, accept that anger is not a solution, and consider other ways the situation can be handled.
- The sixth strategy is to stick with "I" statements. Avoid blaming others or criticizing them for your reaction. For example, you would say, "I am upset because the kitchen isn't clean" rather than saying, "It's your fault I got mad because you didn't clean the kitchen." Taking responsibility for your actions is a key component in anger management.
- The seventh strategy is forgiveness. Holding on to feelings of negativity prevents you from moving forward in a positive way. Finding ways to let go and move forward are important to ensure that you are not harboring anger that will only hold you back.
- The eighth strategy is to utilize humor as a tool to reduce and expel tension. Being able to lighten the mood and laugh dispels anger and hurt feelings. It's important to remember to use positive humor rather than sarcasm in these situations, as the latter can breed anger and make situations worse by causing others to feel hurt.
- The ninth strategy is to use relaxation techniques to dispel anger. Relaxation practices can be as simple as listening to music, using a journal to write down feelings, and practicing yoga or meditation, among other things.
- The tenth strategy for anger management is the ability to control your anger and willingness to ask for help. Sometimes anger issues seem incredibly out of control and too big to handle alone. When this is the case, an important step is to seek help.

Stress Management Techniques:

Stress is something that everyone deals with on a near-daily basis. Stress can be considered chemical, emotional, or physical. There are several causes of stress.

There is no standardized way to predict or know an individual's exact stress level. Different individuals handle stressors in different ways and can cope better or worse under those stressors than others.

Stress can manifest itself in many ways that affect an individual's overall health and wellness. People may develop anxiety, headaches, an inability to sleep properly, or problems in focus or concentration. They may experience depression, lose their appetite, develop anger issues, or have moments of angry outbursts. Studies have shown that stress on the body can also exacerbate existing health issues such as asthma, high blood pressure, symptoms of depression, and fibromyalgia, just to name a few.

There is no one way to eliminate stress. However, there are a variety of ways to manage it. Since stress has both internal and external factors, a variety of methods can be used to help reduce the effects of stress on the body. Activities that include exercise, meditation, yoga, and time for yourself are some of the ways individuals can manage stress levels and decompress from the stressors they deal with in their daily lives. It's also important to set aside time with family and friends to increase a balance of work, life, and social activity.

Sometimes, individuals find it difficult to manage or cope with life stressors on their own. When this is the case, it's important to see your doctor to discuss the issue. Individuals may consider counseling or structured courses on meditation and relaxation as a means to cope.

Contracting and Goal Setting Techniques:

Contracting and goal setting techniques are based on the social worker and client's joint decision to put a written agreement into place that will act as a guide or road map from where they're starting to where they would ultimately like to end up. This may include overcoming challenges or achieving specific goals in the individual's life. Doing so must be done in a way that allows the individual to accept responsibility, take charge regarding the improvements or achievements they attempt to reach, and actively participate in reaching those goals.

Partializing Techniques:

Partializing techniques refer to a planned approach that uses small steps or actions in order to achieve the desired goals. Social workers and clients work together to assess the client's ability to set and reach attainable goals.

Task-Centered Approaches:

In the field of social work, a task-centered approach or model is designed to be a short-term way to approach problem solving. Usually, social workers will first identify target problems with their client, collaborate in setting goals for that problem or problems, develop a task-centered action plan, and execute it. They will then evaluate the results when that task action plan has been fulfilled and assess any remaining needs that the client may still have.

Psychoeducational Approaches:

A psychoeducational approach uses a balance of education and clinical influences to deal with an underlying emotional trauma. This approach is most often used with children. It can lower the chances of an individual's emotional relapse associated with the trauma. Also, it is more likely that they will stick to their treatment plan. This approach improves quality of life, social understanding, and engages the individual in their rehabilitation and treatment in an active and positive way.

Types of Interventions That Social Workers Use

As a social worker, you can use different types of interventions to meet the individual needs of different people. These types include cognitive and behavioral interventions, strengths-based interventions, and crisis interventions.

Cognitive and Behavioral Interventions

Cognitive intervention refers to therapy-based approaches that address a client's psychological issues. These approaches help social workers analyze a client's thoughts, experiences, memories, and senses, so the social worker can understand the overall problem and find solutions for it.

Behavioral intervention addresses a client's physical health, in much the same way that cognitive intervention addresses mental health. You can use behavioral intervention to help instill certain behaviors, like being able to set up and follow regular daily routines, create reminders to stay on task, take breaks to collect oneself or decompress, and use positive reinforcement or personal affirmations.

When you use cognitive or behavioral interventions, it is important to get a clear idea of the client's problem or problems that need to be addressed. This enables you to develop a comprehensive plan to achieve a resolution. Understand that your plan needs to be somewhat flexible. Flexibility ensures that the client makes real progress in a lasting way. It also helps you ensure that dismissal from an intervention does not occur until the client's issue has been properly addressed and resolved.

Strengths-Based Interventions

In strengths-based interventions, social workers recognize that the client has existing strengths and resources that can be used to help them reach their goals. In this type of intervention, social workers positively establish expectations with the client. They also make sure the client and their family (and/or their support circle) feel that they are involved in making decisions regarding the client's treatment. By ensuring this, social workers will help the client feel that they are part of the solution and actively involved in the choices being made in the client's life. It will also help the client feel that they are building a foundation that will empower them once they are no longer in a structured, facilitated intervention. Empowerment and recovery happen by helping people develop their personal strengths with a focus on their overall health and well-being.

Crisis Interventions

In crisis interventions, a social worker assists a client during a crisis. Examples of crises include natural disasters, confrontations, and terrorism. The goals of crisis intervention are to discover the issue that caused the trauma, assess the impact that the trauma had on the client, assist the client by developing an intervention plan, and help the client recover and cope with the trauma. That way, the client can get back to their best self as quickly and effectively as possible.

Crisis intervention is typically a seven-step process. The steps are as follows:

- Get through the initial danger of the crisis.
- Establish a relationship with the client going through the crisis.
- Identify the problems that led to or caused the crisis.
- Help the client explore their feelings and encourage them to discuss what led to the crisis.
- Work with the client to explore different strategies that they can use to cope with the feelings that led to this crisis, or other feelings that could lead to another crisis.
- Work with the client to create an action plan. This plan should help them restore their health and wellness to a point where they're healthy again and coping well.
- Establish follow-up strategies to avoid a future crisis and ensure that the client maintains the coping frameworks they developed.

Therapies and Models Used for Individual Client Intervention in Social Work

There are different therapies and models social workers can use in individual (or one-on-one) client interventions. Below are the main forms of therapy approaches used for individual therapies. Choose the option that's best for the intervention and your client's needs.

Cognitive Behavioral Therapy

Social workers who believe feelings and thoughts influence behavior use cognitive behavioral therapy to help identify dangerous, self-destructive thoughts or behaviors. This line of therapy is best for clients with mental health concerns.

Crisis Intervention Model

The crisis intervention model helps clients who are experiencing a crisis or who have suffered a trauma. Specifically, this line of therapeutic intervention can help victims of domestic violence or rape trauma, or people who need interventions to stop self-harm.

Narrative Therapy

In narrative therapy, social workers help individuals separate themselves from their problems. This process helps clients understand that they are not their problems. It also shows clients that it's possible to change their circumstances if they look at life through a different perspective.

Problem-Solving Model

Social workers use the problem-solving model to help clients identify a problem they would like to solve, create an action plan to find a solution, and then work toward that goal together. To work toward the goal, the social worker and client use strategies that can be changed as needed until the problem is resolved.

Solution-Focused Therapy

Social workers use solution-focused therapy to help clients use their own strengths and abilities to solve their own problems. This form of therapy allows the client to feel actively involved in the solution. It also helps clients develop a sense of pride and fulfillment because they can solve problems using themselves as the resource.

Task-Centered Practice

Task-centered practice breaks down a client's problem into smaller, more manageable tasks. This helps the client better their life, gain control over their life, and improve their self-view. By having goals that are easier to reach and more manageable, the client does not become overwhelmed and does not feel helpless about solving the problem.

Intervention Processes and Techniques for Use Within Larger Systems

Some forms of social work occur on a small scale and are performed one-on-one. Other forms of social work occur in larger systems and are performed through group work, community organizations, and social laws and acts. Intervention processes and techniques in larger systems may look different from those in smaller systems. For example, there are techniques that can be adjusted to fit the needs of a larger group. Additionally, in large groups or group therapies, social workers may need to set both individual and team goals. The approaches for conducting interventions within larger systems are described in more depth below.

Group Work

Group work is a learning method that is put into place when social workers work with multiple people. Studies show that in some circumstances, there is validity in using such an approach rather than working with clients individually.

One way to use this technique is to let individuals assemble in groups for a set period. During that time, they can discuss and collaborate on the work or goal that they're trying to meet. This allows people to express differences of opinion in a structured way.

The group work technique has great merit. It combines a variety of thoughts and ideas, so individuals can discuss a commonly held problem or goal. When people unite to collaborate, they get the opportunity to exchange ideas with each other. Ultimately, that provides people the chance to create a solution they could not have come up with on their own.

There are five stages in group work. These stages are as follows:

- Forming.
- Storming.
- Norming.
- Performing.
- Adjourning.

In any form of group work, it's important to remember that everyone involved needs to feel heard, to be given the opportunity to express their thoughts and views, and to feel validated. To build a cohesive unit, at the beginning of the group therapy, set group expectations and terms for giving feedback. Identify and resolve cracks in the group's cohesion when they occur. That way, the cracks can be repaired, and the group can progress.

Group work can be used for a variety of clients. Such groups include but are not limited to the following:

- Advocacy groups—Individuals who work together to promote a shared cause or interest. This advocacy can be for self-interest or in the interest of others. The group work can focus on self-empowerment or attempt to promote social change.
- Educational groups—A group that is taught by an educated and certified professional who uses a proven set of techniques or methods to teach the group.
- Mutual aid groups—A group that is specifically composed of those with a shared experience or condition. Such groups are informal and designed so people can support one another and exchange information. Facilitators may be people who share the experience or condition, or they may be professionals who help bring such individuals together.
- Psychoeducational groups—A group led by a professional who uses education and psychosocial aspects to address issues and provide support.
- Psychotherapy or counseling groups—A group setting that is facilitated by a professional who uses a set psychiatric approach to deal with psychosocial issues.

Family Therapy Interventions

Social workers can use family therapy intervention for a single family or small groups of individuals within a family. They can also use this intervention for family structures that involve immediate family members as well as extended family that either preside with or are closely intertwined with the immediate family.

When social workers conduct family therapy, they can choose from a few types of therapy. The most used types in this scenario are structural therapy, strategic therapy, systemic therapy, narrative therapy, transgenerational therapy, communication therapy, psychoeducational therapy, and relationship or marriage counseling. Definitions of some of these therapies are listed below.

- In structural family therapy, a social worker develops an understanding of how a particular family is structured, how the individual family members interact with one another, and how the family works. The therapy breaks down the family's hierarchy, relationships, and the various boundaries within the family. Once the social worker understands those aspects, they can help restructure the family in a way that will benefit them as a whole.

- In strategic family therapy, a social worker examines family members and any defined patterns of interaction that exist. This form of therapy is solution based. The idea is to identify problems within the family that are solvable and to set goals and create strategies to help family members achieve those goals. Ultimately, the aim is to help the individual family members think strategically, so they can meet their goals and develop plans and solutions for future problems.

- In systemic family therapy, a social worker uses a belief system to drive the therapy process. This form of therapy is based on the idea that the characteristics of a family and the relationships between those characteristics play key roles in how the family construct behaves and operates. The key to this form of therapy is to understand the roles within the family dynamic by using sociocultural beliefs and perceptions that family members have. It is important to be able to use cultural context to change behavioral patterns and promote solutions that are both helpful and sustainable for the whole family. This form of therapy can be broken into five key steps: deconstruct the problem, identify patterns within the family, explore beliefs and understand the explanations of those beliefs, dissect emotions and attachments within the family construct, and explore contextual factors.

- In narrative family therapy, a social worker structures therapy around the idea that every person has their own individual stories to tell throughout their life. These stories help shape that person. Narrative family therapy helps separate the person or people from the problem they are encountering. It enables them to rely on their own skills and abilities to see the problem objectively. That way, they don't feel like their story shapes how they should be dealing with that problem or finding its solution.

- In transgenerational therapy, a social worker uses a family's past issues or difficulties as a way to foreshadow future conflicts. This approach is valuable because it helps families use solutions to past problems for future problems. Families can also dismiss strategies that have proven to be ineffective in the family dynamic.

Client Engagement and Motivation in the Intervention Process

Engaging clients is an essential part of successfully helping them achieve their goals and gain better control and more independence throughout an intervention. There are ten common motivational strategies that social workers use to help clients reach goals and develop skills they can use once they achieve success.

Here are explanations of these ten strategies:

1. Use a planner or calendar to help clients set goals and deadlines, organize appointments, and note various tasks that they need to do in a set time frame.
2. Set realistic goals, and make sure clients can meet them. Goals that are too large can seem unattainable and therefore result in regression during the intervention process.
3. Provide rationale to clients to help them understand *why* they are going through the intervention. This set goal can then be met and reviewed at the next appointment.
4. Create a system of accountability. The client should know that they are accountable for their actions or inactions.
5. Create a measure of progress to show clients what their goals are, what they've been able to accomplish so far, and how much they have left to achieve before they reach their goal.
6. Develop a system that enables the client to correlate previous habits and routines with the new habits and routines being created. For example, if the client feels energized after having dinner, they could develop a new routine where they do their homework immediately after dinner. They can then correlate how doing their homework directly after their meal helps them focus.
7. Optimize your client's work environment by asking them to identify things that motivate them in an environment. When possible, they should move their place of work to a new environment if the present environment isn't working for them.
8. Build a system of rewards. Having clients work with you to develop a reward system encourages them to progress toward their goals during the intervention process.

Everyone likes to receive a reward, and rewards further build a sense of achievement.

9. Loosen the time constraints on a client's tasks or goals. Some clients find that they can more successfully complete tasks or achieve goals when they feel less pressure to do so. Setting criteria that work for each individual client is an important part of their success.
10. Use a timer. When clients know they have a set period of time to get something done, as well as an official stop and start time, this can greatly motivate them to complete assignments and meet goals.

Not every client is excited, engaged, or goal-oriented in an intervention or treatment plan. For clients who feel deterred by the intervention process, social workers may need to use different tools to engage them. The use of rational strategies, motivational interviewing, and client-controlled treatment that is based on a client-centered approach can all be helpful when dealing with an unengaged client.

If social workers are working with clients who are not voluntarily participating, it is important that social workers strive to stay calm, listen to their clients, inform clients that the social worker's role is to help, express how they can work through the situation and come out successful on the other side, and ensure they establish and maintain professional boundaries. Social workers must also use safety precautions, use tools to deescalate situations, and remind clients that controlling their emotions and refraining from explosive behavior will bring them one step closer to exiting the program.

One of the easiest ways to engage clients is by asking them a list of questions. The questions should give the client the opportunity to express their thoughts, feelings, and, at times, actions in a constructive way.

The Role of Feedback, Active Listening, and Nonverbal Communication in Interventions

During an intervention, feedback is a particularly important tool for social workers to use. Clients should be encouraged to provide feedback and provide it openly, whether it is positive or negative. The information gathered in feedback should help inform social workers as to which intervention processes and techniques have a positive effect and work for clients, and which are ineffective.

When a social worker receives feedback, it is important for them to be an active listener and observer. Active listening helps clients feel like they're being understood and heard. It also helps social workers gain perspective and insight on a client's point of view or situation.

To receive feedback effectively, social workers should listen to feedback when it's given and let clients express their feedback in a way that allows them to feel heard and not interrupted. Pay attention to how you react to feedback, both in one-on-one conversations and in group settings. Be open to hearing what your clients are saying in their feedback. Make sure you understand the message they are trying to express. Take the time to reflect on the information you've been given, and then make choices on what changes will best benefit the most people. Make sure you follow up on feedback that you have received, too.

Having good communication skills is in many ways central to a social work career. Although verbal communication is important to master, it's also important to be skilled at nonverbal communication. This can include facial expressions, avoiding or making eye contact, body language, gesturing, and physical touch. Understanding these signs can be key to understanding how individuals truly feel.

The following are types and aspects of nonverbal communication:

- Inconsistencies—Nonverbal communication typically supports what a client verbally expresses, but not always. Look out for inconsistencies between what is spoken and what is nonverbally communicated. For example, a client may tell you they are really happy about something, but their facial expressions could show disgust, which indicates how they really feel.
- Nonverbal signals within a group—In group sessions, nonverbal communications are not always reliable. Other catalysts within the group can affect communication reactions. For example, if two people in a group are upset with each other, the two may shoot dirty looks at each other while discussing a group project, even if the project was well executed and successfully completed.
- Instincts—Your own gut feelings and personal instincts can be an important nonverbal cue. Your instincts may alert you when something is off or doesn't make sense.
- Eye contact or lack of eye contact—Eye contact can be an important part of nonverbal communication. Notice whether a client actively avoids eye contact, or if they're actively involved in the conversation and making eye contact with the person who is speaking.
- Facial expressions—Some clients can conceal their thoughts or feelings and maintain a poker face, so to speak, that is void of emotion or doesn't give anything away. On the other hand, some clients are incredibly expressive. These people can say a lot without ever having to say a word because their thoughts or feelings are so thoroughly conveyed by the expression on their faces.
- Posture and gestures—A client's posture and gestures can support or throw off how you interpret their verbal cues. Their posture may be relaxed, and they may be sitting forward and up straight to stay focused and engaged. Alternatively, a client's posture might be strained and tight to express stress or anxiety.
- Touch and physical contact—The way a client initiates physical contact and how they receive physical contact from others can be important nonverbal cues. Pay

attention to whether clients seem comfortable with being touched, or if they reciprocate when someone else touches them.

- Intensity—Intensity refers to how a person seems outwardly. Individuals might seem calm and collected, or they might seem angry and express a great deal of outward rage.
- Timing—The amount of time before a nonverbal cue is expressed or exhibited plays into how that nonverbal cue is interpreted by others. An example of timing is when a client responds before you've even finished a question, or when it takes several seconds for a client to respond to you because they weren't paying attention or were splitting their focus.
- Sounds—Sounds are also a form of nonverbal communication. Sounds may express care, concern, or joy, among other emotions.
- Tone of voice—A tone of voice can project feelings of interest, excitement, confidence, strain, and anxiety. Tone can reveal a lot about what a client is talking about and how they feel about what they're saying. For example, a young girl who is delivering a eulogy at her father's funeral might speak with cracks in her voice. She might also speak in a high pitch as she describes how wonderful her father was. In other words, her distress and anguish may be heard in her tone of voice.

Placement Options Based on the Level of Care Required

Individuals can be placed in group homes, assisted living facilities, residential treatment facilities, residential care facilities, skilled nursing facilities, or acute rehab units, as well as other related facilities.

Placement is based on the needs of the individual. Some individuals may be adults with mental health challenges, like a person who has Down syndrome. Someone with mental health challenges may be able to take care of themselves independently but may need some support to ensure they buy groceries, pay their bills, and address health issues. For these individuals, a small, independent and group living home may be a good option. These options would allow clients to live independently, or with roommates. A home health aide or other supervisory individual can also check in on clients at regular intervals.

Alcoholics and other substance abusers may be admitted to an inpatient rehab program for a set duration. Upon leaving rehab, the client may be sent to a sober living facility or home for a time, to help them maintain sobriety and transition into normal life again. Such programs typically involve outpatient therapy or a 12-step program as well.

Older clients who need assistance but can still manage to live in their homes may receive home health services. Those who cannot live alone anymore may be considered for assisted living, residential care facilities, or skilled nursing facilities.

The placement provided and the services received depend on several factors, including the following:

- What type of facility a client is being sent to.
- The reason and duration of their stay.
- The client's ability to complete daily living activities or the amount of help they require for such tasks.
- The client's mental faculties and competency.
- The severity of the client's addiction.
- Intensity of care or rehab services needed.

Discharge, Aftercare, and Follow-Up Planning

Discharge, aftercare, and follow-up planning are all steps to independence. It is highly encouraged that social workers do not abandon their clients while they still require services. This is because clients can experience adverse reactions to changing social workers or dealing with other stressors.

Discharge can happen for many reasons. The most common reasons include a client having met their goals and no longer needing services, a client choosing to continue services with another service provider, or a client requiring a different amount of care than what is currently being provided. If a social worker leaves an agency or organization, the client will be discharged from their care and placed with another social worker. As part of the discharge process, it is typically the responsibility of the social worker to arrange for a client's aftercare and follow-up services.

Discharge starts by creating a discharge plan, which should contain the following points:

- Where the individual, group, or family will reside.
    - This details whether clients need to be sent to a long-term care facility or hospital, or whether they will be discharged home.
- Follow-up care that will be put into place.
    - This may include outpatient care, outpatient counseling, or outside services that may come into the home.
- Other needs.
    - These encompass needs that ensure clients can continue to function and improve once they are discharged from services or care.

Aftercare refers to the support that a client receives after they leave treatment or services. Aftercare may consist of support services and resources, which help prevent relapses into past negative behaviors.

Follow-up refers to when a social worker periodically checks in on discharged clients to ensure they have been able to stay on track after their discharge. This can include checking on a client's physical or mental well-being, addressing any needs the client may have, or helping clients directly (if this becomes necessary).

Case Management in Social Work

One of the key duties that social workers carry out is case management. In case management, a social worker has many responsibilities. All these responsibilities focus on taking care of the client, facilitating resources and treatment, and ensuring the overall care and networking of clients and communities. These responsibilities are broken down below.

Social Worker Responsibilities

- Allocate resources both formally and informally.
- Provide community care.
- Ensure community involvement.
- Provide spiritual enrichment and support.
  - Churches.
  - Ministries.
  - Chaplin.
- Provide counseling.
  - Individual counseling.
  - Children's counseling.
  - Family counseling.
- Support individuals and families.
- Ensure psychological, social, and mental well-being.

Case Management Responsibilities

- Ensure resources are available.
- Manage financial support.
  - Work sources.
  - Temporary Assistance for Needy Families (TANF) program.
  - Women, Infants, and Children (WIC) program.
- Use best practices.
- Navigate individuals and clients through processes.
- Involve patients and clients in care, treatment, and service plans.
- Work with health coverage.
- Assist with acquiring health coverage.
- Provide treatment and services.
  - 12-step programs.
  - Addiction recovery.
  - Inpatient addiction recovery programs.
  - Outpatient addiction recovery programs.

Joint Responsibilities of Case Workers and Social Workers

- Lead advocacy.
    - Housing programs and resources.
    - Legal services.
    - Free clinics.
    - Family reunification.
- Uphold values.
- Provide coordination.
- Provide support.
- Provide self-care driven assistance.
- Provide job coaching.
    - Continued education.
    - Connection to potential employers.
    - Internship facilitation.
- Teach life classes.
    - Relationship.
    - Parenting.
    - Decision-making.
    - Independent living.

Community Resources and Involvement

Community resources and involvement in the field of social work can be important tools for addressing common issues. Community resources and involvement might include the following:

- Interagency collaboration.
- Child, youth, and family outreach.
- Volunteer programs.
- Intergenerational programs.
- Senior centers.
- Community centers.
- Employment programs.
- Job training programs.
- Nutrition programs.
- Healthy living programs.
- Legal services.
- Transportation services.
- Housing programs.
- Case management programs.
- Home care programs or services.

- Respite care programs or services.

These are only some of the possible community resources that may be available in a community. Programs such as Early Head Start, Head Start, Boys & Girls Clubs, the WIC program, the Supplemental Nutrition Assistance Program, and the Housing Choice Voucher program are just a few of the community resources individuals and families can use for assistance. Substance abuse centers and hotlines in an individual's community, battered women and children centers, and homeless shelters can also serve as resources.

Chapter 5: Professional Relationships, Values, and Ethics

Professional Values and Ethical Issues

Social workers must follow a set of core principles. These core principles are incredibly important when guiding social workers through the minefield of social work.

These six core principles are factored into typical ethics policies:

1. Service—Social workers are bound to help individuals and communities identify their needs and address social issues.
2. Social justice—Social workers are bound to promote social justice.
3. Dignity and worth of the person—Social workers are responsible for respecting the intrinsic dignity and worth of the person.
4. Importance of human relationships—Social workers understand and realize the importance of human relationships.
5. Integrity—Social workers must conduct themselves in a manner that is trustworthy.
6. Competence—Social workers must practice in the area where they possess competence and understanding. They must continue to develop their skill base and further enhance their professional experience.

Accreditation and Licensing for Social Workers

To be a practicing social worker, an individual must meet a set of requirements established by the state or province they want to practice in. These requirements include being educated through an accredited social work education program, passing a licensing exam, and receiving a license to practice social work.

Education typically involves a bachelor's degree, master's degree, advanced generalist degree, or a clinical certification that's applicable to a particular social work program.

Once you have obtained your license, you will need to maintain and renew your social work license through continued education, which is facilitated through most reputable agencies.

Social Workers and Ethics Codes

The vast field of social work covers an array of areas that involve personal interactions and dealings with the public. Social workers, therefore, encounter numerous legal and ethical issues in their line of work. For that reason, the National Association of Social Workers has established a code of ethics. It gives social workers guidelines for ethical and legal matters as they pertain to clients, coworkers, and practical settings. It outlines the acceptable behavior and conduct that social workers must abide by to practice in the field. The Association of Social Work Boards, along with each local, province, and state social work board, maintain this code of ethics.

Every social worker is held to a set of ethical standards. Those ethical standards include ethical responsibility to their clients, to colleagues, to the social work board, to their work in practical settings, and to the field of social work as a profession.

Ethical responsibility to colleagues means to treat them with respect, keep shared information confidential, collaborate and consult with them in the interests of a client, and make client referrals when a colleague has more expertise that can help that client. It also pertains to a social worker's responsibility to avoid sexual harassment and address the impairment, incompetence, or unethical conduct of colleagues.

Ethical responsibilities in practical settings pertain to supervision, consultations, education, training, continued education, staff development, performance evaluations, client records, billing, client transfers, administration, commitments to their employers, and disputes in labor management.

Ethical responsibility as a professional social worker refers to professional competence, private conduct, avoiding discrimination, dishonesty, fraud, deception, impairment, misrepresentation, and solicitations, and acknowledging responsibility and credit in a professional capacity.

Ethical responsibilities in regard to the field of social work as a profession refer to professional integrity, evaluation, research, and social welfare.

Client Rights

Aside from knowing your ethical and legal responsibilities as a social worker, you must also know and understand the legal rights of clients. An extensive code of ethics exists for all social workers, but the following list includes some of the most important key rights that clients have. Social workers must make their clients aware of these rights. Social workers themselves should know them and must not violate them.

Here are some of the client rights:

- Confidentiality and privacy

- Informed consent
- Access to services
- Self-determination
- Service plans
- Options for alternative services
- Referrals to alternative services
- The right to refuse services
- The right to terminate services

The rights to confidentiality and privacy are two sides of the same coin. These require social workers to inform their clients of how their information will be used and under what circumstances it will be shared.

The right to access services refers to a client's right to know all of the programs that are offered through their local social services. Social workers are required to disclose all offered services and not just the ones they feel the client might qualify for.

The right to access records means that the client has the right to request and gain access to their personal records, under normal circumstances. Exceptions to this rule apply if the release of records is made by a client who does not possess the mental capacities to advocate on their own behalf or if the social worker can show with validity that the release of the records and information could cause harm to the client.

The right of informed consent means that the client must be presented with all the necessary information about a service or treatment to make an informed decision. The information must include the details of the treatment or service and the side effects or the risks involved. Furthermore, it requires that the client signs a form, which essentially states that they understand the treatment or service, have been informed of the effects, and agree to go through with the service or treatment.

Clients have the right to be presented with services and treatment. The right of self-determination is the client's right to be given the support to accept or decline those services as they see fit. Even involuntary social service clients, who exist due to court orders, parental enrollment, or other such assignment, still have the right to self-determination unless they are legally ruled incompetent to advocate for themselves or otherwise mentally unfit to make their own decisions.

Service plan rights mean that a client has the right to know how involved they can be in the development and application of their services or treatment plans.

The right to alternative services and referrals is a client's right to be informed of services offered through other facilities or providers and the right to be referred to those alternative programs.

The right to refuse services applies to the client's rights to refuse services, medications, and treatments, except when court ordered. They should also be informed of the possible consequences of doing so.

The right to terminate services is a client's right to be told what the policies are with regard to terminating services or treatments and their ability to do so within the guidelines of those policies.

Evaluation and research rights are in place because several social service agencies involve clients in evaluation and research activities. When this is the case, social workers should inform clients about their policies and procedures about these activities, and how the client's information will be protected if used in such circumstances.

Models of Supervision and the Ethical Responsibility of Supervisors and Managers

There are different positions within social work. Social work supervisors oversee multiple social workers and their cases. Typically, social work supervisors operate under one of five models of supervision:

1. Directive
2. Alternative
3. Collaborative
4. Nondirective
5. Creative

Here are some of the key ethical issues a social work supervisor will face:

- Informed consent – It occurs when the individual or individuals involved are aware of the possible consequences or outcomes and choose to consent or grant permission with the full knowledge of that information.
- Competency – It is an individual's mental ability to understand the things that are going on and actively participate in their role and decisions pertaining to a situation, decision, or procedure.
- Protection of the public – It is the ability to investigate situations, carry out assessments, and collect necessary information to evaluate a situation and offer assistance and services in the event that a qualifying situation or environment is discovered. They have the right to step in and take action if policies, plans, and actions are not conducted and the situation persists in a way that endangers themselves, others, or the public.
- Accurate representation to the public – It is the action of representing the public in a genuine and truthful way. It puts the needs and interests of the public first and adequately advocates on their behalf.

- Confidentiality – It is the act of keeping information private, only to use it or share it in a legal and ethical manner with permitted parties or persons.
- Documentation and record keeping – It is when the materials or resources used to provide official information or evidence must be recorded in a legal capacity. Documentation can include paper notes, digital notes, digital recordings, or any other approved method in one's field.
- Boundary issues and multiple relationships – Boundary issues in social work occur when there are potential or actual conflicts of interest between a social worker and a client. These conflicts can include anything that crosses a social worker and client's professional life with the social worker's personal life. Similarly, multiple relationships, also known as dual relationships, refer to a social worker having a therapeutic role in a client's life when the client is also a student, friend, family member, employee, business associate, or anyone that has a personal connection to the therapist. This undoubtedly causes a significant conflict of interest.
- Diversity – Diversity refers to race, ethnicity, national origin, color, social class, religious or spiritual affiliations, status of immigration, gender, sexual orientation, gender identity, marital status, or disability status.
- Self-determination – It is a client's right to make their own decisions and choices. It is an important point to respect and abide by, especially to encourage client engagement and cooperation. When it comes to self-determination, social workers have the task of being a support system in addition to their typical role.
    - This is done by offering choices to clients, honoring the choices the client makes, setting small goals or projects for clients to meet, following-up on their decision making and progress, offering opportunities when able, and highlighting and encouraging the client's strengths.
    - Ethically, it is important for social workers to inform clients of their rights as well as any information they may need in a clear and well-informed manner. These rights include confidentiality and privacy rights, informed consent, access to services, access to records, service plans, their options for alternative services, the right to review services, and their right to start grievance procedures.

A Supervisor's Purpose and the Types of Roles They May Play

Supervisors have typically completed more schooling and continued education than those beneath them. Their role is to use that information to help social workers who assign case work. They must then oversee this case work.

Social work supervisors include the following:

- Administrative supervisors
- Educational supervisors
- Clinical supervisors
- Supportive supervisors

Client/Social Worker Legal and Ethical Professional Boundaries

It is important to set professional boundaries, especially in social work, where interactions are incredibly personal and oftentimes invasive. The key boundaries of social work include the following:

- Client focus – Make the needs of the client your central focus when making decisions regarding them and their lives.
- Self-disclosure – Refrain from sharing personal details about yourself with clients.
- Dual relationships – Avoid any kind of outside or personal relationships with clients. They cannot be related to you, you cannot provide outside support to them, and you cannot employ a client.
- Work within your competence – Know your professional limitations and what you are personally capable of. Use the resources of other professionals, ask for advice, or find other support in the event that you are out of your depth.
- Look after yourself – It is your responsibility to make sure you are fit to do your job. This includes managing your emotional health and life stresses.

The points listed above as well as your code of ethics are a firm foundation that will help ensure a balance in your professional career. There are gray areas in the profession of social work. For instance, social workers may disclose personal information as a means of strengthening their professional relationship on a therapeutic level to develop trust and understanding.

The professional and ethical boundaries that social workers need to maintain in their profession are for the benefit of both the social worker and their client. To help maintain those professional boundaries, social workers are encouraged to do the following:

- Increase their awareness of countertransference on the part of the social worker.
- Cope with client transference head on if and when it begins.
- Pay attention to clients during coaching and note any resistance to that guidance.
- Look out for clues that point to anxiety or resistance.
- Practice self-reflection.

Ethical Issues That May Arise in the Field of Social Work

- Obligations to minors
- Boundaries in a therapeutic capacity
- Personal, moral, and religious beliefs and boundaries
- The right to self-determination
- Privacy
- Confidentiality

Identifying and Resolving Issues of Ethics

At one time or another, most social workers will face an ethical dilemma. How you deal with it can say a lot about your professional ethics and your personal morality. So, when facing such an issue, it's important to ask these questions:

1. Who is involved?
2. What action is required?
3. Is the action ethical or unethical?
4. Are there legal issues to consider?
5. Do any additional standards need to be applied?
6. In what context does this occur?
7. What is the purpose of taking such action?
8. Are there alternative actions that can be considered and possibly taken? If so, why or why not?
9. What conflicts can arise?
10. Are there other moral, ethical, or legal dilemmas?
11. Who is responsible for making these decisions?
12. Does another party need to be involved in this process?
13. What are the ways to resolve any and all issues that may have arisen?
14. What choice was made to resolve the issue?

The United States state and federal legislations that may apply here include the following:

- Act to Promote Public Health Through Workplace Safety for Social Workers – H3864
- Boni Frederick Bill, Kentucky – SB59
- Social Worker Safety Bill, West Virginia – SB2566
- Teri Zenner Social Work Safety Act – H1490
- Occupational Safety and Health Act of 1970

"Red Flag" Behaviors in Social Worker–Client Relationships That Can Indicate Ethical and Legal Violations

It's important for social workers to maintain professional boundaries with clients. In fact, it's a key part of their code of ethics. As such, it's important to learn what types of behaviors are "red flags" to help you judge whether a relationship may be crossing the line and violating those boundaries. These violations include the following behaviors from a social worker:

- Giving clients their personal contact information
    - Home address
    - Home phone number or personal cell phone number
    - Personal email address
    - Social media account contact information

- Communicating with clients by text message on personal or company cell phones
- Being overly friendly or affectionate with clients, giving hugs, giving kisses, rubbing shoulders, or using personal contact to greet, comfort, or support clients
- Spending excessive amounts of time on the phone with a client (This can be during work hours, personal time, or both.)
- Dressing provocatively when seeing a client or clients
- Spending excessive amounts of time with a client, both scheduled and nonscheduled
- Talking excessively about a particular client, or frequently relating to a client
- Sharing personal details and experiences with a client
- Giving personal financial contributions to a client or paying for things not covered by the agency
- Using drugs or alcohol with clients
- Coworkers noticing a personal relationship with the client
- Client's family and friends noticing the relationship

The Legal and Ethical Issues of Death and Dying in Social Work

When it comes to death and dying, end-of-life decisions are important. In fact, there are key legal and ethical issues that occur for end-of-life care. These cover the patient's ability to make decisions for themselves, their right to refuse or withhold treatment, and the right to withdraw life-sustaining support.

Ethics in Regard to Research

In the world of social work, research and statistics are sometimes collected and analyzed to assist in developing better practices and procedures, gain understanding, and better understand situations and situational occurrences. This research is important, but it is even more important that such personal and invasive work is conducted in an ethical and legal manner.

To do this, there are important principles to follow:

- Ensure that the individuals, groups, or communities that are studied are protected both during and after the research.
- Ensure that participants who are vital to the scientific studies and activities are mentored and supported in an effective and ethical manner.
- Ensure that clear, apparent, and implicit conflicts of interest are handled in an ethical and legal manner.
- Conduct yourself in an ethical and professional manner when working with other professionals and those in other fields of work or study.
- Ensure that any problems that occur in research or in research data are properly, ethically, and legally managed.

- Ensure that authorships and publications are conducted and executed by reliable and respected individuals or parties.
- Contribute to the peer-review process in a responsible, ethical, and legal manner.
- Ensure that you understand the meaning and forms of research misconduct and that you prevent research misconduct in an ethical and legal way.

In social work, there are a wide array of research practices that may be used. These practices include the following:

- Action research – It is conducted by studying a community and assessing its needs. The aim is to develop a specialized program that will meet those needs.
- Community-based participatory research – It uses a collaboration of all stakeholders across the board to identify issues, research and design changes, implement effective change, and achieve goals. It also involves the community and professionals to contribute the skills and perspectives needed.
- Control group – It is an identical group of people used to compare those you will be serving against.
- Double-blind studies – It is a study where both the subject and the researcher are not aware of whether the subject has received a placebo or the treatment. This is done to ensure that the treatment and care are the same across the board and prevent unconscious bias from affecting the results.
- Field study – It is the collection of raw data or information. Such information is collected outside a lab or formal research setting.
- Longitudinal study – It is research that is conducted repeatedly over a set period of time. Such studies can be done over short or long periods and focus on observation.
- Mixed methods – It is the process of mixing multiple methods of research together to obtain a more comprehensive and detailed analysis.
- Focus group – It is a small group, similar in demographic, who answers research associated questions to gauge how those in a similar situation would most likely respond.
- Pilot study – It tests a new idea or project on a small scale. Such studies can help analyze the effectiveness of a project, its cost, the community response, any possible drawbacks, overall performance, and likelihood of success on a large scale before such a project is launched to full capacity.

Social Workers, Professional Development, Risks, and Developing Protocols

Social workers will be sent into a variety of situations and environments. It is therefore important that social workers are able to assess risk and safety.

Vital knowledge and skills that a social worker needs to possess include the following:

- Risk assessment – This is used to determine whether a client is potentially violent or has a propensity for violence.
- Plan for safety – These are the procedures and actions that are supposed to be followed when with a client or transporting a client.
- Verbal de-escalation techniques – These are used to defuse or de-escalate a situation that is potentially or actually explosive.
- Nonviolent self-defense – A training that is specially tailored for mental health professionals or those working with individuals with mental health issues who may be unaware or not in control of their mental faculties. These clients may therefore act irrationally or violently in a way that they are not in control of. Such training is designed to protect the individual without causing lethal harm to the other person, and in many cases to subdue the individual to eliminate the active threat or danger.

Here are more general guidelines put into place for social workers and client safety:

- Develop or encourage a safe climate when meeting.
- Have set, uniform policies in each division of an agency to ensure that all employees are trained and respond in the approved and accepted manner for a given situation.
- Adequately fulfill the needs of staff.
- Develop comprehensive safety procedures for office visits, home visits, and public or community visits.
- Create safety procedures pertaining to weapons, substance abuse, and other perceived threats.

It is important to take steps to keep social workers, support staff, administrators, and guests safe. Protocols need to be put in place for everyone's overall safety. When it comes to the safety of social workers and clients, it is important to do these steps:

- Check new or proposed client records for individuals with a history of violence.
- Regularly check current client records for a propensity for violent behavior, aggression, or overly impulsive outbursts.
- Put in place systems that alert staff members of a dangerous situation or client.
- Require special training and continued re-education regarding potentially violent clients.
- Have a set protocol for when security should be alerted, when the police should be involved, and when and how the office or facility should be evacuated in the event that it becomes dangerous for staff and guests.

Professional Standards

Professional standards in this context are the set practices, ethics, and behavior of a social work group. Such professional standards include the following:

- Accountability
- Confidentiality
- Fiduciary duties
- Honesty
- Integrity
- Law abidance
- Loyalty
- Objectivity
- Transparency

Confidentiality in Social Work

Confidentiality is an important part of social work. However, it does not always apply. This is because social workers are required to report anything that signals imminent harm to others, including clients.

The elements of client reports in the social work system include demographic information, intake material, assessments, quarterly reviews, reassessing, service plan goals, discharge plans, releases of information, referrals, and correspondence.

Here are the six principles to adhere to when breaching confidentiality in social work:

1. Justify the purpose for a breach in confidentiality.
2. Refrain from using information that can identify the client unless it is required.
3. Ensure that only the necessary client information is shared.
4. Identifiable client information should strictly be released on a need-to-know basis.
5. Every individual with access to identifiable client information needs to know the rules of confidentiality and abide by them.
6. Understand the law and ensure compliance.

Client information and records are of course composed and seen by the social worker and also typically seen by the social worker's supervisor. Additionally, any colleague that has a reasonable need to know the client's information will also have access to it. Most often, this information includes any client concerns, the goals that the client and social worker have set, the plan on how those goals should be reached, professional records that follow the client and their progress, and compliance and effectiveness of the services being used.

Record Keeping in the Social Work Field

Record keeping is an important part of taking care of each client in a social worker's caseload. This is, in part, exceedingly important because sometimes cases are handed off to other social workers. This can be especially true when a social worker goes on vacation, takes maternity leave, is otherwise on leave, or leaves an agency permanently.

Ensuring that clear, decisive, and detailed records are kept is all for the overall benefit of the client. It allows anyone who may need to see their records to know what assessments have been done and what issues were determined. They can also find out what plans were put into place, what services, treatment, or assistance was provided, how much progress has been made to reach set goals, where in the discharge process a client may be, what follow-up arrangements have been made, and so on.

Typically, social workers' records are kept for at least six years; however, if the client is a minor, most states require that the records be kept for at least six years after the child reaches their eighteenth birthday.

Many social work agencies and organizations adhere to eight principles for social work record keeping. Here are those eight principles:

- Accountability
- Transparency
- Integrity
- Protection
- Compliance
- Accessibility
- Retention
- Disposition

Professional Development and Use of Self in Social Work

Professional development refers to the wide range of ways in which individuals improve and expand their professional competencies, knowledge, skill base, and effectiveness in their positions. Use of self refers to the targeted and level-headed use of the knowledge and skills they already possess. Therefore, professional development and use of self are using the skills that you have as a social worker and the expansion of those skills and abilities through further education and training.

Client and Social Worker Principles and Techniques of System Relationships

System relationships refer to the professional relationships between social workers and their clients. The foundation for that relationship is to have a clear understanding of the professional relationship and outline of services to be established.

Social workers provide support and services to help a client through a situation, assist them in gaining independence, connect them to needed services, and support them as they seek services and assistance.

Development and Organization in Social Work

Social work is about helping others by assessing their individual needs, using available resources to offer them assistance and support for those needs, and ultimately helping individuals to a point of self-sustainability. To this end, organizations are created to meet the needs of individuals, couples, families, groups, and communities. Such organizations are structured in different ways to provide for their target audiences and communities. Organizations can include, on their own or in combination, these elements:

- Advisory boards
- Board of directors
- Bureaucracy
- Consensus models
- For-profit organizations
- Mission statements
- Non-profit organizations
- Organizational charts
- Organizational cultures

Organizations and How Their Social Workers are Taken Care Of

It is important that social work organizations and agencies maintain a specific level of educated, well-trained, and professional staff. This is important to maintain a well-run, high-performing, ethically-based, and quality service providing agency.

To ensure that the social workers employed at each agency are sufficiently taken care of is part of making things run well. It also ensures that the social workers stay with the agency. Here are some of the things agencies can do to help their social workers stay up to date on their practical methods of social work and ensure they don't get burnt out:

- Continue education and training from reputable and current sources.
- Offer or require that social workers meet with a counselor or psychologist at regular intervals to check in.
- Provide emotional support.
- Keep caseloads to a realistically manageable level.
- Ensure adequate supervision and case support.
- Be honest with staff.
- Keep the agency as organized as possible.
- Allow for clear and concise communication.
- Address issues in a compassionate and empathetic way.
- Insist that social workers practice self-care and ensure that breaks or vacations are taken.

Self-care is probably one of the key factors in avoiding burnout and maintaining overall health and wellness as a social worker. While self-care does include eating right, exercising, and getting a healthy amount of sleep, there are other elements as well. Self-care is about maintaining physical health and wellness, mental health and wellness, and emotional health and wellness.

Such care eliminates burnout, gives a healthy outlet to pent-up stress, and alleviates emotional stress. Social workers are required to be very empathetic and compassionate in their field, which can often take a serious toll if not handled properly. In fact, it is said that as part of the self-care process, social workers should ensure that they do these:

- Take adequate breaks.
- Set professional short-term goals to reach and take short breaks once each goal is met.
- Don't take on new commitments unless they have the time to accommodate them while still maintaining self-care.
- Ensure they have a healthy support system.
- Connect with their emotions, let themselves feel, and then let those emotions go in a healthy way.
- Always be mindful of themselves and their needs.

The Dynamics of Social Worker and Client Relationships within the System

Social workers face an array of possible problems on a daily basis. These issues can include encounters with differing personalities and difficult issues that need to be addressed. Social workers must be able to deal with individuals from different backgrounds, cultures, and religions. The problems they need to solve will be just as different and diverse as the people involved. Cultural competencies will play a major role in that interaction and the social worker's ability to help in an effective way.

Social workers and clients develop a professional relationship that is closer than most other types of professional relationships. As such, it's important to set and maintain boundaries. A positive relationship is required for clients to trust the social workers they are working with and for social workers to facilitate services and help the client in a healthy way.

This positive social worker and client relationship is an important factor in the client's overall performance in services and programs, as well as in their ability to meet goals, complete intervention plans, and successfully leave the system.

Social workers must be attentive, as some clients do not always want help; sometimes, they are only looking for sympathy rather than actual support and help. To help a client, they must genuinely want the assistance; Otherwise, intervention planning, services, and other such assistance will be wasted.

Social workers are facilitators. They are there to assist in the intervention process, track client progress, set additional goals if needed, and advocate for clients.

Social workers are problem solvers, advocates, brokers, change agents, counselors, and mediators. They wear multiple hats and juggle multiple roles within agencies.

Positive and Safe Work Environments as a Social Worker

There are a few key points to have and maintain a positive and safe work environment as a social worker:

- Ensure good communication.
- Listen to supervisors, professional peers, and other associates.
- Recognize and appreciate hard work.
- Show trust.
- Enjoy the job and find fun in what you do.
- Lead the way for others.

Time Management and Social Work

Time management is important in any profession, but managing time as a social worker is key in balancing caseloads and ensuring the even distribution of time and attention to all clients. There are many methods that social workers can use to keep themselves organized and ensure that they manage their time as efficiently as possible.

Here are some ways of keeping yourself organized:

- Make to-do lists for tasks that need to be completed.
- Have one designated day each week in which you only take absolutely necessary calls or reply to essential emails so you can focus on writing up reports and completing paperwork.
- Have a routine of taking notes during phone calls or meetings about what is said so you can refer back to those notes for important information.
- Make referrals immediately once needs are established.
- Have a goal for the end of each day to look forward to.
- Reflect on yourself, your personality, and your approach in regard to time management.

Test 1: Questions

(1) Twenty-seven-year-old Alex is in a phase of self-discovery. He explores various career paths while he seeks to define his identity and role in society. According to Erik Erikson's human growth and development theory, what stage is Alex most likely in?

(A) Infant and toddler.

(B) Young child.

(C) Young adult.

(D) Middle-aged adult.

(2) Sarah reflects on her life's successes and adventures. Although she worries about deteriorating physical health, she is happy and gratified by the relationships she has cultivated. According to Erikson's theory, which stage of human growth and development is Sarah most likely in?

(A) Teenage years.

(B) Older adult.

(C) Older child.

(D) Young adult.

(3) Mia displays remarkable wisdom and curiosity for a five-year-old. Her parents have noticed her keen ability to observe and imitate her family members and favorite cartoon characters. After Mia witnesses her parents compliment her sister's musical ability, she tries to play the piano independently to win her parents' approval. Which human development theory best describes Mia's actions?

(A) Bandura's social learning theory.

(B) Bowlby's attachment theory.

(C) Erikson's psychosocial development theory.

(D) Freud's psychosexual development theory.

(4) Kiara is confrontational and always blames others when challenges arise. She does not attempt to manage her anger. Which of the following signs shows that she is a perpetrator of abuse?

(A) She shifts responsibility onto others in a confrontational way.

(B) She makes genuine efforts to address and control her anger.

(C) She consistently apologizes and seeks resolution when conflicts arise.

(D) She seeks professional help and support to manage her emotions.

(5) Three-year-old Emily has been attending the same daycare facility for a while. Miss Laura, Emily's primary caretaker, recently took a week off. During this time, Emily would cry for several hours and appear distraught after dropoff. She turned down comfort from the other caregivers and seemed distant for the rest of the day. When Miss Laura returned, Emily initially ignored her. She later displayed signs of anger and rejection toward her. Which fundamental idea of John Bowlby's attachment theory best describes Emily's actions while Miss Laura was away?

(A) First key point: Children have a natural need to form bonds with their primary caregivers from birth.

(B) Second key point: From birth until age five, an infant's attachment and bonding are most important.

(C) Third key point: Maternal neglect during the first five years of life might have long-lasting consequences.

(D) Fourth key point: Distress has several levels depending on how temporarily connected you are to your primary attachment source.

(6) A social worker is working with 7-year-old Samantha who consistently displays intense distress when separated from her primary caregiver and struggles to be consoled upon the caregiver's return. According to John Bowlby's stages of attachment, Samantha is likely exhibiting behaviors from which of the following stages?

(A) Secure Attachment.

(B) Ambivalent Attachment.

(C) Avoidant Attachment.

(D) Disorganized Attachment.

(7) Ten-year-old Sarah and her family recently relocated. She will attend a new school where no one knows her. Sarah boldly engages in discussion with her peers and eagerly participates in extracurricular activities. Which fundamental idea of John Bowlby's attachment theory relates to Sarah's successful integration into her new school and neighborhood?

(A) The consequences of parental neglect over time.

(B) The importance of forming bonds in the first two years of life.

(C) The creation of an internal workable model.

(D) The phases of distress that a person goes through when temporarily separated.

(8) Forty-year-old Mark grapples with loneliness and a pervasive lack of happiness. He questions his contribution to his family, impact on society, and sense of belonging. According to Erik Erikson, which stage of development is Mark most likely experiencing?

(A) Identity vs. role confusion.

(B) Generativity vs. stagnation.

(C) Intimacy vs. isolation.

(D) Ego integrity vs. despair.

(9) At age sixteen, Emma explores diverse hobbies and interests while she seeks to build personal connections with her family, friends, and classmates. This is part of an effort to better understand herself and her identity. Which phase of Erik Erikson's psychological development most accurately sums up Emma's current stage?

(A) Trust vs. mistrust.

(B) Initiative vs. guilt.

(C) Identity vs. role confusion.

(D) Intimacy vs. isolation.

(10) Despite her recent retirement, Sarah contends with profound sorrow and emptiness. Her beloved husband of more than four decades has passed, which ended a relationship that blossomed during their high school years. According to Erik Erikson's theory, which stage of development is Sarah most likely experiencing?

(A) Generativity vs. stagnation.

(B) Intimacy vs. isolation.

(C) Identity vs. role confusion.

(D) Ego integrity vs. despair.

(11) Alex has just started preschool. He shows a growing interest in asserting his independence and taking control of his life. His parents are uncertain about the potential impact of granting him substantial freedom. Where in Sigmund Freud's evolution is Alex most likely to be?

(A) Oral.

(B) Anal.

(C) Phallic.

(D) Latency.

(12) Mia, a sixteen-year-old high school student, is going through a period of self-discovery. She spends a lot of time reading, researching various topics, talking with her peers, and participating in community activities. According to Jean Piaget, which stage of cognitive development is Mia most likely in?

(A) Sensorimotor stage.

(B) Preoperational stage.

(C) Concrete operational stage.

(D) Formal operational stage.

(13) Jacob is a gifted artist. He has an enormous desire to form deep relationships with other people. He frequently feels uneasy and uncertain when he expresses his feelings because he fears rejection. According to Erik Erikson's theory, which stage of psychological development is Jacob most likely going through?

(A) Trust vs. mistrust.

(B) Autonomy vs. shame.

(C) Intimacy vs. isolation.

(D) Ego integrity vs. despair.

(14) Emily recently took an early retirement from her long-term job. She is currently in a period of reflection. She contemplates her life and scrutinizes her past interactions. She questions whether she has lived a fulfilling life. According to Erik Erikson, which stage of psychosocial development is Emily likely to be going through?

(A) Industry vs. inferiority.

(B) Identity vs. role confusion.

(C) Generativity vs. stagnation.

(D) Ego integrity vs. despair.

(15) Seven-year-old Liam has just started school. He constantly asks questions, explores fresh ideas, and shows a deep curiosity and drive to learn. He likes to make up complicated stories and characters while he plays pretend with his friends, expresses himself through sketching and storytelling, and engages in imaginative play. According to Jean Piaget's theory, what stage of cognitive development is Liam likely going through?

(A) Sensorimotor stage.

(B) Preoperational stage.

(C) Concrete operational stage.

(D) Formal operational stage.

(16) Mrs. Johnson is eighty-five and resides in a nursing home. She remains actively engaged in her community. She places a high value on her friendships and family and readily imparts her wisdom to young individuals seeking guidance. According to Erik Erikson's theory, what stage of cognitive development is Mrs. Johnson most likely to go through?

(A) Intimacy vs. isolation.

(B) Generativity vs. stagnation.

(C) Ego integrity vs. despair.

(D) Identity vs. role confusion.

(17) Linda lost her job earlier this year due to her company's downsizing. She has been skipping meals due to financial constraints. This has resulted in inadequate calorie intake. Which of the six basic needs is Linda NOT currently meeting?

(A) Water.

(B) Sleep.

(C) Food.

(D) Human interaction.

(18) Liam tries to manage his stress and dissatisfaction. His inability to control his thoughts and actions negatively impacts his overall well-being. What aspect of Liam's health and well-being might be problematic?

(A) Mental health and wellness.

(B) Emotional health and wellness.

(C) Physical health and wellness.

(D) Social health and wellness.

(19) Which of the following is not one of the six basic needs?

(A) Safety.

(B) Autonomy.

(C) Novelty.

(D) Affection.

(20) Sarah experiences mood swings and feels aimless. She questions whether her lack of exposure to unique circumstances has led to her emotional problems. Which of the following should Sarah try to restore her equilibrium?

(A) Food.

(B) Human interaction.

(C) Novelty.

(D) Water.

(21) Lily is Sarah and Ethan's newborn daughter and their first child. They have read about the value of attachment and bonding in a child's growth. They remain uncertain about how their early attachment to Lily will influence her future emotional and social development. Which of the following statements best exemplifies the idea of attachment and bonding?

(A) Lily needs alone time in her first year to gain independence.

(B) Lily's brain and hormones need bonding with her parents for normal development.

(C) Early attachment will not affect Lily's future behavior or communication.

(D) Lily's parents should ensure strong communication during adolescence.

(22) Aiden and Liam are twin boys, but they live separately and experience distinct parenting styles. Aiden is brought up in a home where he receives consistent affection, praise for his accomplishments, and regular discipline. Liam has a parent who is less supportive and affectionate and more judgmental. The boys exhibit divergent behaviors and attitudes as they age. Liam is frequently insecure, reluctant to take risks, and has self-esteem issues. Aiden is self-assured, tries new things, and has a positive sense of self. Which of the following best describes Aiden and Liam's differences?

(A) Aiden is naturally confident, while Liam's nervousness is from external factors.

(B) Aiden's behavior is temporary, but Liam's stems from parenting.

(C) Aiden's behavior mirrors his parents' relationship, which is irrelevant to Liam's behavior.

(D) Aiden's growth results from supportive parenting, while a less nurturing upbringing causes Liam's difficulties.

(23) Emma and Mark have a son named Ethan. Their family's dynamics evolve as Ethan ages. Ethan's grandparents become increasingly involved in his life, while Emma and Mark focus more on their professional lives. Because of his desire for independence, Ethan occasionally pushes established behavioral limits. Where do Emma, Mark, and Ethan seem to be in the family life cycle theory?

(A) Stage one.

(B) Stage three.

(C) Stage four.

(D) Stage six.

(24) James and Sarah have been married for over two decades. Their two children recently left home to attend college. They experience a range of emotions as empty nesters. They concentrate on one another, rethink their partnership, and make plans. Where are Sarah and James in the family life cycle theory?

(A) Stage two.

(B) Stage four.

(C) Stage five.

(D) Stage six.

(25) Sixteen-year-old Michael faces physical limitations due to a medical condition. The use of a wheelchair occasionally restricts his participation in certain activities. Despite his disability, Michael is adamant about doing well in school and achieving his goals. He benefits from strong parental involvement and a supportive home environment that bolsters his confidence and resilience. How will his disability impact Michael's family?

(A) Michael's disability will not impact his family.

(B) Michael's family might experience financial hardship due to the cost of accommodating Michael's condition.

(C) As Michael's family joins disability advocacy groups, their social life will advance.

(D) Michael's household will have more opportunities to socialize in public.

(26) Ethan and Liam are identical twin boys. Due to a developmental issue, Ethan needs ongoing care and support. As the boys grow, their parents observe changes in their behavior. Ethan struggles with social interactions, and Liam demonstrates age-appropriate social abilities and habits. Given the information, what explains Ethan's behavior?

(A) Ethan's challenges result from a lack of bonding with his parents.

(B) Ethan exhibits conduct that is typical of all children who struggle with developmental issues.

(C) The abuse Ethan experienced while in foster care led to his behavior.

(D) Ethan's behavior is consistent with a typical response to his parents' love and care.

(27) Emma is going through a challenging phase marked by worry and grief. She has become less social, and her academic performance has declined. Her conduct has changed, and her parents are concerned for her well-being. Will Emma's mental health impact her family as they support her during this challenging time?

(A) Emma's mental health challenges will not impact her family.

(B) Emma's openness about her challenges will benefit her parents' mental health.

(C) Emma's family members might worry and feel upset because of her mental health challenges.

(D) Emma's mental health difficulties will make the family closer together.

(28) Maria fulfills the role of the primary caregiver for her elderly mother, who has Alzheimer's. Maria contends with pervasive sentiments of isolation while she encounters difficulties seeking external assistance. What might occur if Maria does not prioritize her well-being or receive support?

(A) Maria's duties as a caregiver will become easier.

(B) Maria will experience less pressure and loneliness.

(C) Maria's mother's condition will improve.

(D) Maria may experience burnout and adverse mental and physical health effects.

(29) Fifteen-year-old Sarah has moved in and out of foster care since age six. Her frequent transitions between foster families have made the establishment of trusting relationships with her current, caring family challenging. She exhibits aggression and an aversion to physical touch. How does John Bowlby's attachment theory account for Sarah's behavior?

(A) Sarah's early years of inadequate attachment bonding made it difficult for her to develop healthy attachments and caused her to avoid physical contact.

(B) Sarah protects herself aggressively after the trauma she experienced while in foster care.

(C) Sarah is a healthy, happy child who exhibits the standard reluctance to physical touch that all foster children demonstrate.

(D) Sarah's aggressive behavior is brought on by traumatic memories and a sense of displacement from her foster care. She misses her birth family and her previous foster parents.

(30) The Anderson family has just relocated. The two children experience stress because they have to attend a new school. The Andersons' difficult circumstances and family dynamic can be characterized as which of the following?

(A) The Andersons are a nuclear family, and their children feel uprooted.

(B) The Andersons are a large family, and the challenging circumstance is the birth of a new child.

(C) Moving to a new home or school poses a challenging circumstance for the single-parent Anderson family.

(D) The stressful circumstance for the Anderson family is caused by separation or divorce.

(31) Lisa and Mark have been married for five years. They do not want to have children. Spending time together is a priority, and they encourage one another in their personal and professional endeavors. Which element creates a happy and healthy family dynamic for couples like Lisa and Mark?

(A) To be financially secure.

(B) To reside with relatives other than parents in an extended family.

(C) To add a new child or infant to the family to promote joy and happiness.

(D) To prioritize quality time together and maintain a healthy connection.

(32) Lisa has been under a lot of stress and pressure at work because of an increased workload and the demands from her superiors. She often yells at her spouse about unimportant issues rather than directly confronting her feelings. Which psychological protection mechanism is Lisa displaying in her actions?

(A) Denial.

(B) Repression.

(C) Projection.

(D) Displacement.

(33) Jack's recent breakup has left him heartbroken and depressed. He spends significant time working out to cope with his emotions. Which psychological protection is Jack currently employing?

(A) Regression.

(B) Rationalization.

(C) Sublimation.

(D) Repression.

(34) Sarah experiences stress at work due to her substantial workload and deadline pressures. She suffers from regular migraines, insomnia, and anxiety. What kind of stress is Sarah most likely experiencing?

(A) Acute stress.

(B) Episodic stress.

(C) Chronic stress.

(D) Trauma-induced stress.

(35) John recently survived a fatal car collision. Since then, he has been restless, terrified, and emotionally numb. What type of trauma is John experiencing?

(A) Acute trauma.

(B) Complex trauma.

(C) Episodic trauma.

(D) Chronic trauma.

(36) Susan has experienced previous domestic abuse. She grapples with anxiety and depression. She engages in risky behaviors such as binge drinking to cope with her emotions. Why do some people who have been exposed to violence partake in such risky activities?

(A) They engage in risky behaviors to feel euphoria.

(B) They engage in risky behaviors to break the cycle of violence.

(C) They engage in risky behaviors to cope with the trauma.

(D) They engage in risky behaviors to deal with mental health problems.

(37) Why might economic factors affect a person's use of alcohol, drug abuse, or violence?

(A) Economic conditions may result in increased social support.

(B) Economic factors might result in better mental health.

(C) Economic issues could be significant stressors and trigger poor coping mechanisms.

(D) Economic conditions may result in a decrease in drug abuse propensities.

(38) At five years old, Jamie was abandoned by her birth parents and placed in foster care. She was never adopted because of a heart problem and spent much of her time alone. Initially, Jamie would cry when she needed attention or was hungry. At nine months, she stopped crying when left alone. Jamie responds with hostility when her foster parents attempt to show affection. How do Jamie's actions fit into John Bowlby's attachment theory?

(A) Jamie's first five years saw insufficient attachment bonding. Consequently, she is touch-averse and cannot form healthy bonds with her foster parents.

(B) Jamie does not want others to touch her because she was molested in foster care. She defends herself in an age-appropriate way.

(C) Jamie is a well-behaved young person in good health. All foster parents experience these common responses when they adopt a child from foster care.

(D) Jamie longs for her biological parents. She is displaced in foster care, devastated by memories of abandonment, and exhibits expected behavioral outbursts.

(39) What is the main objective of trauma-informed treatment?

(A) To provide prompt medical attention for bodily wounds brought on by trauma.

(B) To deal with the consequences of trauma and lessen long-term harm.

(C) To remove people from circumstances that can cause traumatic reactions.

(D) To help people learn coping skills that will help them avoid future trauma.

(40) What method of trauma-informed care is recommended by the CDC, OPHPR, and NCTIC?

(A) To handle trauma with a single approach.

(B) To act quickly and decisively in a public health emergency.

(C) To manage the situation with care and compassion.

(D) To encourage people to deal with trauma without seeking professional assistance.

(41) Ten-year-old Emily was referred to a social worker due to concerning signs observed by adults at her school. She consistently wears soiled and damaged clothing. She is underweight and often experiences stomach pains. Which of the following assumptions is most likely accurate?

(A) Emma has experienced physical abuse.

(B) Emma is being physically neglected.

(C) Emma is a victim of emotional abuse.

(D) Emma's parents are abusing their mental health.

(42) A child protection officer is investigating a report of possible child abuse. The child is showing extreme dread, social seclusion, and a tendency for self-harm. The officer learns that the child has been exposed to dangerous conditions at home. She also learned that his parents have a history of drug abuse. What is the child most likely experiencing?

(A) He experiences physical abuse.

(B) He has experienced sexual assault.

(C) He experiences emotional abuse and psychological neglect.

(D) He suffers from both parental substance addiction and physical neglect.

(43) Emily receives counseling from Dianna, but she does not talk at all. She avoids eye contact and shies away from developing relationships, especially with therapists and social workers. She also avoids being touched by anybody, even her foster siblings. Dianna thinks Emily might have been abused sexually. What might be holding Emily back from reporting the abuse?

(A) Emily worries that no one will believe her.

(B) Emily holds herself responsible for the abuse.

(C) Emily is physically mistreated.

(D) Emily acts destructively toward herself due to emotional abuse.

(44) Maria appears to be a devoted parent. She shows love for them in public and is actively involved in their lives. However, she frequently criticizes them and calls them her greatest mistake when they are in private. Is Maria abusive?

(A) Maria is not abusive toward her children. She is only stressed.

(B) Maria calls her children names because they do not listen to her. She is not abusive.

(C) Maria abuses her children verbally and emotionally.

(D) Maria does not care about her children.

(45) Mark is highly regarded in his community for his humble lifestyle and consistent volunteer work, even though he may not contribute significant resources. Mark has privately been inflicting emotional abuse on his wife, Lisa, for an extended period. Lisa does not recognize that Mark's repeated hurtful comments about her body, affluent parents, and well-off friends indicate an abusive relationship. She loves him deeply and isolates herself from people he disapproves of to please him. Why does Mark abuse Lisa?

(A) Mark's impulsive and temperamental disposition is the leading cause of his abusive tendencies.

(B) Mark mistreats Lisa because she does not give him enough attention.

(C) Mark's mistreatment of Lisa results from his jealousy and low self-esteem.

(D) Mark abuses Lisa because he takes drugs.

(46) People who mistreat, abuse, or take advantage of others frequently exhibit specific traits. These include which of the following?

(A) Lack of self-assurance and self-confidence.

(B) Pride, jealousy, and envy.

(C) Apathy and absent-mindedness.

(D) Attention-seeking, narcissism, and kindness.

(47) Ethan's parents consistently prioritize their desires over his needs. They show a lack of genuine interest in him. They only seem to pay attention when he falls ill or cries due to hunger. Ethan's mother expresses affection when he is unwell, so he often pretends to be sick to gain loving attention. Which of the following best describes this situation?

(A) Ethan's parents are not deliberately neglectful, but they are not attentive.

(B) Ethan's parents' decision to put their needs ahead of their child's demonstrates that they give their child proper care.

(C) Ethan's parents work very hard, so they cannot give Ethan as much attention as he wants.

(D) Ethan takes advantage of his parents.

(48) Marie is a mother of two young children. She is married to John, who has recently displayed signs of irritability and emotional distance. He often disregards her and avoids communication. Following a heated argument, John's frustration escalated to the point where he physically harmed Marie. He then sincerely expressed remorse for his actions and endeavored to demonstrate his love and support. He attributed his outburst to work-related stress and assured her of his intent to address and change his behavior. Which phase of the abusive relationship cycle does this situation fit into?

(A) Stage one: Tension-building.

(B) Stage two: Abuse and violence.

(C) Stage three: Reconciliation.

(D) Stage four: Calm.

(49) Lisa and Mark have been married for five years. Mark used to be friendly and caring but has lately become more critical of Lisa. He regularly intimidates her and mistreats her emotionally. Mark makes suicide or self-harm threats whenever Lisa tries to speak up for herself. Lisa feels confined and terrified to leave. Which phase of the abusive relationship cycle does this situation fit into?

(A) Stage one: Tension-building.

(B) Stage two: Abuse and violence.

(C) Stage three: Reconciliation.

(D) Stage four: Calm.

(50) Sarah frequently abuses her daughter, Emma, and her husband, John, when she abuses alcohol. Emma tries to distance herself from her mother by playing video games. She also avoids social situations and experiences anxiety when engaging with others. What part does Emma play in the dynamics of the family?

(A) The enabler.

(B) The hero.

(C) The scapegoat.

(D) The lost child.

(51) David and Lisa are drug addicts. Their relationship is declining. They frequently get into intense confrontations while ignoring the needs of their children. Their drug use endangers the children. What are the children in this home experiencing?

(A) Physical and emotional abuse.

(B) Emotional and psychological abuse.

(C) Neglect.

(D) Psychological abuse and neglect.

(52) What does current research suggest about the connection between abuse and addiction?

(A) Addiction and abuse are separate problems with no connection.

(B) Abuse and addiction are behaviors that mutually reinforce one another.

(C) Addiction reduces the likelihood of abuse and acts as a protective factor against it.

(D) All of the above.

(53) Michelle's battle with alcohol addiction has led to a significant deterioration in her behavior. She often directs angry insults toward her children and neglects their essential needs. Her husband, Mark, supports Michelle's addiction by protecting her and justifying her actions. The oldest child, Emily, takes on extra responsibilities to stabilize things at home. Based on the above, what roles are Emily and Mark playing in the family?

(A) Emily is the hero, and Mark is the enabler.

(B) Emily is the enabler, and Mark is the hero.

(C) Both Mark and Emily are enablers.

(D) Mark is an enabler, and Emily is selfish.

(54) How does the cycle of abuse often play out by stage in abusive relationships?

(A) Mounting stress, violence, atonement, serenity.

(B) Honeymoon phase, tension-building, violence, reconciliation.

(C) Tension-building, violence, honeymoon phase, reconciliation.

(D) Reconciliation, honeymoon phase, violence, tension-building.

(55) James is ignoring the risks associated with substance abuse. He appears to think about the substance obsessively and consistently denies having an addiction when questioned. What type of addiction symptoms is James exhibiting?

(A) Overdosage symptoms.

(B) Behavioral symptoms.

(C) Psychological symptoms.

(D) Physical symptoms.

(56) Which of the following are indications of drug abuse?

(A) Tiredness and bloodshot eyes.

(B) Slurred speech and dilated pupils.

(C) Decline in physical health and odd bodily odors.

(D) Sudden loss of weight.

(57) Michael is counseling David, who appears to be battling substance abuse. He has observed David shiver, feel confused, and experience hallucinations. What do these signals tell Michael?

(A) David is experiencing addiction.

(B) David is experiencing an overdose.

(C) David is experiencing symptoms of drug withdrawal.

(D) David is experiencing psychological challenges.

(58) Maria and Sarah are sisters who experienced prejudice because of their ethnicity while growing up in a socioeconomically disadvantaged environment. Maria performed well in school and found a well-paying job. Sarah experienced unemployment and lacked access to healthcare. What do the sisters' differing experiences demonstrate about the impact of an individual's background?

(A) People from similar backgrounds may experience varied outcomes and opportunities.

(B) Discrimination and socioeconomic environments may impact academic success, but they do not affect employment prospects.

(C) A person's development is unaffected by socioeconomic environment or discrimination.

(D) Socioeconomic environments and discrimination impact a person's growth differently.

(59) Which of the following statements best describes social justice?

(A) Social justice means treating everyone similarly under the law.

(B) Social justice entails giving everyone equal access to resources and opportunities.

(C) Social justice refers to feelings of inclusiveness and multiculturalism.

(D) Social justice aims to promote local economic growth and stability.

(60) How might preconceived notions about gender, sexual orientation, race, and ethnicity affect an individual's development?

(A) Preconceived notions affect an individual's personality and degree of success.

(B) Preconceived notions affect an individual's mental health, but not their physical health.

(C) Preconceived notions do not affect an individual's actions or beliefs.

(D) Preconceived notions only affect an individual's financial situation.

(61) What is poverty?

(A) Poverty is defined as limited access to essential medical services.

(B) Poverty results from a lack of resources and failure to meet basic needs.

(C) Poverty is when people struggle to find decent work.

(D) Poverty is defined as living in unsafe areas of a city or neighborhood.

(62) How does poverty affect the overall well-being of communities?

(A) Poverty increases the likelihood of domestic violence and crime.

(B) Poverty increases social services and community participation.

(C) Poverty makes it easier for people to access health care and education.

(D) Poverty does not affect the socioeconomic status of the community.

(63) How does culture influence an individual's personality and behavior?

(A) Culture influences a person's self-assurance, external expression, and values.

(B) Culture influences a person's physical characteristics and appearance.

(C) Culture does not influence a person's attitude or behavior.

(D) Culture influences ancestry and biology.

(64) What is the difference between race and ethnicity?

(A) Race is associated with shared history and tradition. Ethnicity is associated with physical characteristics.

(B) Ethnicity is related to cultural dynamics. Ethnic identity is specific to a society.

(C) Race has cultural significance. Ethnic identity focuses on biological relationships.

(D) Race emphasizes physical characteristics. Ethnicity emphasizes culture and beliefs.

(65) A social worker interacts with people from different ethnic origins. She takes the time to reflect on her presumptions, prejudices, and aspirations to ensure positive interactions. Which principle of culturally sensitive social work practice is she following?

(A) Morals and principles.

(B) Self-awareness.

(C) Cultural sensitivity.

(D) Communication and language.

(66) Mark tries to understand and respect his client's cultural beliefs and customs to provide culturally relevant interventions. Which of the following does Mark demonstrate?

(A) Cross-cultural competencies.

(B) Advocacy and empowerment.

(C) Diverse workforce.

(D) Leading with cultural competence in mind.

(67) Sarah is preparing for her multicultural group internship. She participates in seminars and workshops to learn more about various cultures and how they affect individuals and communities. Which social work practice principle is Sarah trying to implement?

(A) Service provision.

(B) Training for professionals.

(C) Ethics and principles.

(D) Cultural sensitivity.

(68) Alex just adopted they/them pronouns and a gender-neutral name after struggling with gender identity. Due to the lack of support from their friends and family, they suffer from low self-esteem, loneliness, and despair. What aspect of gender identity and expression is Alex exploring?

(A) Sexual preference.

(B) Gender identity.

(C) Gender expression.

(D) Gender roles.

(69) Jamie, a transgender person, has transitioned from male to female. Although content with how she expresses her gender, she encounters stigma and discrimination at work and in her community. Jamie continues to advocate for transgender rights despite these obstacles. What facet of a person's identity does Jamie accept and support?

(A) Gender roles.

(B) Gender expression.

(C) Sexual orientation.

(D) Gender identity.

(70) Emily is counseling a family to cope with financial difficulties and marital issues. Which growth and development theory area will allow Emily to grasp and address these issues successfully?

(A) Feminist theory.

(B) Family life cycle.

(C) Principles of human genetics.

(D) Communication theories and styles.

(71) Jane's client has expressed concern about their personal information potentially being shared with third parties. Jane is committed to addressing these concerns and providing reassurance. Which of the following best describes the principle that Jane should emphasize?

(A) Eligibility criteria.

(B) Informed consent.

(C) Privileged communication.

(D) Just cause.

(72) Tom needs help navigating the complex healthcare system to find the services he needs. His social worker helps him find and use resources. This process is best described as which of the following?

(A) Advocacy.

(B) Accessibility.

(C) Case management.

(D) Community development.

(73) Sarah helps a new social worker, Emily, manage her first cases. Emily often asks Sarah for advice and benefits from her knowledge. This relationship can best be described as:

(A) Cultural competence.

(B) Networking.

(C) Mentorship.

(D) Co-dependency.

(74) During an evaluation, Michael discovers that his client plans to harm others. Which of the following is appropriate in this situation?

(A) Keep the information confidential at all costs.

(B) Share the information only if the client consents.

(C) Release the information for the safety of others.

(D) Wait for explicit instructions from a supervisor.

(75) A social worker monitors the effectiveness of a program that helps young people with drug problems. Which of the following methods would he most likely not implement?

(A) Assess progress made over time in the program.

(B) Use mystery shoppers to evaluate progress firsthand.

(C) Increase the budget for administrative tasks.

(D) Conduct follow-up surveys.

(76) Lisa is assigned to monitor thirty families' needs, assessments, interventions, and other related services. What does this describe?

(A) Case management.

(B) Accessibility.

(C) Caseload.

(D) Core social work values.

(77) James finds himself in a situation where one of the core values of social work conflicts with another. Which of the following best describes this situation?

(A) Ethical practice dilemma.

(B) Vulnerable population.

(C) Global assessment of functioning.

(D) Generalist practice.

(78) Emily assesses an elderly client to determine her ability to perform daily tasks like cooking and cleaning. What assessment does she make?

(A) Needs assessment.

(B) Functional assessment.

(C) Global assessment of functioning.

(D) Employment assessment.

(79) Social workers work with residents of a small rural community to identify needs, develop resources, and build connections. Which term best describes this process?

(A) Indirect practice.

(B) Advocacy.

(C) Community development.

(D) Eligibility criteria.

(80) Which of the following core values of social work focus on a commitment to learning and understanding different cultures, and how do they affect personal identity?

(A) Social justice.

(B) Integrity.

(C) Importance of human relationships.

(D) Cultural competence.

(81) Martha entered counseling because she struggled with depression. During a session, her therapist tried to repeat what Martha said in their own words to ensure understanding. This technique is known as:

(A) Reframing.

(B) Confrontation.

(C) Paraphrasing.

(D) Active listening.

(82) John has been feeling tired and stressed. During his biopsychosocial assessment, his family history revealed a history of mental illness. This would be part of which aspect of his assessment?

(A) Biological.

(B) Social.

(C) Psychological.

(D) Diversity perspective.

(83) Samantha assesses a family. She notices that the parents are warm and caring but do not set clear boundaries for their children. Which of the following best describes the parents?

(A) They are liberal.

(B) They are more interested in their own lives.

(C) They want their children to experience the world without boundaries.

(D) They are neglectful.

(84) A social worker assesses a family where domestic violence is suspected. How can they get more information?

(A) Ask about the child's school grades.

(B) Inquire about family hobbies.

(C) Question how arguments are settled.

(D) Ask about family income.

(85) Tim's social worker is helping him set goals for treatment. He actively helps to shape the plan and prioritize his needs. This collaboration is meant to:

(A) Minimize the social worker's responsibilities.

(B) Prioritize the most important things first.

(C) Focus only on Tim's unhealthy behaviors.

(D) Reject Tim's personal information.

(86) What is essential in assessing a parent with intellectual impairments?

(A) The parent's recreational activities.

(B) The parent's ability to assess a child's situation and respond accordingly.

(C) The parent's employment status.

(D) The parent's educational background.

(87) Lisa observes that the children in a household are well-fed, clothed, and sheltered, but the parents are harsh and critical in their guidance. This could lead to concerns about whether:

(A) The basic care needs of the children are met.

(B) The children are in a safe environment.

(C) The children are provided positive and age-appropriate guidance.

(D) The parents are affectionate toward the children.

(88) What would a social worker look for during an assessment involving parents and children to understand the parent-child relationship?

(A) The parents' income level.

(B) The parents' employment history.

(C) The way the parent talks to the child.

(D) The parents' community profile.

(89) Emily's son avoided school and showed extreme irritability. After a thorough evaluation, he was diagnosed with ADHD. Which characteristics did Emily's son most likely exhibit?

(A) Difficulty paying attention.

(B) Obsession with a particular body type.

(C) Constant feelings of sadness.

(D) Multiple panic attacks.

(90) James' therapist often mirrors his feelings and expressions during counseling to build rapport. This technique is an example of:

(A) Confrontation.

(B) Reflecting.

(C) Open-ended questions.

(D) Summarizing.

(91) Emma counsels a family in which the parents are warm but unable to set realistic limits for their children. She would probably be concerned about which of the following?

(A) The parents' affection toward the children.

(B) The parents' community and recreational activities.

(C) The parents' guidance and boundary-setting.

(D) The parents' health conditions.

(92) Tom's therapist often encourages him to express himself more openly by asking questions that cannot be answered with a simple "yes" or "no." This technique is called:

(A) Confrontation.

(B) Open-ended questioning.

(C) Summarizing.

(D) Paraphrasing.

(93) Dr. Lewis prescribes a mood stabilizer for a depressed patient. What should Dr. Lewis provide with the prescription?

(A) A complete treatment plan.

(B) A list of possible side effects.

(C) An assessment of anxiety.

(D) A cultural competence test.

(94) A client is involved in setting treatment goals. They experience enhanced focus, success, and self-assurance because the social worker requires them to set goals one or two at a time to keep things manageable. This approach is designed to:

(A) Focus only on immediate problems.

(B) Reduce the likelihood of feeling overwhelmed.

(C) Ignore long-term planning.

(D) Concentrate on the social worker's agenda.

(95) In a biopsychosocial assessment, information about a client's age, marital status, race, and community profile is classified into which of the following categories?

(A) Background and current functioning.

(B) Impressions, assessments, and recommendations.

(C) Basic information.

(D) Presenting the problem.

(96) A social worker evaluates a family with suspected substance abuse issues. Which of the following would a social worker focus on in the biological portion of a biopsychosocial assessment?

(A) Employment status.

(B) Community involvement.

(C) Use of drugs or alcohol.

(D) Educational background.

(97) During a biopsychosocial assessment, a social worker notices that their client often mentions feeling overwhelmed by work stress. What part of the biopsychosocial assessment would this information be part of?

(A) Biological.

(B) Psychological.

(C) Social.

(D) Chemical.

(98) Joseph was in therapy to deal with events in his past relationships. What kind of therapy is he likely to receive?

(A) Cognitive behavioral therapy.

(B) Dialectical behavior therapy.

(C) Psychodynamic therapy.

(D) Humanistic therapy.

(99) Elizabeth's client is a child who plays and dances but does not speak. The child never talks to anyone she does not know or has not met. Elizabeth suspects the child has ASD. Which of the following led her to that conclusion?

(A) The child's lack of communication with others.

(B) The child's refusal to talk with others.

(C) The child's shyness.

(D) The child's inability to form bonds with people who are not known.

(100) A social worker wants to determine whether the warm behavior of the mother toward her children is genuine. A social worker can seek an opinion from/using which of the following?

(A) The child's medical records only.

(B) Extended family, friends, educators, and healthcare professionals.

(C) The child's educational background only.

(D) The child's financial records.

(101) A social worker helps their client set treatment goals. Which of the following is not usually included in the treatment plan?

(A) A client's personal information.

(B) A client's favorite hobbies.

(C) A detailed list or diagnosis of current issues or problems.

(D) Measurable objectives to meet those goals.

(102) A parent-child assessment finds that a child rejects their parent's love. What should be the primary concern of the social worker?

(A) The child's education.

(B) The parent-child relationship.

(C) The child's financial support.

(D) The parent's employment status.

(103) Mark met with a client in a confidential, safe, and supportive environment. What kind of therapy does this describe?

(A) Method of treatment.

(B) Counseling intervention.

(C) Behavior plan.

(D) Consideration of culture.

(104) A therapist works with couples where one partner feels threatened by the other. What specific question could the therapist ask to learn about possible domestic violence?

(A) What hobbies do you enjoy together?

(B) What happens when your partner gets upset or angry?

(C) How long have you been married?

(D) What is your joint income?

(105) A client's account is incoherent. What counseling technique could be used to verify the client's narrative?

(A) Reframing.

(B) Paraphrasing.

(C) Active listening.

(D) Confrontation.

(106) A client frequently breaches boundaries established by a social worker. Which technique should the social worker employ?

(A) Role-play.

(B) Limit-setting techniques.

(C) Self-monitoring.

(D) Harm reduction.

(107) Cindy counsels a client struggling with substance abuse. Which of these techniques is the most non-judgmental approach Cindy can use to help the client?

(A) Limit setting techniques.

(B) Role-play.

(C) Harm reduction techniques.

(D) Role modeling technique.

(108) Two colleagues are facing a disagreement at work. They decide to find a solution that satisfies both parties equally. Which conflict resolution method are they likely using?

(A) Avoidance.

(B) Competing.

(C) Collaborating.

(D) Accommodating.

(109) Sarah is a social worker using role-play with a client. What should she do at the end of the role-play session?

(A) Assign homework.

(B) Have a discussion and decompress.

(C) Set new goals.

(D) Evaluate progress.

(110) A social worker using the trauma-informed care method wants to assure the client that they control the process. Which principle is the social worker focusing on?

(A) Safety.

(B) Choice.

(C) Collaboration.

(D) Empowerment.

(111) James has a hard time controlling his emotions. A social worker teaches him how to take care of his mental health. What aspect of self-care is being addressed?

(A) Physical.

(B) Emotional.

(C) Psychological.

(D) Relational.

(112) A social worker teaches new behaviors through imitation in a group counseling session. Which method are they employing?

(A) Role-play.

(B) Role modeling technique.

(C) Limit setting.

(D) Harm reduction techniques.

(113) A client is undergoing anger management therapy. Their social worker employs a method that allows the client to express their feelings while minimizing damaging behavior. Which approach is most likely being used?

(A) Limit setting techniques.

(B) Role-play.

(C) Self-monitoring.

(D) Conflict resolution methods.

(114) A social worker prioritizes interventions encouraging healthy food consumption, participating in exercise activities, and seeking help when needed. What are the main goals of these self-care techniques?

(A) Spiritual.

(B) Relational.

(C) Physical.

(D) Professional.

(115) During a conflict, Tom decides to step back and avoid arguing. What strategy of conflict resolution is he employing?

(A) Competing.

(B) Avoidance.

(C) Collaborating.

(D) Compromising.

(116) A community launches a safe ride program and provides therapies like methadone. These strategies are examples of:

(A) Role modeling techniques.

(B) Limit-setting techniques.

(C) Conflict resolution methods.

(D) Harm reduction techniques.

(117) Rachel works with a social worker to improve a particular undesirable behavior. Together, they establish goals and track progress. Which approach is being used?

(A) Self-monitoring techniques.

(B) Role modeling techniques.

(C) Conflict resolution methods.

(D) Trauma-informed care methods.

(118) Mary sticks to her position during a heated exchange without considering the opposing party's point of view. Which method of resolving disputes is Mary using?

(A) Collaboration.

(B) Competition.

(C) Accommodation.

(D) Compromise.

(119) Tom helps his clients regain control after trauma by giving them the necessary tools. Which trauma-informed care principle is he emphasizing?

(A) Safety.

(B) Trustworthiness.

(C) Collaboration.

(D) Empowerment.

(120) When James and his spouse argue, he reacts quickly and with rage. What technique for controlling his anger could he employ to respond more rationally?

(A) Immediate reaction.

(B) Blaming others.

(C) Think before you speak.

(D) Use sarcasm to lighten the mood.

(121) Sarah experiences headaches and nervousness. She feels overburdened at work. What is the recommended strategy for reducing her stress?

(A) Increase work hours.

(B) Ignore the stress.

(C) Meditate and exercise.

(D) Keep emotions bottled up.

(122) Tom and his social worker are developing a roadmap for his life goals. What approach are they using?

(A) Anger management.

(B) Contracting and goal setting.

(C) Cognitive intervention.

(D) Crisis intervention.

(123) A corporation must deal with an employee who exhibits frequent angry outbursts. Which of the following is a way to help the worker?

(A) Encourage yelling to release anger.

(B) Ignore the problem.

(C) Encourage humor as a tool to reduce tension.

(D) Hold on to feelings of negativity.

(124) A child is undergoing trauma therapy that combines educational and clinical methods. Which technique is being used?

(A) Crisis intervention.

(B) Psychoeducational approach.

(C) Behavioral intervention.

(D) Strengths-based strategy.

(125) Michael is trying to overcome a problem in a short-term manner with the help of his social worker. What approach is being used?

(A) Psychoeducational approach.

(B) Task-centered approach.

(C) Contracting and goal setting.

(D) Crisis intervention.

(126) Susan wants to improve her ability to cope with anger by practicing yoga and meditation. What does success depend upon with this strategy?

(A) The application of relaxation techniques.

(B) A focus on causation and blame of others.

(C) The ability to hold on to feelings of negativity.

(D) The use of sarcasm.

(127) A social worker and a client break down a big goal into small, attainable steps. What technique is being employed?

(A) Anger management.

(B) Partializing technique.

(C) Crisis intervention.

(D) Strengths-based approach.

(128) A therapist focuses on a patient's thoughts, memories, and experiences to resolve psychological issues. What type of intervention is this?

(A) Cognitive intervention.

(B) Behavioral intervention.

(C) Crisis intervention.

(D) Contracting and goal setting.

(129) Jack struggles with high blood pressure. How might stress affect his existing health issue?

(A) It will cure the issue.

(B) It will not have any effect.

(C) It can exacerbate the issue.

(D) It will make the issue disappear.

(130) A social worker helps individuals build on their strengths and actively involves them in treatment decisions. What strategy is being used?

(A) Cognitive and behavioral intervention.

(B) Strengths-based and empowerment approach.

(C) Contracting and goal setting.

(D) Task-centered approach.

(131) An organization wants employees to set and follow regular daily routines and benefit from positive reinforcement. What kind of strategy might this refer to?

(A) Crisis intervention.

(B) Behavioral intervention.

(C) Contracting and goal setting.

(D) Strengths-based strategy.

(132) Jessica struggles with anxiety and frequently experiences self-critical thoughts. Which treatment approach is best for her situation?

(A) Crisis intervention model.

(B) Cognitive behavioral therapy.

(C) Task-centered practice.

(D) Solution-focused therapy.

(133) After a natural disaster, a community is in immediate need of help. Which model would social workers most likely employ?

(A) Narrative therapy.

(B) Solution-focused therapy.

(C) Cognitive behavioral therapy.

(D) Crisis intervention model.

(134) Tim's family has persistent disagreements that appear to be rooted in their cultural heritage and belief systems. What kind of family therapy is appropriate for them?

(A) Strategic family therapy.

(B) Narrative family therapy.

(C) Systemic family therapy.

(D) Structural family therapy.

(135) Michelle is determined to confront her problems proactively and seeks assistance to achieve her goals. Which therapeutic method places the most significant emphasis on the client's strengths?

(A) Task-centered practice.

(B) Cognitive behavioral therapy.

(C) Solution-focused therapy.

(D) Crisis intervention model.

(136) A group of individuals with a common illness unite to support each other. What type of group is this?

(A) Psychoeducational group.

(B) Mutual aid group.

(C) Advocacy group.

(D) Educational group.

(137) In a group therapy session, members experience conflicts and misunderstandings. What stage of group development is this?

(A) Forming.

(B) Storming.

(C) Norming.

(D) Performing.

(138) Mary feels overwhelmed by a complex problem. Her social worker is helping her break the problem down into smaller tasks. What therapy is being used?

(A) Task-centered practice.

(B) Solution-focused therapy.

(C) Crisis intervention model.

(D) Narrative therapy.

(139) A couple is experiencing communication issues and wishes to understand their family dynamics better. Which therapy might be most effective?

(A) Strategic family therapy.

(B) Structural family therapy.

(C) Transgenerational therapy.

(D) Psychoeducational therapy.

(140) An organization attempts to empower local communities to enact social change. What type of group are they most likely forming?

(A) Advocacy groups.

(B) Educational groups.

(C) Mutual aid groups.

(D) Psychotherapy or counseling groups.

(141) James struggles to cope with the trauma of a violent crime. What type of therapy is most appropriate for him?

(A) Narrative therapy.

(B) Crisis intervention model.

(C) Family systems therapy.

(D) Problem-solving model.

(142) During family therapy, the therapist explores past issues that may foreshadow future conflicts. What approach is the therapist using?

(A) Transgenerational therapy.

(B) Strategic family therapy.

(C) Structural family therapy.

(D) Systemic family therapy.

(143) Emily feels trapped by her problems and cannot imagine improvement. Which therapy would help her view her issues as separate from herself?

(A) Narrative therapy.

(B) Solution-focused therapy.

(C) Task-centered practice.

(D) Problem-solving model.

(144) Sarah's client often feels overwhelmed by significant goals. What strategy should she use to ensure success in the intervention process?

(A) Set unrealistically high goals to challenge the client.

(B) Create realistic and attainable goals.

(C) Ignore the client's concerns and push for progress.

(D) Suggest that the client does not set any goals.

(145) James notices that his client often seems more focused after dinner. What approach could James suggest to this client?

(A) Avoid doing homework after dinner.

(B) Do homework immediately after dinner.

(C) Only have dinner after completing all homework.

(D) Skip dinner to have more time for homework.

(146) Jane is a dedicated social worker known for her involvement in the promotion of social justice and advocacy for the rights of marginalized individuals. She boldly challenges systemic inequality and advocates for socially conscious policy change. What basic moral principle does Jane exemplify in her actions?

(A) Service.

(B) Dignity and worth of the person.

(C) Social justice.

(D) Importance of interpersonal relationships.

(147) Nathan is an experienced social worker. He is well-versed in many aspects of social work and constantly seeks opportunities to learn and improve. What basic moral principle is evident in Nathan's character?

(A) Competence.

(B) Integrity.

(C) Worth and dignity.

(D) Value of interpersonal relationships.

(148) Hannah aspires to become a social worker and is keen to begin her career. She has completed a master's degree in social work from an accredited program and now prepares for her licensing exam. What is the primary purpose of the licensure examination for social workers?

(A) Verify eligibility for ongoing education.

(B) Ensure foundational skills and knowledge.

(C) Evaluate specialized professional skills.

(D) Facilitate social work education programs.

(149) Sophia is a dedicated social worker who loves her job. Her colleague, Jack, appears to react inappropriately to a vulnerable client. Sophia believes that Jack's actions are harmful to the client and violate ethical standards. What is the appropriate course of action in this situation?

(A) Sophia should talk directly to Jack about her concerns.

(B) Sophia should ignore the situation and focus on her clients.

(C) Sophia should report her concerns to her superior.

(D) Sophia should share her concerns with colleagues and seek their opinions.

(150) What is the primary purpose of the National Association of Social Workers (NASW) code of ethics?

(A) It determines rules for social interaction.

(B) It guides ethical and legal issues in social work.

(C) It explains what social work professionals do.

(D) It supports social workers in financial need.

(151) Elena is counseling Alex, who grapples with drug-related issues. Elena discovers that Alex is unaware of the potential risks associated with the treatment process. What essential right must Elena consider?

(A) Right to do her job.

(B) Right to informed consent.

(C) Right to other assistance.

(D) Right to discontinue service.

(152) What decisions can clients make in social work?

(A) To avail of any service they want.

(B) To refuse any service except one ordered by a court.

(C) To access their records.

(D) To access new services or referrals.

(153) John leads a team of social workers. He grants his team autonomy and involves them in decision-making. Recently, John encountered a situation where a team member made a decision that was not safe. What moral issue does John face in this situation?

(A) Public safety.

(B) Successful public representation.

(C) A wide variety of boundary conditions and relationships.

(D) Diversity.

(154) What are clients' rights to self-determination in social work?

(A) The right of consumers to avail of all services provided.

(B) The right to refuse any service except as ordered by the court.

(C) The consumer's right to request access to personal records.

(D) The client's right to be notified of new services and referrals.

(155) How should case managers approach decision-making in social work?

(A) Case managers should encourage client involvement by providing options and goal-setting.

(B) Case managers should advocate for equitable public representation.

(C) Case managers should ensure diversity in client interactions.

(D) Case managers should record client communications.

(156) A client who used to confide in Emily now shows signs of resistance to her direction. What action should Emily take to support the client while maintaining proper professional boundaries?

(A) She should share information about herself to build trust.

(B) She should seek advice from other professionals to address client objections.

(C) She should create an external support system for the client.

(D) She should provide emotional support to the client.

(157) A social worker faces a complex ethical dilemma in which a minor desires to make a medical decision that goes against her parents' wishes. Which of the following should the social worker prioritize?

(A) Support the parents' desire to maintain family unity.

(B) Seek advice from colleagues without disclosing any client information.

(C) Consider a minor's legal and moral capacity to take responsibility for their decisions.

(D) Refer the matter to another employee.

(158) Elena has cultivated deep connections with her clients. She frequently extends her communication beyond regular working hours. In addition to providing emotional support, Elena shares her personal experiences and provides significant financial assistance to her clients. What red flag behavior is Elena exhibiting?

(A) She shows empathy.

(B) She shares personal information and experiences with the client.

(C) She spends additional time on the phone with the client.

(D) She is friendly.

(159) A social worker is engaged in research to develop tailored programs to address a community's specific needs. She actively collaborates with community members and colleagues to identify issues, implement meaningful changes, and ensure the active involvement of all stakeholders in working towards their shared goals. What research exercise is she using?

(A) Action research.

(B) Field studies.

(C) Longitudinal studies.

(D) Mixed methods.

(160) Emily prepares for a home visit with a client with a history of aggression and sudden outbursts. Which skills will ensure Emily's safety during this visit?

(A) De-escalation techniques.

(B) Risk assessment and safety planning.

(C) The review of patient records for a history of drug abuse.

(D) Security measures for public or community tourism.

(161) A social worker routinely conducts home visits for her clients. Which of the following precautions should she take to ensure her safety during these visits?

(A) Carry a small gift for the client's children.

(B) Wear casual clothing to blend in.

(C) Inform a colleague about the visit's location and expected duration.

(D) Avoid discussions about sensitive topics.

(162) Sarah's client has expressed an intention to harm herself and others. According to professional standards, how should Sarah proceed?

(A) Respect the client's privacy and provide emotional support.

(B) Report the client's intentions to the proper authorities.

(C) Encourage the patient to seek alternative treatment.

(D) Get permission from the client before doing anything.

(163) Which principle guides the sharing of client information and tangible records in social work while maintaining confidentiality?

(A) The transparency principle.

(B) The need-to-know principle.

(C) The accountability principle.

(D) The law-abiding principle.

(164) Which principle of social work record keeping ensures that records of actual and interventional client interactions are maintained properly and accurately?

(A) Accountability.

(B) Transparency.

(C) Integrity.

(D) Protection.

(165) Which term refers to the ongoing development of professional skills, knowledge, effectiveness, and existing knowledge in social work?

(A) Reflective practice.

(B) Self-awareness.

(C) Professional development.

(D) Ethical competence.

(166) Which term refers to relationships in which social workers aim to establish a clear understanding with clients? Assume there are clearly defined tasks that provide support and facilitate the client's journey to independence.

(A) Personal relationships.

(B) Informal partnership.

(C) Employee collaboration.

(D) Structural relationships.

(167) Which basic social work principle assesses individual needs, utilizes available resources, and provides support and assistance to individuals, families, groups, and communities to achieve self-sufficiency?

(A) Empowerment.

(B) Advocacy.

(C) Collaboration.

(D) Development.

(168) A dedicated volunteer social worker at a busy non-profit organization tirelessly assists individuals in the community. She currently struggles with exhaustion and is overwhelmed due to her demanding workload. What should she do to stay healthy?

(A) Set small goals.

(B) Avoid emotional attachment to tasks.

(C) Rest after 8 hours of work.

(D) Take on additional work to keep busy.

(169) Alex is actively involved in a community group that supports individuals from diverse backgrounds. Among those he assists is Maya, who hails from a unique culture and holds strong personal beliefs. Maya turns to Alex for guidance when she faces challenges within her family. What is the most critical thing Alex should do to assist Maya?

(A) Share other people's problems with Maya.

(B) Concentrate only on what Maya believes.

(C) Respect Maya's culture and beliefs.

(D) Act quickly without asking Maya.

(170) Maria is a volunteer social worker. She aims to work well with her colleagues and treat them with respect. Her boss told her she was doing a great job and helping the company succeed. How has Maria managed to gain the appreciation of her boss?

(A) Through her respect for her colleagues.

(B) By effectively completing her tasks.

(C) By performing hard work.

(D) By following a strict schedule.

Test 1: Answers and Explanations

(1) (C) Young adult.

Erickson's theory defines young adulthood as people aged eighteen to thirty-five. According to this theory, young adults act out in various ways as they learn their place in the world.

(2) (B) Older adult.

Individuals aged sixty-five or older fall into the category of older adults, as described by Erikson's theory of human growth and development.

(3) (A) Bandura's social learning theory.

The notion that our actions and preferences are influenced by what we observe in others is a fundamental principle of Bandura's social learning theory.

(4) (A) She shifts responsibility onto others in a confrontational way.

Kiara constantly blames others for her behavior and issues. Instead of working on herself, she confronts others. The behavior reflects a lack of accountability for one's actions and the habit of blaming others.

(5) (D) Fourth key point: Distress has several levels depending on how temporarily connected you are to your primary attachment source.

Initially, she cries (protest). Subsequently, she becomes quiet and disengaged (despair). Upon Miss Laura's return, she reacts with agitation and rejection (a demonstration of separation anxiety).

(6) (B) Ambivalent Attachment.

John Bowlby described different attachment styles based on how children respond to separation from their primary caregivers. Ambivalent Attachment is characterized by intense dependence on the caregiver. Children with this type of attachment typically become very distressed when the caregiver leaves and are not easily consoled upon the caregiver's return. They might also display clinginess and difficulty exploring their environment confidently.

(7) (C) The creation of an internal workable model.

Sarah easily integrated into her new school and community, which could be attributed to her strong bond with her caregiver during her childhood. This close relationship likely contributed to her heightened self-esteem and overall well-being.

(8) (B) Generativity vs. stagnation.

Individuals like Mark navigate the generativity vs. stagnation stage between the ages of forty and sixty-five. During this phase, they are concerned with positively impacting the world, seeking comfort, and striving to discover their sense of purpose. Mark challenges are characteristic of this stage, where individuals might feel overlooked and struggle to recognize the significance of their efforts.

(9) (C) Identity vs. role confusion.

Teenagers have the potential to nurture and strengthen their sense of loyalty during the stage of identity vs. role confusion, which spans from age twelve to eighteen.

(10) (D) Ego integrity vs. despair.

Erikson's theory posits that individuals aged sixty-five and older encounter the stage of ego integrity vs. despair. During this phase, people reflect on their lives and may feel wiser and more fulfilled (ego integrity) or depressed and regretful (despair).

(11) (B) Anal.

Children go through the anal stage of development between the ages of one and three. During this period, they focus on mastering control over bodily functions and asserting individuality.

(12) (D) Formal operational stage.

According to Jean Piaget's theory, Mia is most likely in the formal operational stage of cognitive development. Adolescents advance during this stage by strengthening their ability to reason logically, think abstractly, and consider possible outcomes. Through her participation in reading, research, peer discussions, and community activities, Mia has shown that she is capable of sophisticated thought and problem-solving.

(13) (C) Intimacy vs. isolation.

According to Erikson's theory, Jacob is probably in the intimacy vs. isolation stage of psychological development. Young adults seek committed relationships during this stage but may also be concerned about rejection or abandonment.

(14) (C) Generativity vs. stagnation.

According to Erik Erikson, Emily is likely in the generativity vs. stagnation stage of psychosocial development. Adults in their middle years reflect on their accomplishments and contributions to society at this time. They might consider the importance of their life experiences and wonder if they have lived fulfilling lives. Emily's assessment of her life's achievements and sense of purpose demonstrates her dedication to generativity.

(15) (B) Preoperational stage.

Between the ages of two and seven, children experience the preoperational stage of development. As reflected in Liam's behavior, youngsters in this stage start to think symbolically and engage in imaginative play. Liam's imaginative storytelling aligns with this stage's emphasis on symbolic reasoning and representation through words or drawings.

(16) (C) Ego integrity vs. despair.

Individuals aged sixty-five and older navigate the ego integrity vs. Positive reflection during this stage can lead to a profound sense of fulfillment, wisdom, and self-acceptance.

(17) (C) Food.

Linda skips meals to save money, which suggests she does not satisfy her basic food needs. The body needs proper nutrients to work, develop, and heal. Linda's insufficient dietary intake is probably hurting her overall well-being and health.

(18) (B) Emotional health and wellness.

Liam may encounter difficulties managing his emotions and behavior. Regulating our actions, emotions, and thoughts is essential for our emotional well-being. Struggles in this regard can also have repercussions on other aspects of our health.

(19) (C) Novelty.

The six basic needs model lists these needs for human development: Love/Affection, Safety/Security, Autonomy/Independence, Self-worth, Emotional nurturance, and Stimulation.

(20) (C) Novelty.

People with unvarying routines might not experience a deep sense of self-satisfaction. Introducing new experiences into her life may contribute to Sarah's overall well-being and boost her happiness.

(21) (B) Lily's brain and hormones need bonding with her parents for normal development.

When Lily is in her parents' company, it enhances her brain and body coordination and creates a sense of safety and love. This special bond with her parents is critical in shaping Lily's emotional well-being, relationships with friends, and overall development.

(22) (D) Aiden's growth results from supportive parenting, while a less nurturing upbringing causes Liam's difficulties.

Aiden and Liam exhibit contrasting actions and attitudes because of the different parenting styles that they experience.

(23) (B) Stage three.

They are in stage three of the family life cycle, which revolves around parenting children from birth through adolescence.

(24) (C) Stage five.

According to the family life cycle theory, Sarah and James are in stage five, the empty nest stage. Parents who have transitioned from active child-rearing to self-focus and aging preparation experience various emotions in this phase.

(25) (B) Michael's family might experience financial hardship due to the cost of accommodating Michael's condition.

Disabilities can have a substantial financial impact on families. In Michael's case, his family may need to pay for specialized equipment, accessible accommodation, and continued medical treatment.

(26) (A) Ethan's challenges result from a lack of bonding with his parents.

Ethan's developmental handicap might have hampered his capacity to establish trusting relationships with his parents during his early years. As seen in Ethan's behavior, insufficient attachment bonding can cause problems with social interactions.

(27) (C) Emma's family members might worry and feel upset because of her mental health challenges.

Mental health challenges often affect the family and friends of those who struggle. Emma's anxiety and sadness may cause stress and emotional difficulties for her loved ones.

(28) (D) Maria may experience burnout and adverse mental and physical health effects.

Maria risks burnout if she disregards her well-being while caring for her elderly mother. She should prioritize her health and seek a support network to share her caregiving responsibilities.

(29) (A) Sarah's early years of inadequate attachment bonding made it difficult for her to develop healthy attachments and caused her to avoid physical contact.

Sarah struggles to build dependable relationships and shies away from physical touch since she did not have many secure attachments during her early years. According to Bowlby's attachment theory, the strength of early attachments might affect a person's capacity to connect with others later in life.

(30) (A) The Andersons are a nuclear family, and their children feel uprooted.

The recent relocation of the Anderson family has caused the children to feel stressed. This is most likely because they feel uprooted and bereft of their friends.

(31) (D) To prioritize quality time together and maintain a healthy connection.

This couple's happy and healthy family dynamic depends on spending quality time together and fostering a deep relationship. This strengthens their bond and helps them in their personal and professional activities.

(32) (D) Displacement.

Lisa is utilizing the displacement psychological defense mechanism. This allows her to release tension by expressing herself in a risk-free setting.

(33) (C) Sublimation.

Jack is using the psychological defense tactic of sublimation. Negative emotions or experiences can be transformed into positive actions or behaviors through this process.

(34) (C) Chronic stress.

Chronic stress is brought on by long-lasting circumstances that put persistent pressure on the body and mind.

(35) (A) Acute trauma.

A recent and dramatic occurrence can result in acute trauma. This can cause sensations of anxiety, terror, and emotional numbness.

(36) (C) They engage in risky behaviors to cope with the trauma.

Some people who have experienced violence may turn to dangerous habits like binge drinking to deal with the emotional pain brought on by the trauma they suffered. These practices may momentarily ease their emotional suffering.

(37) (C) Economic issues could be significant stressors and trigger poor coping mechanisms.

Economic stresses can trigger unhealthy coping strategies like alcoholism, drug misuse, or violence. Individuals may engage in these behaviors to cope when they experience extreme stress or depression and cannot find healthy outlets.

(38) (A) Jamie's first five years saw insufficient attachment bonding. Consequently, she is touch-averse and cannot form healthy bonds with her foster parents.

Bowlby proposed that during early childhood, the quality of a child's attachment to their caregivers plays a critical role. In Jamie's case, she did not form strong attachments in her early years, which led to difficulties forming close relationships. She exhibits discomfort with physical contact and reacts negatively when affection is expressed.

(39) (B) To deal with the consequences of trauma and lessen long-term harm.

Trauma-informed care places paramount importance on ensuring the safety and emotional well-being of individuals who have experienced trauma. It seeks to mitigate the long-term effects of these traumatic experiences and empower individuals to regain a sense of normalcy in their lives. It creates a supportive and understanding environment where individuals develop tools and resilience.

(40) (C) To manage the situation with care and compassion.

According to the CDC, OPHPR, and NCTIC, trauma-informed care should be handled with care and compassion. Professionals who respond to public health emergencies or trauma incidents should demonstrate understanding and support for those impacted by trauma.

(41) (B) Emma is being physically neglected.

Emma routinely wears dirty and faded clothes, is underweight, and complains of stomach aches. These are all symptoms of physical neglect.

(42) (C) He experiences emotional abuse and psychological neglect.

All of these are signs of emotional abuse and inadequate care.

(43) (A) Emily worries that no one will believe her.

Most sexual abuse survivors never reveal what happened to them because they think nobody will believe them. Emily most likely thinks that if she reports the assault, it will not be taken seriously.

(44) (C) Maria abuses her children verbally and emotionally.

Name-calling, criticism, and belittlement towards another individual is abuse. Maria's behavior constitutes child abuse.

(45) (C) Mark's mistreatment of Lisa results from his jealousy and low self-esteem.

Mark does not like Lisa to spend time with her wealthy acquaintances. This indicates that he may be jealous of her status, which may be the source of his abuse.

(46) (B) Pride, jealousy, and envy.

People who mistreat others are often prideful, jealous, and envious. They may also be attention-seeking and narcissistic but are rarely kind or absent-minded.

(47) (A) Ethan's parents are not deliberately neglectful, but they are not attentive.

Ethan's parents ignore him when he is in good health. However, they worry for him when he is sick. This means that they are not being deliberately neglectful. They are most likely absent-minded. Regardless, they are neglecting Ethan.

(48) (C) Stage three Reconciliation.

Reconciliation occurs when the abuser expresses remorse and shows affection after the violent act (stage two).

(49) (B) Stage two: Abuse and violence.

Mark's mistreatment of Lisa is typical of stage two in the abusive relationship cycle.

(50) (D) The lost child.

Emma assumes the role of the lost child in this family dynamic.

(51) (C) Neglect.

David and Lisa do not prioritize the needs of their children.

(52) (B) Abuse and addiction are behaviors that mutually reinforce one another.

Abusive circumstances might encourage persons to use addictive substances as a coping mechanism. This can result in a vicious cycle of toxic behavior in families.

(53) (C) Both Mark and Emily are enablers.

He does not intervene when Emily is abusive or neglectful, which shows that he supports her behavior. Emily aids Michelle by covering up her mistakes and managing her responsibilities.

(54) (C) Tension-building, violence, honeymoon phase, reconciliation.

The abuse cycle often consists of four stages: tension-building, violent acts, honeymoon phase, and reconciliation.

(55) (B) Behavioral symptoms.

James is displaying behavioral symptoms of addiction. Behavioral symptoms are changes in behavior and actions caused by substance abuse.

(56) (B) Slurred speech and dilated pupils.

Drugs that slow the body down, such as opioids or sedatives, are associated with slurred speech. It is also typical for stimulants like amphetamines to cause dilated pupils.

(57) (C) David is experiencing symptoms of drug withdrawal.

These are common symptoms of alcohol or drug withdrawal.

(58) (A) People from similar backgrounds may experience varied outcomes and opportunities.

Maria and Sarah come from the same backgrounds but end up experiencing different paths.

(59) (B) Social justice entails giving everyone equal access to resources and opportunities.

For example, a foster child in a socioeconomically depressed neighborhood must be given the same opportunities as a child born into a wealthy family.

(60) (B) Preconceived notions affect an individual's mental health, but not their physical health.

Preconceived notions create internal assumptions that may be rooted in incorrect information. They can influence an individual's thinking and lead to faulty decision-making.

(61) (B) Poverty results from a lack of resources and failure to meet basic needs.

An individual experiencing poverty does not have enough of what they need to meet a basic standard of living.

(62) (A) Poverty increases the likelihood of domestic violence and crime.

Poverty is associated with a greater likelihood of domestic violence and crime. Individuals who lack essential resources are prone to frustration and desperation.

(63) (A) Culture influences a person's self-assurance, external expression, and values.

Culture shapes how people behave and what they believe in. It is the invisible force that guides their values and self-esteem.

(64) (D) Race emphasizes physical characteristics. Ethnicity emphasizes culture and beliefs.

Race considers physical traits, like skin color, hair type, and other external features. Ethnicities relate to cultures, such as the things believed in, languages spoken, and traditions followed.

(65) (B) Self-awareness.

The social worker's consideration of her occasional irrational thoughts demonstrates her self-awareness. She actively works to acknowledge and appreciate every individual she assists, regardless of their circumstances. This reflects her understanding of the significance of her actions and words on others and emphasizes her commitment to fairness and righteousness.

(66) (A) Cross-cultural competencies.

Mark invests time in understanding diverse cultures and various approaches to different tasks. This commitment enables him to provide well-informed advice and support when needed.

(67) (D) Cultural sensitivity.

Sarah demonstrates cultural sensitivity through her proactive investment of time in learning about various cultures. Her commitment to participating in seminars and workshops centered on cultural influence illustrates her dedication to staying well-informed. This strategy guarantees that when she extends assistance to individuals from diverse backgrounds, she will better understand their requirements and will be able to provide more effective support.

(68) (C) Gender expression.

Gender expression is the way individuals showcase their gender identity outwardly. This includes things like their clothing choices, demeanor, actions, and preferred pronouns. In Alex's situation, their decision to use specific pronouns and a gender-neutral name indicates that they have given heavy consideration to how they wish to portray their gender to the world.

(69) (D) Gender identity.

Gender identity describes a person's internal concept of their gender, which may or may not match the gender assigned to them at birth.

(70) (B) Family life cycle.

Emily should use her knowledge of the family life cycle to assist this family. The term family life cycle refers to the various stages and changes a family undergoes over time. This includes a range of experiences, including financial hardships and relationship struggles, which significantly impact the family's dynamics and overall well-being.

(71) (C) Privileged communication.

Privileged communication is an exchange of information protected by law from disclosure. An example of such a conversation is between a social worker and a client. This allows individuals to openly express their concerns and emotions without worrying that their information will be disclosed to others.

(72) (C) Case management.

The social worker simplifies complex requirements and ensures that Tom receives the care he needs by identifying his specific requirements.

(73) (C) Mentorship.

In a mentoring relationship, an individual coaches a recruit and aids in the development of specialized knowledge and abilities.

(74) (C) Release the information for the safety of others.

The social worker must balance the responsibility of confidentiality with the duty to warn and protect others if the client plans to cause harm. In this case, disclosing knowledge for others' safety is the appropriate course of action. Michael's decision to disclose information follows a legal and ethical framework that prioritizes others' protection over confidentiality.

(75) (C) Increase the budget for administrative tasks.

Evaluating program effectiveness focuses on determining how well the program achieves its goals. Methods such as benchmarking progress, using mystery shoppers, and conducting follow-up studies directly relate to understanding the program's impact. Increases in executive appropriations are not tied to program progress or performance evaluations and are unlikely to be used.

(76) (C) Caseload.

A social worker's caseload is the total number of open cases they manage at any time. Organizational, time-management, and prioritization abilities are necessary to manage workloads. It is a vital component of social work practice and must be balanced to ensure that each client is given the time and care they need.

(77) (A) Ethical practice dilemma.

Ethical practice dilemmas arise when a conflict exists between two or more ethical principles or values. They emphasize the complexity of applying ethical principles, judgment, and honesty.

(78) (B) Functional assessment.

These evaluations may examine a person's physical, mental, or emotional capacity. They are essential to determine a person's level of independence, point to areas where help may be required, and create interventions to support the client to maintain or regain independence in daily life.

(79) (C) Community development.

The social workers use community development to identify members' needs and foster connections. This strategy attempts to improve community well-being and ensure services are tailored to the community's unique needs and preferences.

(80) (D) Cultural competence.

A fundamental social work principle is cultural competence, which includes awareness of how various cultures affect an individual's sense of self. This comprises self-awareness, understanding the dynamics of cultural interaction, cultural knowledge, and the capacity to adapt abilities to the cultural environment, in addition to awareness and acceptance of cultural differences.

(81) (C) Paraphrasing.

Counselors employ the communication strategy of paraphrasing to comprehend a client's feelings and thoughts better. Through new wording, the listener better understands the speaker's message. The process promotes effective communication, builds rapport, and fosters a supportive relationship between the client and therapist.

(82) (A) Biological.

A biopsychosocial assessment considers biological, psychological, and social factors. Mental disorders in a client's family are categorized as biological aspects. This draws attention to a hereditary propensity that may factor in this client's exhaustion and stress.

(83) (C) They want their children to experience the world without boundaries.

A lack of limits can lead to children acting out and becoming confused. Children benefit from clear boundaries because they may better grasp what is expected of them, feel safer, and learn self-discipline.

(84) (C) Question how arguments are settled.

Evaluating family dispute resolution provides insights into family dynamics, communication patterns, aggression, and power dynamics. This information aids social workers to assess the safety of family members, especially children, and to devise appropriate interventions.

(85) (B) Prioritize the most important things first.

The process will tailor Tim's rehabilitation or therapy to his unique needs and values by actively involving him in setting goals and priorities. This client-centered approach allows the social worker to personalize Tim's support according to his priorities. Tim's participation in decision-making enhances the alignment with his personal goals and boosts his motivation and dedication. It increases his rehabilitation's overall effectiveness.

(86) (B) The parent's ability to assess a child's situation and respond accordingly.

The capacity to understand a situation and respond appropriately to a child is a vital consideration when evaluating a parent with developmental difficulties. This directly affects the parent's capacity to raise and care for the child. It entails being aware of the child's physical and emotional signs. Lack of awareness might make it difficult for parents to nurture and care for their children adequately.

(87) (C) The children are provided positive and age-appropriate guidance.

Recognizing this concern allows the social worker to address it through education, support, or intervention that promotes a healthier parent-child relationship.

(88) (C) The way the parent talks to the child.

During a social worker's assessment of a parent or caregiver's communication with a child, they evaluate if the adult communicates appropriately for the child's age and understanding. This includes showing respect, sensitivity, and knowledge to make the child feel valued and heard during the conversation.

(89) (A) Difficulty paying attention.

A hallmark of deficit disorder is difficulty focusing. The symptoms of Emily's son fit this diagnosis, and regulating these traits would be the primary goal of treatment.

(90) (B) Reflecting.

The therapeutic practice of reflecting involves mirroring the client's emotions and facial expressions. It consists of repeating the patient's words back to them exactly as they said them. This way, the speaker can hear their thoughts and focus on their words and emotions. This method promotes transparency, trust, and emotional expression, which helps James heal and allows for a greater understanding of particular issues.

(91) (C) The parents' guidance and boundary-setting.

Concerns regarding leadership and limits might arise from Emma's evaluation of this household. Children need boundaries to learn responsibility, self-control, and sound judgment.

(92) (B) Open-ended questioning,

Open-ended questions, as opposed to simple yes or no inquiries, play a significant role in therapy by fostering a climate in which clients feel encouraged to delve into their emotions and thoughts. These questions enable therapists to better understand their clients' experiences and emotions by prompting more elaborate and nuanced responses. This aids in the therapeutic process and contributes to a richer and more insightful dialogue between therapist and client.

(93) (B) A list of possible side effects.

A list of potential side effects should be provided when a drug is prescribed so the patient knows what to anticipate and look out for.

(94) (B) Reduce the likelihood of feeling overwhelmed.

The social worker helps the client through what would otherwise feel like an impossible procedure by reducing goals into smaller, attainable steps. The client experiences enhanced focus, success, and self-assurance in response to this strategy, which makes the entire treatment or rehabilitation process more approachable and attainable.

(95) (C) Basic information.

Demographic details, including age, marital status, race, and neighborhood profile, are included in the baseline data for the biopsychosocial assessment. This data provides contextual background to aid in comprehending the client's social and cultural milieu. It serves as the framework for a more thorough evaluation.

(96) (C) Use of drugs or alcohol.

When assessing a family's suspected drug involvement, the social worker would focus on drug or alcohol use during the biological side of the assessment. This includes any physical or health-related effects of substance use.

(97) (C) Social.

Work-related stress is a key aspect of the social domain in the biopsychosocial assessment. It arises when individuals feel overwhelmed by demanding responsibilities or challenging tasks. The assessment explores the client's social functioning, especially their ability to manage work-related stress. Understanding effective coping strategies for work-related stress can enhance resilience and uncover potential triggers for treatment.

(98) (C) Psychodynamic therapy.

Psychodynamic therapy aims to study how unconscious processes and past experiences affect present-day behavior. It can help identify patterns contributing to problems and enable targeted action to encourage change. Other therapies, such as cognitive-behavioral or dialectical behavior therapy, might not consider past connections and specific life events.

(99) (A) The child's lack of communication with others.

Communication and social difficulties are vital signs of ASD. Since it interferes with social contact, a child with an autism spectrum condition is likely to have trouble communicating with others. Individuals on the autism spectrum have a difficult time in social situations.

(100) (B) Extended family, friends, educators, and healthcare professionals.

Opinions are likely to be sought from various sources, including family, friends, teachers, and health professionals, to confirm the integrity of the mother's behavior. They could provide a factual account of how the mother interacts with her children.

(101) (B) A client's favorite hobbies.

Personal information, present difficulties or issues, and quantifiable goals are frequently included in therapy plans. Clients' preferred hobbies are only included if they directly connect to the therapeutic objectives. Although hobbies may be covered during therapy, they are not usually a part of the official treatment schedule.

(102) (B) The parent-child relationship.

The parent-child relationship is likely to be the social worker's top concern if it is discovered that a child is rejecting the affection shown to them by a parent. This behavior may be a sign of mistrust, apprehension, or disengagement. It is important to comprehend the dynamics of this interaction to create interventions that satisfy the needs of both the child and the parent.

(103) (B) Counseling intervention.

Counseling is most effective when it takes place in a private, secure, and encouraging setting. Through the development of trust between the therapist and the patient, this method enables the patient to discuss private difficulties without the fear of being judged or betrayed.

(104) (B) What happens when your partner gets upset or angry?

By discovering how the client's partner responds when angry or disturbed, the therapist might discover whether domestic violence is likely to occur. This would enable the therapist to determine whether this behavior poses a threat.

(105) (D) Confrontation.

Confrontational counseling involves directly addressing a client's inconsistencies without criticism. It encourages clients to reflect on their contradictions. The counselor may highlight disparities between their statements and actions or conflicting assertions. This approach can lead to a better understanding of underlying issues and foster a more open and honest therapeutic relationship.

(106) (B) Limit setting techniques.

This strategy creates distinct and firm boundaries between the professional and the customer. It ensures that each party abides by the terms and conditions of their arrangement. It encourages courteous and healthy interaction. This is critical to social work.

(107) (C) Harm reduction techniques.

Harm reduction techniques aim to meet people where they are in their substance usage without passing judgment. Instead of promoting abstinence, the strategy focuses on reducing the harmful effects of substance abuse. It recognizes that complete cessation might not be possible for everyone immediately and instead strives to reduce harm and improve safety. Although they might be helpful in some therapeutic settings, the alternative approaches to substance abuse are not instantly compatible with them.

(108) (C) Collaborating.

Working together to create a solution that satisfies both parties equally is the goal of the conflict resolution technique known as collaboration. It requires open communication, respect for one another, and an openness to consider one another's needs and concerns. There are other approaches to addressing disagreement, but they do not support the objective of equally gratifying each party.

(109) (B) Have a discussion and decompress.

The client and social worker must discuss and decompress after every role-playing session. This will allow both to discuss any emotions that might have cropped up during role-play and share their thoughts. They can then analyze their role-playing session and use these learnings to improve in their next session.

(110) (B) Choice.

This aims to empower the client to make their own decisions. In this line of therapy, the client chooses how they want their therapy to proceed. The client has a voice and an active involvement in their mental healthcare and makes educated decisions about their treatment.

(111) (C) Psychological.

Recognizing and responding to our own needs, establishing boundaries, and engaging in activities that promote physical, emotional, and mental health are all examples of psychological aspects of self-care. In this case, the social worker is teaching James to focus on promoting his mental well-being.

(112) (B) Role modeling technique.

Social workers use modeling to demonstrate beneficial behaviors by displaying and performing during sessions. The social worker uses this method to foster resolution.

(113) (B) Role-play.

Role-playing is a therapeutic technique where clients act out scenarios to practice new behaviors, enhance communication skills, gain insight into emotions, and increase empathy. This helps clients build confidence and apply these skills in real-life situations.

(114) (C) Physical.

This practice prioritizes body care and the preservation of physical health, which plays a critical role in overall well-being. It includes proper nutrition, physical activity, adequate rest, and seeking medical attention when necessary.

(115) (B) Avoidance.

A person may step back and refrain from participating in a disagreement as part of the avoidance approach of conflict resolution. The avoidance strategy is used when a person assesses the problem as minor or there are more consequences to disagreement than benefits.

(116) (D) Harm reduction techniques.

Harm reduction techniques aim to lessen the harmful effects of behaviors like substance abuse. These strategies aim not to eliminate behaviors but to acknowledge reality and reduce risks.

(117) (A) Self-monitoring techniques.

By self-monitoring, an individual actively sets and monitors objectives while collaborating with a social worker to address problematic behavior. The social worker helps the person identify behavioral patterns and make intentional changes.

(118) (B) Competition.

A heavy emphasis on one's interests and concerns at the expense of others characterizes the competing conflict resolution technique. This strategy frequently leads to a lose-lose outcome.

(119) (D) Empowerment.

One of the guiding principles of trauma-informed care is empowerment, which aims to give clients back control of their lives after experiencing trauma. By giving his clients the tools, assurance, and support they need to take control of their healing and rehabilitation, Tom hopes to empower them.

(120) (C) Think before you speak.

This is a valuable anger management technique. James can respond more rationally and constructively by pausing and considering his feelings and thoughts before reacting. This approach promotes better communication and can help prevent further escalation of conflicts.

(121) (C) Meditate and exercise.

Exercise and meditation are effective stress-reduction techniques. Meditation improves focus by soothing the mind and promoting a peaceful mindset. Exercise can improve physical well-being by releasing endorphins, which naturally improve mood.

(122) (B) Contracting and goal setting.

Using the contracting and goal-setting technique, the client and social worker jointly create a detailed plan to reach specific targets. During this process, objectives are identified, attainable targets are created, and the actions to get there are determined. It gives the healing process structure and direction.

(123) (C) Encourage humor as a tool to reduce tension.

In a professional environment, encouraging humor can be a helpful tactic for reducing stress and hostility. Humor may diffuse potentially explosive situations, create a pleasant environment, and lighten the mood.

(124) (B) Psychoeducational approach.

The psychoeducational approach combines clinical therapy and education to help individuals to comprehend and overcome trauma. This approach entails teaching survivors about the psychological impacts of trauma and providing therapeutic interventions to help them manage and heal. It equips people with the knowledge and abilities to comprehend their conditions and actively participate in their recovery.

(125) (B) Task-centered approach.

In social work, the task-centered approach is a brief problem-solving method. It helps clients tackle specific issues by dividing them into manageable tasks. This approach highlights collaboration between the client and the social worker. It determines clear and achievable goals and systematically addresses problems within a limited timeframe.

(126) (A) The application of relaxation techniques.

Relaxation techniques, such as yoga and meditation, effectively reduce stress and promote inner peace.

(127) (B) Partializing technique.

Partializing approaches divide vast or complex issues and objectives into smaller, more manageable components or phases. The ultimate aim is to make success more accessible. This technique boosts confidence and reduces feelings of overwhelm.

(128) (A) Cognitive intervention.

Cognitive intervention addresses psychological disorders by examining an individual's thoughts, beliefs, memories, and cognitive processes. This approach explores the connection between thoughts and emotions. It identifies and corrects distorted or dysfunctional thinking patterns that can lead to emotional distress or behavioral issues. Therapists concentrate on these cognitive aspects to help patients develop healthier thought patterns and coping strategies.

(129) (C) It can exacerbate the issue.

High blood pressure and stress can have dangerous physiological impacts on the body. Jack should avoid further stress, which may aggravate his preexisting health problem. Stress triggers the body's fight-or-flight reaction. It can cause the body to release chemicals like cortisol, which increase heart rate and restrict blood vessels.

(130) (B) Strengths-based and empowerment approach.

The strengths-based and empowerment approach focuses on finding and improving a person's natural talents, resources, abilities, and strengths. This approach focuses on a person's strengths rather than their weaknesses.

(131) (B) Behavioral intervention.

A behavioral intervention aims to change particular behaviors through routine establishment, positive reinforcement, and systematic approaches to change. It focuses on observable behaviors and uses techniques to strengthen desired behavioral patterns.

(132) (B) Cognitive behavioral therapy.

Cognitive behavioral therapy (CBT) is a widely used approach that addresses anxiety and unhelpful thought patterns. CBT helps individuals identify and challenge their incorrect or irrational thoughts and beliefs. It also teaches them to think more realistically and positively.

(133) (D) Crisis intervention model.

The crisis intervention model was created to provide quick assistance and support following a crisis or traumatic occurrence. It emphasizes stabilization, determination of urgent needs, provision of emotional support, and coordination of resources and services to aid survival and recovery.

(134) (C) Systemic family therapy.

Systemic family therapy aims to understand a family's underlying systems, patterns, and dynamics. It takes into account cultural backgrounds and ingrained belief systems. This enables the therapist to explore deeply ingrained issues and collaborate with the family to gain insight into and resolve conflicts within the context of their unique system and cultural heritage.

(135) (C) Solution-focused therapy.

Solution-focused therapy would help Michelle build on her strengths and help her identify solutions.

(136) (B) Mutual aid group.

A mutual aid group consists of individuals who share similar struggles or experiences. They come together to support, motivate, and understand one another. Members share their experiences, acquire coping strategies, and receive emotional support. This fosters a sense of belonging and empowerment.

(137) (B) Storming.

The second stage of group growth is storming. It is frequently marked by group members' disputes, misunderstandings, and rivalry. Members may challenge one another, the group's goal, or leadership as they seek to define their roles and expectations.

(138) (A) Task-centered practice.

By dividing a significant problem into manageable goals and activities, clients can systematically address each component and reduce overwhelming feelings.

(139) (B) Structural family therapy.

Structural family therapy enables the therapist to examine the family's organizational structure, spot troubling tendencies, and collaborate with family members to enhance relationships and communication within the family system.

(140) (A) Advocacy groups.

Advocacy groups promote empowerment and bring about change at the local level.

(141) (B) Crisis intervention model.

The crisis intervention model is designed to provide immediate support and assistance to individuals who have experienced a traumatic event.

(142) (A) Transgenerational therapy.

Transgenerational therapy mainly examines and comprehends the patterns, conflicts, and problems passed down through generations. It is centered on investigating historical family difficulties and their impact on present and future generations.

(143) (A) Narrative therapy.

Narrative therapy is a strategy that helps individuals view their problems as separate from themselves. It focuses on life stories and encourages individuals to rewrite them in alignment with their values and goals. This approach allows them to gain a fresh perspective by detaching their difficulties from their identity. It promotes empowerment and control and enables a more objective analysis of issues.

(144) (B) Create realistic and attainable goals.

Creating reasonable and achievable goals would be the most appropriate action for a client who frequently feels overwhelmed by ambitious targets.

(145) (B) Do homework immediately after dinner.

Establishing a routine that fits the client's natural rhythm is sensible. This may result in more fruitful and effective study sessions.

(146) (C) Social justice.

Jane is a champion of social justice. She shows that she wants to make the world better for everyone, particularly those who have been mistreated.

(147) (A) Competence.

Nathan's strong desire for excellence in his work drives him to continually acquire new skills and enhance his ability to assist others.

(148) (B) Ensure foundational skills and knowledge.

A licensure exam ensures that a social worker has the skills and knowledge necessary to help others.

(149) (C) Sophia should report her concerns to her superior.

When faced with ethical concerns about inappropriate behavior, the most appropriate action is to report the concern to a supervisor or government official.

(150) (B) It guides ethical and legal issues in social work.

The National Association of Social Workers (NASW) code of ethics outlines acceptable practices and conduct for social workers with clients, colleagues, and practical settings. The code of ethics is not concerned with statutory regulations, professional role descriptions, or financial support but focuses on promoting ethics in social work.

(151) (B) Right to informed consent.

The right to informed consent means that clients must be given complete information about a service or treatment so they can make informed decisions. This includes the details of a treatment or service, potential side effects, and associated risks. Elena needs to ensure Alex fully understands the implications of the treatment plan before moving forward.

(152) (B) To refuse any service except one ordered by a court.

In social work, the right to self-determination refers to the freedom of the client to accept or refuse services or treatment as they see fit. This empowers clients to make decisions in their own best interests. This right does not apply when court orders are involved.

(153) (A) Public Safety.

If a team member makes an unsafe decision, the primary moral concern is the safety and well-being of the public. Autonomy and empowerment are valuable, and they also come with the responsibility of ensuring that ethical guidelines and standards are upheld to protect the public's safety.

(154) (B) The right to refuse any service except as ordered by the court.

Self-determination means the client can decide which services they wish to pursue. The only exception is when a court orders a client to participate in a particular service.

(155) (A) Case managers should encourage client involvement by providing options and goal-setting.

For managers in social work, decision-making revolves around assisting clients by providing them with practical strategies and establishing clear, measurable goals. The primary focus is to empower clients and facilitate their progress toward positive outcomes.

(156) (C) She should create an external support system for the client.

Creating a network to support the client without Emily's direct involvement will accomplish two objectives: The client will retain access to care and resources. Emily will be able to maintain an appropriate professional rapport with the client.

(157) (C) Consider a minor's legal and moral capacity to take responsibility for their decisions.

When faced with ethical dilemmas involving minors, social workers should prioritize the minor's right to self-determination. Seeking advice and considering family unity is essential, but a minor's moral responsibility for autonomy takes precedence. Contextualized intervention is not a complete solution and may not address the ethical issue adequately.

(158) (B) She shares personal information and experiences with the client.

By sharing personal experiences, Elena is blurring the professional boundaries, which can jeopardize her objectivity and professionalism. Over time, this can lead to ethical dilemmas and potential harm to the therapeutic relationship. Boundaries are necessary to protect both the client and the social worker and to ensure the professional nature of the relationship is maintained.

(159) (A) Action research.

Her research approach, which involves the identification of community needs and the development of plans to meet those needs, is consistent with the concept of action research. This approach focuses on practical change based on research and includes collaboration with stakeholders.

(160) (A) De-escalation techniques.

Given the client's history of aggression and outbursts, Emily must be able to calm stressful situations and protect herself from injury. Nonviolent self-defense training is essential for the management of clients with behavior problems.

(161) (C) Inform a colleague about the visit's location and expected duration.

The most fundamental safety precaution for a social worker during home visits is to ensure someone else knows their whereabouts. By informing a colleague about the location of a visit and how long they expect to be there, the social worker establishes a safety net. If something were to go wrong, someone would be aware of their location and could act accordingly.

(162) (B) Report the client's intentions to the proper authorities.

When a client expresses an intent to harm themselves or others, social workers should report this information immediately to ensure the safety of the client and others.

(163) (B) The need-to-know principle.

The need-to-know principle states that identifiable patient information should only be disclosed to individuals with a legitimate and vital justification.

(164) (C) Integrity.

The principle of integrity in maintaining social work records emphasizes the importance of accurate and truthful records of actual transactions, scrutiny, independence, and internal improvement. This ensures that the information recorded is reliable, accurate, consistent, and essential to patient care.

(165) (C) Professional development.

As with any professional journey, social workers must continuously learn, develop, and upgrade skills. This process is called professional development. Reflective practice involves self-examination of practices and experiences. Self-awareness focuses on being able to understand personal feelings and behavior. Ethical competence refers to the ability to solve complex ethical dilemmas.

(166) (D) Structural relationships.

Social work revolves around preparing the client for success. This is accomplished by creating a structural relationship comprising clearly defined roles, expectations, and tasks. Personal connections, unofficial alliances, and inter-office cooperation are all beneficial, but they refer to different notions.

(167) (D) Development.

This is the concept of fostering positive change at various levels.

(168) (A) Set small goals.

Given its emotional demands, the field of social work causes a real risk of burnout. Social workers should set small goals so they can be achieved quickly. They should refuel, consider their accomplishments, and manage the emotional strain of their work throughout the month.

(169) (C) Respect Maya's culture and beliefs.

Alex should treat Maya's culture and beliefs with respect. This helps build trust and makes Maya feel valued.

(170) (A) Through her respect for her colleagues.

Maria prioritizes teamwork and demonstrates respect for her colleagues. This fosters a positive work environment that ultimately benefits the organization. Her dedication to these values did not go unnoticed, as her boss recognized her significant contributions and commended her for a job well done.

Test 2: Questions

(1) Maria is 32. When she was young, she developed a rare medical condition that led to her physical appearance resembling that of a 12-year-old. Although her chronological age is 32, her body development is at the older child stage. According to human development stages, what challenges does Maria face due to her unique growth condition?

(A) Cognitive challenges and difficulty understanding complex concepts.

(B) Emotional difficulties when trying to process emotions and feelings.

(C) Challenges related to her physical appearance.

(D) Health concerns as she enters her middle adult stage.

(2) Jamie has just completed fifth grade. His personality is beginning to shift. He has started to form opinions. According to this scenario, what stage of human growth is Jamie in?

(A) Young child stage.

(B) Older child stage.

(C) Adolescent years.

(D) Young adult stage.

(3) Allie is five. She speaks, talks, walks, and eats like her mother. Which of the following theories resonates with Allie's behavior?

(A) John Bowlby's attachment theory.

(B) Erik Erikson's psychosocial development theory.

(C) Albert Bandura's social learning theory.

(D) Jean Piaget's cognitive development theory.

(4) Bandura's social learning theory focuses on how a child develops behaviors through their experiences. Which of the following scenarios depicts the social learning theory that he proposed?

(A) Sally has had a white teddy since she was a toddler. It is always with her, whether eating, watching TV, or sleeping.

(B) Henry was brought up under the care of his nanny. She was a loving and devoted woman who never let him out of her sight. He grew up to be an extremely caring, amiable child.

(C) Amanda sees that her parents become happy when they drink orange juice, so she brings them a glass of orange juice to elicit a happy response.

(D) George is three. His mom lets him make small decisions like what clothes to wear and what activities to participate in. She believes this will help him develop a sense of independence.

(5) Carol worries that her one-year-old will mimic her bad habits. Her husband does not think the child is old enough to mimic bad habits. Should Carol refrain from exhibiting bad habits when in the baby's presence at this stage of development?

(A) The first 18 months are not critical for the child's mental growth. It is okay not to be careful in front of the one-year-old.

(B) The first 18 months significantly impact a child's cognitive and mental abilities. It is important to be diligent from infancy.

(C) Carol can wait until the child is 24 months old before stopping her bad habits.

(D) Children are not likely to imitate behaviors at this young age. Parents can focus on addressing bad habits later when the child is more receptive to learning.

(6) Camilla is separated from her mother a few months after birth. She is raised by her nanny and with time grows attached to her. She meets her mother when she turns five but does not feel connected to her and calls for her nanny. How does John Bowlby's Attachment theory describe her behavior?

(A) Camilla's primary caregiver has been her nanny since infancy. The attachment she feels toward her nanny is not something she learned.

(B) Camilla is dependent on her nanny, and her attachment to her is the reason for her behavior.

(C) Camilla observed her nanny for five years and imitated her reactions when she met her mother.

(D) Camilla is entirely dependent on her nanny. A bond like this instills a sense of confidence in her when her nanny is beside her.

(7) Hailey was five when she was removed from her mother's custody. As she grew older, she became bitter and cold toward her father and everyone around her. How does John Bowlby's attachment theory explain this behavior?

(A) Hailey's overall growth depended on her mother. After her bond with her mother was damaged, her behavior became aggressive and cold.

(B) Hailey observed how others interacted with her father and imitated the same behavior toward him.

(C) Hailey suffered from maternal deprivation during the initial years of her life, which resulted in lifelong bitterness.

(D) Hailey behaved aggressively toward everyone to gain attention.

(8) Hannah is six years old. Her mother is away and she in her grandmother's care for six months. For the first few weeks, Hannah shows extreme resentment, refuses to eat, and expresses anger at everything. After a few weeks, she becomes uninterested in her favorite activities. According to Bowlby's theory, what behaviors will Hannah express in the third stage of separation?

(A) She will protest her mother's absence and refuse to respond to anyone else.

(B) She will enter the despair stage, where she will become outwardly calmer but remain upset by her mother's absence. She will withdraw from engaging in activities.

(C) She will gradually re-engage with those around her and show anger or resentment toward her mother upon her return.

(D) She will become completely detached and refuse to engage with her mother or show affection or attention upon her return.

(9) Which of the following is not a mental correlation children form with their mothers, according to John Bowlby's Attachment Theory?

(A) They recognize their favorite toys and activities.

(B) They judge the reliability of their mother's presence and care.

(C) They assess their own worth and importance based on maternal interactions.

(D) They evaluate strangers' trustworthiness in their mother's absence.

(10) Henry is Sally's firstborn. He is three years old. Sally has to leave him for two weeks. How will Henry likely respond to Sally's absence?

(A) Henry will recover from this limited separation without suffering long-term harm.

(B) Henry will protest and show distress over his mother's absence.

(C) Henry will become outwardly calm and quiet while being inwardly upset about the absence of his mother.

(D) Henry will show great disappointment and refrain from engaging with anyone.

(11) Jane is a newborn whose mother died at birth. She was brought up by her aunt, who has a daughter named Rachel. Jane was neglected from infancy and grew up to be completely independent without trusting anybody. Rachel, however, grew up to be a secure person who feels confident while around others. According to Erik Erikson's psychosocial development theory, which of the following might be the cause of Jane's personality?

(A) Lack of consistent and responsible caregivers during her early life.

(B) Genetic predisposition to skepticism and mistrust.

(C) Overprotection and excessive care from her aunt.

(D) Strong influence from her cousin Rachel's personality.

(12) Jennifer is a new mother who is skeptical of almost everything. Her baby is now two years old, but she never lets him out of her sight. Jennifer cares for him without allowing assistance from anyone, and she does not allow him to make any decisions. According to stage 2 in Erikson's theory, what might the child experience?

(A) He will develop complete mistrust in people surrounding him, including his mother.

(B) He will lack self-esteem and confidence due to a lack of control over his choices.

(C) He will struggle to interact with peers and will not work well with others.

(D) He will not be able to adjust to new environments.

(13) Sarah used to be homeschooled by her mother. She formed no friendships through the age of five. She seemed to lack the ability to make friends when she was enrolled in a school at six. How does Erik Erikson's theory explain this situation?

(A) Sarah's genetic predisposition affects her ability to make friends.

(B) Sarah lacked exposure to peer interaction during her early years.

(C) Sarah's mother provided excessive freedom and choices while homeschooling.

(D) Sarah's guilt about attending school at age six inhibits her social interactions.

(14) Brian is seven years old. His mother and father have full-time jobs outside of the home and run a business from home. Although they provide Brian with everything he might need, they do not have adequate time to show support and encouragement when it comes to his everyday achievements. According to Eric Erikson's psychosocial developmental theory, how might this affect Brian's school performance?

(A) Brian will perform well to gain praise and attention from his parents.

(B) Brian may struggle due to feelings of self-doubt and inferiority.

(C) Brian will develop excellent leadership skills and will be very responsible.

(D) His school performance will not be affected.

(15) According to Erik Erikson's theory, which of the following best represents the stage during which it is critical to focus on healthy encouragement and positive reinforcement?

(A) Trust vs. mistrust stage.

(B) Autonomy vs. shame stage.

(C) Identity vs. role confusion stage.

(D) Initiative vs. guilt stage.

(16) Mark is 25-years-old. Since high school, he has been wary of people and cautious when forming new relationships. He continues to isolate himself, and his group of friends keeps getting smaller. How does Erik Erikson's theory explain his behavior?

(A) Mark has been unable to make connections in healthy ways, which has resulted in feelings of isolation and a lifelong struggle with loneliness.

(B) Mark has had a lot of healthy connections over the years, but he is giving himself a break and distancing from everyone to self-reflect.

(C) Mark never got the support and encouragement he needed from his relationships.

(D) Mark lacks self-identity and cannot find people who resonate with his ideas.

(17) Jack has always been an irresponsible adult. He went through a divorce during his thirties because he was an undependable partner. He is now 45 and continues not to prioritize others. He feels that his life has no meaning. How does Erik Erikson's theory explain Jack's thoughts and behavior during this stage in his life?

(A) He could not make close and personal relationships during his early life, which made him become thoughtless.

(B) His mother never gave him love and care, so he became selfish and does not care for others.

(C) He never established close relationships or a sense of nurturing, which makes him think he has a meaningless life.

(D) His relationships never gave him the support and encouragement he needed to self-reflect.

(18) Marline led a prosperous life. She had a happy marriage that yielded children and grandchildren. She thought of herself as a successful woman who led a life full of joyful moments. After her husband's death, she reflected upon how she led her life. Which option below is consistent with Erikson's theory?

(A) She had moments of despair and some moments she regretted.

(B) She was happy about how she had led her life.

(C) She felt she led a meaningless life.

(D) She felt sad after her husband's death and occupied herself tending to others.

(19) James grows up to have a habit of nail-biting, which may have originated when he was an infant. How does Sigmund Freud's psychosexual development theory explain this habit?

(A) A child's sense of self only develops once they reach puberty.

(B) During a child's first year, they put energy into behaviors that bring the most pleasure.

(C) Nail-biting is the result of curiosity and exploration.

(D) Nail-biting is a behavior learned through classical conditioning.

(20) What is the main idea behind Jean Piaget's cognitive development theory?

(A) A person's psychosocial development is organized into eight main stages.

(B) A child's intelligence grows with age.

(C) A child's intelligence depends on forming attachments to their primary caregiver.

(D) A child learns and develops in multiple ways.

(21) Emily works in a daycare. She is responsible for children ages six months to two years old. One of her responsibilities is to promote learning in infants. She is instructed that children in this age group learn through their five senses. According to Jean Piaget's theory, what is this stage called?

(A) The preoperational stage.

(B) The concrete operational stage.

(C) The sensorimotor stage.

(D) The formal concrete operational stage.

(22) Beatrice is a primary school teacher. She teaches children from ages two to seven years of age. She wants to promote learning in her students. According to Piaget's cognitive development theory, which activities should she focus on?

(A) Focus on logical thoughts and help students put events in a sequence and organize them.

(B) Focus on abstract concepts and use concepts, logic, and reason to solve problems.

(C) Focus on symbolism and teach students that things can have multiple meanings.

(D) Focus on teaching students how to sense objects surrounding them.

(23) Sam uses his own logic to make his decisions. He focuses on what will benefit him and his own self-interests. Which of the following theories represents Sam's behavior?

(A) Person-in-environment (PIE) theory.

(B) Rational choice theory.

(C) Ethical dilemma resolution theory.

(D) Psychodynamic theory.

(24) Carl is an Irish social worker who grew up in a village. He works with an NGO to provide water resources to remote areas in different parts of the world. According to the PIE theory, which aspect of Carl's work will likely be influenced by his background and the environment he operates in?

(A) His background knowledge in providing water resources to remote areas in Ireland.

(B) His understanding of remote, local cultures and their customs.

(C) His choice to work as a social worker for the interest of others.

(D) His cognitive ability to optimize water resources.

(25) Emma notices her six-month-old girl cries differently depending on what she wants. For example, if she is hungry, she cries in a specific way. If her diaper needs to be changed, her cry has a distinct tone. Emma's ability to distinguish cries for different needs showcases what?

(A) The development of "baby talk" for effective communication.

(B) The baby's preference for using taste and touch for communication.

(C) An understanding of the infant's nonverbal language through crying.

(D) The early stage of forming simple sentences for communication.

(26) Roxanne is five years old. Her parents are trying to teach her the importance of road safety, why she must wear a seatbelt, and why she should look both ways before crossing the street. Which approach should her parents take to support her growing independence?

(A) Encourage Roxanne to rely on her parents by always holding her hand while she crosses the street.

(B) Allow Roxanne to cross the street without any guidance to test her independence.

(C) Practice the habit of looking both ways before crossing together.

(D) Tell Roxanne she does not need to wear a seatbelt since she is still young.

(27) Maria has two kids. She worries that they will be exposed to drugs and other substances. At what age should Maria start discussing the danger of drugs with her children?

(A) Between ages four to six.

(B) Between ages seven to twelve.

(C) Between ages thirteen to seventeen.

(D) At age 18.

(28) Antonio is 15 years old. His mother controls how he dresses, who he befriends, and how he combs his hair. This creates tension between Antonio and his mother. How should his mother proceed?

(A) Continue controlling Antonio's choices to ensure he follows her guidance.

(B) Give Antonio complete freedom without any guidance or boundaries.

(C) Openly communicate and negotiate boundaries with Antonio and allow him to exercise his preferences within limits.

(D) Ignore Antonio's concerns and continue imposing her own decisions.

(29) Lisa is a 23-year-old who just graduated from college. She landed a great job at a well-reputed company. At times, she finds it challenging to keep up with everything that is going on. At this age, what aspect of her life should Lisa be most concerned with?

(A) Lisa should prioritize earning as much as possible while she is young.

(B) Lisa should get annual medical checkups to take care of her health.

(C) Lisa should maintain a balance between her professional and personal life and avoid over-exerting herself.

(D) Lisa should ignore her body's signals and push herself very hard.

(30) Mark is 45-years-old. There is a history of diabetes in his family. There have been recent changes in his level of productivity. Which action should Mark prioritize at this age?

(A) Mark should focus on his work and save as much money as possible.

(B) Mark should seek immediate medical advice and get regular checkups.

(C) Mark should focus on advancing his career.

(D) Mark should ignore family history, as it has nothing to do with his productivity.

(31) Susan fears that her seventy-year-old mother might have Alzheimer's disease. She occasionally forgets small things and shows disinterest in activities she once loved. How can Susan help maintain her mother's overall health?

(A) Encourage her mother to completely avoid activities to prevent overexertion.

(B) Allow her mother to isolate herself from social interactions to reduce stress.

(C) Encourage her mother to engage in cognitive activities, hobbies, and social interactions.

(D) Advise her mother to stop all physical activities to conserve energy.

(32) Stella is trying to lose weight by minimizing her food intake. She keeps her calories below 1,000/day. Her overall health is declining, and she has started to lose a lot of hair. Should she continue with her diet or make changes?

(A) She should add vitamins to her daily regimen to boost hair growth.

(B) She should increase her food intake to a minimum of 1,200 calories/day.

(C) She should decrease her calorie intake to reach her weight loss goal and then resume regular intake after she has achieved the goal.

(D) She should stay on her current diet plan until she reaches her goal.

(33) A six-month sleep study was conducted on two separate groups. One group slept for five hours every day. The other group slept for eight hours every day. The members of the first group displayed slow responses to daily tasks and were always tired. Members of the other group were more active. How does this demonstrate the importance of sleep for human health?

(A) Sleep is critical for maintaining overall well-being and cognitive function.

(B) Sleep duration has no impact on productivity.

(C) Sleeping less allows more time for task completion.

(D) Sleeping more benefits human health.

(34) Brandon feels overwhelmed all the time. He is finding it extremely difficult to stay connected with his family, spend time with friends, and perform well at work. Which aspect of his health should he focus on?

(A) Physical health.

(B) Mental health.

(C) Emotional health.

(D) Spiritual health.

(35) Camille finds it very hard to control her emotions. She also finds it challenging to communicate how she feels to her loved ones, which affects her behavior. How does her situation relate to the importance of emotional intelligence?

(A) Emotional intelligence has no relation to emotional health.

(B) She needs to start exercising to promote her emotional well-being.

(C) Emotional intelligence plays a huge role in influencing emotional well-being.

(D) Emotional health depends on genes, so she might struggle communicating with her close ones.

(36) Hannah was not concerned about her physical appearance until she started high school. At that stage, she began to compare herself to others negatively. Comments about her appearance negatively affected her. Her friends and family encouraged her, which positively impacted her. How do these experiences reflect the importance of her self-esteem on her self-image?

(A) Negative comments have no impact on self-esteem.

(B) Self-esteem is solely influenced by interactions with family.

(C) Her self-esteem is influenced by the negative and positive feedback she receives from different sources.

(D) Self-esteem is determined solely by personal qualities and strengths.

(37) Jennifer is a new mother who has to choose between her career and childcare. Since she is a single mother, she chooses to pursue a master's degree and leave her baby with her loving grandmother for a year. How will this detachment affect the baby?

(A) The baby will develop a close attachment to her grandmother and find a sense of security in her.

(B) The baby will grow up to be more independent.

(C) The distance will negatively affect the baby's physical health.

(D) The detachment may hinder the baby's cognition and sense of intimacy.

(38) Hannah focuses on forming close bonds with her baby boy. She feels this will have a massive impact on him as he grows older. What impact can a close bond and attachment have on her son?

(A) The close bonds she forms with her child will not impact him as he grows older.

(B) The close feeling he has during infancy will help him build self-confidence and cope with new challenges as he grows older.

(C) The close bond will help him foster new relationships and create his belief system as he grows older.

(D) The close bond can lead to an increased dependency on his mother as he ages.

(39) Maya is new to parenting. She wants to do her very best. Which of the following should she avoid when trying to foster a positive and supportive role as a parent?

(A) Encourage positive behavior.

(B) Be consistent in all her parenting methods.

(C) Spend time with her child.

(D) Keep her parenting style rigid when her child is not listening.

(40) How does a bond created with a child's mother in infancy help in adulthood?

(A) Fosters healthy relationships.

(B) Helps build a sense of self.

(C) Creates a person's own belief system.

(D) Encourages self-confidence.

(41) Rosetta has never lived away from her parents. She moves into her own home at the age of 21. How does the family life cycle theory explain this?

(A) Young adults must move on and have their own families. They need a place to create a life for their children.

(B) It is common for adults in their 20s to leave their parents' house. Rosetta is following societal norms.

(C) Young adults seek independence and a sense of self. This drives Rosetta's decision to move.

(D) Rosetta does not want to be a burden on her parents anymore, so she moves out.

(42) Camilla is now in her 60s. Her children no longer live with her, and she spends most of her time with her husband and close friends. How is this stage of life described through the family life cycle theory?

(A) Her children have families of their own. They have to make adjustments and realign family dynamics.

(B) She is at the stage where she receives support from her children, grandchildren, and close friends.

(C) She is adjusting to an "empty nest" after her children move out and start their own families and careers.

(D) Her children need to focus on their careers, so they move out and leave their parents behind.

(43) Michelle's husband is a chain smoker and a heavy drug user. She sent her children away to protect them from his aggressive behavior. He constantly fights with others and has increasingly become violent. Michelle is unaware that her husband is facing many emotional problems and turns to drugs to find solace. Which of the following catalysts might be associated with his substance abuse?

(A) Negative reinforcement or pain avoidance.

(B) Positive reinforcement or pleasure-seeking.

(C) Emotional stability or adaptability.

(D) Social engagement or peer pressure.

(44) Katie's parents are going through a divorce. The tension in her house is significantly impacting her mental health. What can her parents do to support her?

(A) Advise Katie to spend time with her friends and participate in activities outside the house.

(B) Expedite the divorce so Katie can have peace of mind.

(C) Avoid discussing the divorce in front of Katie to protect her from stress.

(D) Seek professional counseling for Katie and themselves.

(45) Sarah has been caring for her elderly mother for four years. Her mother has Alzheimer's. Sarah feels emotionally drained and isolated most of the time. What should Sarah do in this situation?

(A) Focus on her mother's well-being.

(B) Ensure that all her mother's needs are adequately met. Sarah's needs are secondary.

(C) Seek support from family members and healthcare professionals and take breaks to recharge.

(D) Continue caregiving and do her best to support her mother despite the challenges.

(46) Lisa's family has been experiencing difficulties. Lisa is placed in residential care as a result. Her mother explains why the move is necessary, but Lisa is too young to comprehend her explanation. How will the move affect Lisa?

(A) She will adapt quickly because her mother explained why the move was necessary.

(B) Being in residential care will have no impact on her.

(C) She may exhibit emotional and behavioral changes.

(D) It will affect her emotional and physical health.

(47) The Johnsons are a married couple with two children, Lily and Elliot. Mr. Johnson recently lost his job as a result of downsizing. Mrs. Johnson is now solely responsible for the family's expenses until her husband secures employment. They also have to leave their house for a more affordable option. What stressful situation are the Johnsons facing?

(A) Financial difficulties due to job loss and downsizing.

(B) A move to a new home for better opportunities.

(C) One partner being the sole provider of basic needs.

(D) A move to a bigger house to fit the family's growing needs.

(48) Amy's ten-year marriage ended in a painful divorce. Amy now avoids discussing the separation. Which defense mechanism is she using?

(A) Projection.

(B) Denial.

(C) Sublimation.

(D) Rationalization.

(49) Rob is going through a difficult time at work. To manage that stress, he joins the gym and exercises vigorously for two hours every day. What coping mechanism is Rob using?

(A) He uses all his energy to avoid thinking about the problems at his job.

(B) He turns his negative energy into a positive activity to avoid thinking about the difficulties at his job.

(C) He displaces all his energy so he does not feel frustrated.

(D) He uses the gym as an excuse for his behavior in daily life.

(50) Elliot experienced an abusive childhood. He never resolved his childhood trauma. Despite appearances to the contrary, his trauma still affects him negatively as an adult. Which of the following psychological defense mechanisms is he exhibiting.?

(A) Projection.

(B) Repression.

(C) Displacement.

(D) Sublimation.

(51) Hailey is 17-years-old. She has been behaving in uncharacteristic ways. She stays out late, has befriended much older individuals, and does not respond appropriately to her parents. She blames her parents for every negative thing she experiences. Which psychological defense mechanism is Hailey using?

(A) Projection.

(B) Repression.

(C) Rationalization.

(D) Displacement.

(52) John has two jobs and elderly parents to care for. He does not have time to relax or care for himself and is deeply stressed. Which category of stress is John likely experiencing?

(A) Acute stress.

(B) Chronic stress.

(C) Episodic stress.

(D) Positive stress.

(53) Ellie works best under pressure. It is a habit she developed over time, but now it is difficult to let it go. Whenever she feels stressed, she channels it into something productive and positive. Which stress category represents Ellie's case?

(A) Acute stress.

(B) Chronic stress.

(C) Positive stress.

(D) Episodic stress.

(54) Jake got into a serious car accident. He did not sustain many injuries, but the experience was traumatic. Since the accident, he will not ride in or drive a car. He prefers walking and avoiding high-traffic zones. What do his responses showcase in terms of trauma?

(A) Normal symptoms after experiencing a traumatic car accident.

(B) Acute trauma as a result of a dangerous accident.

(C) Chronic trauma because he is getting the same feeling repeatedly.

(D) Complex trauma because he cannot resume his typical activities.

(55) Emma grew up encountering domestic abuse regularly. When she got older and moved out, she battled anxiety and depression. She found peace in using drugs, alcohol, and other substances. What concept explains Emma's behavior?

(A) The impact of working and having a practical life of her own led her to engage in risky behaviors.

(B) Her family's influence remained evident after she moved out.

(C) Her childhood experience of witnessing violent acts led her to this stage.

(D) Growing up in a dysfunctional environment made her anxious as an adult.

(56) Elliot grew up in a loving family. When he turned 18, he went to college. At 24, he married his high school best friend, Katie. Over time, Katie became very controlling.

She did not permit Elliot to spend time with his parents or friends when he wanted to. Elliot spoke to Katie about her behavior without responding in an abusive way. What does this show about the influence of one's upbringing?

(A) The influence of his belief system and power of decision-making within the family.

(B) The correlation of communication styles and conflict resolution.

(C) The influence a loving family upbringing has on healthy coping mechanisms and communication skills.

(D) The result of traumatic experiences in his childhood.

(57) Relief workers were sent to support flood victims. They were instructed to remain sensitive to the trauma the event may have caused. They prioritized a safe environment and open communication. This approach aligns with which step of the trauma-care approach?

(A) Trustworthiness and transparency.

(B) Peer support.

(C) Empowerment and choice.

(D) Safety.

(58) Cameron lost his wife and was left to care for his three-year-old son alone. He can only afford a part-time nanny who leaves when Cameron gets home. Because he has other responsibilities, he has little time to properly supervise his son at home. What form of neglect is his son experiencing?

(A) The child does not receive the love and care he requires.

(B) The child is not regularly taken to the doctor or dentist.

(C) the child's basic needs, like food, clothing, and shelter, are not provided.

(D) The child is not adequately supervised at home.

(59) James and Abigail are twins. Abigail has a stellar academic record. James does not perform well in school. James is good at sports and spends his free time playing his PlayStation. He is constantly compared to his sister and excessively criticized for not performing as well as she does at school. What effect does this have on James's mental health?

(A) Increased self-esteem and confidence due to sibling rivalry.

(B) Enhanced motivation and academic performance.

(C) Potential negative impact on mental health due to excessive criticism and comparison.

(D) Greater emotional resilience and adaptability.

(60) Child abuse and child neglect are two different concepts. Which of the following is *not* an example of child abuse?

(A) An adult hits a child when they do something wrong.

(B) An adult undermines a child's abilities and does not encourage them to improve.

(C) A caretaker does not provide sufficient basic needs for the child, like food and clothing.

(D) A child is forced to perform laborious jobs.

(61) Sophie is well-spoken, very well-educated, and composed. She handles every client meeting with grace and is remarkably talented when it comes to client acquisition. Her behavior toward her staff is the complete opposite. She belittles and micromanages them. Based on this information, which trait does not describe Sophie?

(A) She has incredibly high self-esteem.

(B) Her behavior is very controlling, with an explosive temper.

(C) She is caring toward her staff.

(D) She exhibits strong professional virtues

(62) Nine-year-old Ethan recently began a new school. He worries about his ability to connect with his classmates and form friendships. He begins to initiate discussions and participate in group activities after being impressed by his neighbor, Alex's, ability to do so. Which human development theory best explains Ethan's actions in this circumstance?

(A) Bandura's social learning theory.

(B) Bowlby's attachment theory.

(C) Erikson's psychosocial development theory.

(D) Freud's psychosexual development theory.

(63) The Wormwoods' Neighbor noticed they do not give their young daughter, Matilda, as much attention as their older son. Matilda is exceptionally talented and endures her parents' chaotic behavior. Which of the following does not indicate that the Wormwoods exhibit risky parenting?

(A) The Wormwoods neglect Matilda's basic needs, such as cooking breakfast and providing clothes.

(B) The Wormwoods prioritize their own expenses before hers.

(C) The Wormwoods are unwilling to support Matilda's dream of becoming a doctor.

(D) The Wormwoods provide structured and consistent routines for Matilda's daily activities.

(64) Hannah married her best friend, Charles. After several months of loving behavior, Hannah became the victim of Charles' passive-aggressive behavior. He refused to communicate with her about the issue, and it eventually became a repetitive issue. After each instance, Charles would apologize for his behavior, but he blamed Hannah for initiating the fights. What does Hannah experience after each cycle of abuse in this relationship?

(A) Charles tries to defuse the situation and avoids communication.

(B) Charles demonstrates extreme behavior, becomes excessively controlling, and inflicts physical abuse.

(C) Charles behaves as if nothing happened, blames Hannah for his behavior, and attempts to manipulate her into thinking she is the perpetrator of abuse.

(D) Everything calms down and returns to normal before the cycle repeats itself.

(65) Jennifer has always been a source of happiness for her family. Her older brother developed a drug addiction at 16. Jennifer often attempts to soothe the tension her brother's addiction creates by making jokes. What family role does she play in this context?

(A) The hero.

(B) The scapegoat.

(C) The enabler.

(D) The mascot.

(66) David was a young boy when his father began engaging in excessive drinking, throwing unprovoked tantrums in front of his family, and refusing to seek any help. David was left with a guilty feeling that led him to think his family would eventually abandon him. Years later, David developed the same drinking pattern as his father. Which cycle of addiction is David exhibiting?

(A) His cycle of addiction is driven by the acceptance of help.

(B) His cycle of addiction is driven by external force and intervention.

(C) The repeating cycle reflects what he suffered as a child.

(D) The repeating cycle is characterized by a lack of remorse and resistance when seeking help.

(67) Charlie is a 22-year-old who attends an out-of-state college. When he returns home for a holiday during his senior year, he demonstrates some unusual behavior. He frequently engages with drug abusers in the area, exhibits no control over his anger, and denies his substance use when confronted. Which of the following signs of addiction does Charlie's behavior depict?

(A) Social.

(B) Behavioral.

(C) Physical.

(D) Psychological.

(68) Myra is a social worker who advocates for the betterment of minorities living in Nevada. She believes everyone should be treated with respect and equality regardless of race, religion, or ethnicity. Her focus aligns with the concepts of:

(A) Socioeconomic and economic justice.

(B) Discrimination and stereotyping awareness.

(C) Gender identity and transgenderism awareness.

(D) Cultural diversity and inclusion.

(69) Antonio is an exchange student studying in New York for a semester. He notices that American culture, beliefs, and languages are unlike those of his native Mexico. Which of the following defines the effects of his behavior and attitude when he meets other students in America?

(A) His ethical belief system, which upholds his moral values.

(B) His ancestral beliefs, culture, and tradition.

(C) His customs, institutions, and achievements, which are specific to Mexico.

(D) The differences in physical characteristics.

(70) Maria works in a multinational corporation. She is committed to advocating for diversity within the company. Her potential new client is from China. She wants to connect with him and demonstrate that the company would value having a Chinese client. She studies Chinese culture and tradition in order to impress him. What can you infer about Maria's social work practices?

(A) Her sheer commitment to reducing any innate biases and stereotypes.

(B) Her efforts to study Chinese culture and tradition.

(C) Her focus on personal advancement within the company.

(D) Her preference to choose clients from China for diversity.

(71) Abel is an aspiring social worker. He prepared for Minnesota examinations for three months and passed with flying colors. The social work board in Minnesota will have to accept and approve the certification he acquired before he can legally practice in the state. What is this final step called?

(A) Accessibility.

(B) Advocacy.

(C) Caseload.

(D) Accreditation.

(72) It was difficult for social workers to serve their communities effectively during the Covid-19 pandemic. High costs and a lack of appropriate infrastructure and resources hindered the remote delivery of services. How might these barriers be categorized?

(A) Lack of accreditation.

(B) Lack of advocacy.

(C) Lack of accessibility.

(D) Excessive caseload.

(73) Jim is a social worker in Arizona. He was contacted by an African-American woman in her mid-twenties named Michelle. Michelle asked for consultation regarding a matter of racial discrimination. She lived in a small town where women of color faced difficulty accessing contraception and experienced substandard medical care. Jim intervened on her behalf and worked to guarantee access to comprehensive medical care for everyone. Which of the following strategies is illustrated by the case mentioned above?

(A) Accreditation.

(B) Advocacy.

(C) Accessibility.

(D) Community development.

(74) Susan, a social worker, is responsible for 29 individuals. Her responsibilities include managing their assessments, planning and executing interventions, arranging required services, managing progress, accessing further needs and requirements, and discharging individuals whose needs have been met and targets have been acquired. Which of the following most closely describes Susan's caseload?

(A) The number of interventions planned by Susan to put into place and execute for her clients.

(B) The number of services that Susan arranged for the individuals she is responsible for and the interventions she planned for them.

(C) The number of individuals or groups that Susan is responsible for within a certain period of time.

(D) The number of individuals or groups Susan is responsible for within a certain period of time and the number of individuals discharged from her services.

(75) A social worker was working on the case of a minor with behavioral problems. He reviewed the processes, protocols, and services available. He further reviewed the client's needs and then worked on coordinating the client's needs with the services available to him. What are the protocols mentioned above known as?

(A) Case management.

(B) Caseload.

(C) Codependency.

(D) Code of ethics.

(76) Which of the following correctly defines the code of ethics followed by a social worker?

(A) A set of rules outlining the protocols that a social worker must abide by and the procedures a social worker has to follow in the case of an ethical dilemma.

(B) A set of rules outlining the protocols that a social worker does not have to abide by and the procedures a social worker can avoid in the case of an ethical dilemma.

(C) A set of rules outlining the protocols that a social worker must abide by and the procedures a social worker can avoid in the case of an ethical dilemma.

(D) A set of rules outlining the protocols that a social worker does not have to abide by and the procedures a social worker has to follow in the case of an ethical dilemma.

(77) Agatha is a middle-aged woman married to a nicotine addict. She has a full-time job and performs most of the household chores. Agatha enables her partner's addiction and covers up for him by shielding him from the consequences. She is the sole bread-earner of the household and gives him money to pay for cigarettes. Which of the following is this case a classic representation of?

(A) Community development.

(B) Confidentiality.

(C) Codependency.

(D) Conflict of interest.

(78) David is part of a small community in Louisiana. The community is underdeveloped and economically stunted due to a lack of infrastructure and resources. A group of social workers approached the community and interacted with the members to assess their needs. They devised plans to develop resources and promote networks within the community to encourage growth and development. Which of the following terms can be used to refer to the services of the social workers?

(A) Confidentiality.

(B) Community development.

(C) Codependency.

(D) Continued education.

(79) Anna just got her accreditation and can legally practice in Mississippi. Her first case is a girl experiencing minor suicidal tendencies. Sonya is a teenager in high school, struggling in her academic and social life. She informed Anna about her issues and requested that her family's contact details remain private. Anna mistakenly disclosed Sonya's private information to a colleague despite her request. Anna committed a breach of:

(A) Confidentiality.

(B) Codependency.

(C) Conflict of interest.

(D) Continued education.

(80) Mark has been an active social worker for many years. Despite having a social work degree and experience, he is pursuing additional education. What is this education known as?

(A) Delayed education.

(B) Higher education.

(C) Secondary education.

(D) Continued education.

(81) Zack was helping a client acquire financial independence. He had been working with her for about two months when his client sent him a connection request on social media. Zack has to decide whether to accept her social media request or not. Which of the following terms can be used to refer to this scenario?

(A) Field of practice.

(B) Evidence-based practice.

(C) Ethical practice dilemma.

(D) Cultural competence.

(82) Which of the following is not a core social work value?

(A) Service.

(B) Confidentiality.

(C) Integrity.

(D) Competence.

(83) Markson's client exhibits aggressive and violent behavior. He uses a scale to assess the client's likelihood of inflicting self-harm, his risk of harming others, his ability to care for himself, and his ability to care for himself while suffering from other issues. Which of the following is Markson practicing?

(A) Functional assessments.

(B) Generalist practice.

(C) Indirect practice.

(D) Global assessment of functioning.

(84) A social worker in Arkansas does not actively engage with clients and people in the community. Instead, she offers her professional services in administrative, consultative, and supervisory roles. Moreover, she does research, policy development, and community development. Which of the following practices do her functions classify as?

(A) Global assessment.

(B) Indirect practice.

(C) Direct practice.

(D) Functional assessment.

(85) Vlad's client exhibits aggressive and violent behavior. He uses a scale to assess the client's likelihood of inflicting self-harm, the risk of harming others, the ability to care for themselves, and the ability to care for themselves while suffering from other issues. What is the assessment of the individual's ability to care for themselves called?

(A) Global assessment of functioning.

(B) Ethical practice.

(C) Functional assessment.

(D) Just cause.

(86) Mr. Willis is an experienced social worker. He works to ensure community development in a small Illinois town. He has to assess the effectiveness of the program he devised. To assess its effectiveness, he assesses and reviews the skills developed by the program, compares the progress over a span of time, and reviews the resources to see if any more need to be allotted. He also documents the objectives and accomplishments achieved to gauge the program's success. Which of the following measures did Mr. Willis forget to execute to assess the program's effectiveness correctly?

(A) He executed all required measures to assess program effectiveness.

(B) He forgot to accommodate for flexibility in the program.

(C) He forgot to ensure accountability.

(D) He forgot to review the resources to see if any more need to be allotted.

(87) Which of the following correctly differentiates implied and informed consent?

(A) Implied consent is a verbal or nonverbal agreement implying the individual's consent to treatment. In contrast, informed consent entails clearly informing the individual of all information they require to make an informed decision.

(B) Implied consent is the delivery of explicit information to the individual, implying the individual's consent to treatment. In contrast, informed consent entails clearly informing the individual of all information they require to make an informed decision.

(C) Implied consent entails clearly informing the individual of all information required to make an informed decision. In contrast, informed consent is a verbal or nonverbal agreement implying the individual's consent to treatment.

(D) Implied consent is the delivery of explicit information to the individual, implying the individual's consent to treatment. In contrast, informed consent is a verbal or nonverbal agreement implying the individual's consent to treatment.

(88) Frankie is exercising privileged communication with her client. It entails communication being protected by both ethics and law. However, some conditions or circumstances allow Frankie to disclose the information discussed during privileged communication. Which of the following circumstances do not allow Frankie to disclose the information discussed during privileged communication?

(A) When the client is suspected of harming themselves.

(B) When Frankie wants to discuss case details with her family members.

(C) When the client is likely to harm someone.

(D) When the client consents to Frankie sharing her private information with others.

(89) Abbey is helping a client rehabilitate after suffering a significant injury and becoming disabled. She assessed the client's living situation, mental and physical health, financial status, and education. Once the information was confirmed and it was determined that assistance was required, what was Abbey's next course of action?

(A) To form an intervention plan.

(B) To discharge the client.

(C) To determine the effectiveness of programs.

(D) To network.

(90) Sarah was assigned the task of interviewing clients to assess whether intervening was valid. During the interview, she practiced active listening, engagement, interpretation, prompts, reflection, confrontation, and empathy. What are these elements referred to as?

(A) Assessment criteria.

(B) Elements of biopsychosocial assessment.

(C) Assessment strategies.

(D) Interviewing or counseling techniques.

(91) Max is helping a homeless individual rehabilitate and acquire financial independence. Before devising a plan, he assesses each individual to determine their needs and requirements. He asks each individual the following questions:

- Are you suffering from any medical conditions (diagnosed or undiagnosed)?
- Do you use drugs or alcohol?
- Does/Did anyone abuse alcohol or drugs in your family?
- Is there a history of any mental illnesses in your family?

Which of the following assessments can these questions be classified as?

(A) Biological assessment.

(B) Psychological assessment.

(C) Social assessment.

(D) Interpersonal assessment.

(92) Tessa's client is an underaged child exhibiting unusual behavior in school and poor academic performance. She asks the child the following questions:

- Do you have any close friends at school?
- Who are you closest to in your family?
- How much family support do you have?
- Are there any issues at home?

What kind of assessment is the social worker conducting?

(A) Psychological assessment.

(B) Social assessment.

(C) Interpersonal assessment.

(D) Social and psychological assessment.

(93) Susan's client requires rehabilitation and aims to acquire financial independence. Susan plans to assess the individual's circumstances to gauge their needs and requirements. Susan arranges an interview with the person to devise a plan accordingly. She asks the individual the following questions:

- Do you have a history of any diagnosed or undiagnosed medical conditions?
- Have you ever visited a therapist or counselor before?
- Is there any history of drug or alcohol abuse in your family?
- Do you experience anxiety?

Which of the following assessments can these questions be classified as?

(A) Social assessment.

(B) Biological assessment.

(C) Psychological assessment.

(D) Biological and psychological assessments.

(94) Ms. Bailey is a family social worker. She recently received a complaint regarding an unsafe family environment and possible danger to the children. She put the information received from the agency regarding the family into chronological order. Why did she do so?

(A) It will allow Ms. Bailey to analyze any early indicators of abuse or negligence and highlight any emerging patterns raising concern.

(B) It will allow Ms. Bailey to get a good picture of the family and present a well-structured report to her supervisor.

(C) It will allow Ms. Bailey to discharge the family without intervention or planning.

(D) It will allow Ms. Bailey to take leave and work with other clients or individuals in the community.

(95) Peterson is a family social worker. He approached the parents of one particular family and asked them the following questions:

- How do you manage your anger?
- Do you ever experience confusion while performing daily tasks?
- What do you do when you are at home with your children and you feel anxious or overworked?

Which of the following factors is Peterson assessing by asking the above questions?

(A) Domestic abuse.

(B) Mental health issues of the child.

(C) Mental health issues of the parent.

(D) Parent-child relations.

(96) Amelia was introduced to a troubled teenager in the foster system. Her initial assessment indicated the need for intervention. However, Amelia needs to follow specific protocols before devising an intervention plan. Which of the following factors should Amelia consider before planning client intervention?

(A) Assess whether the parents are ready to change and open to help from a social worker.

(B) Assess the teenager's mental health and gauge whether they can be discharged.

(C) Assess the parent's behavior with the child at home.

(D) Assess whether the client is ready to change and open to help from a social worker.

(97) Parker arranged a meeting with a client before devising an intervention plan for them. The client sought financial independence after a long spell of unemployment due to personal reasons. Parker asked her the following questions:

- What kind of unhealthy behaviors do you indulge in?
- What are you willing to do to eliminate or change these unhealthy habits?
- What are your expectations from this interaction?

What purpose do these questions serve?

(A) These questions ensure that Parker and the client become friends.

(B) These questions allow Parker and the client to set goals for the treatment plan.

(C) These questions ensure that Parker and the client develop a close relationship.

(D) These questions allow Parker and the client to get to know each other.

(98) Marcia has been working with a client for a week. Her assessments indicate the need for an intervention. What should Marcia's next step be?

(A) Discharge the client.

(B) Develop a personal bond with the client.

(C) Plan the intervention.

(D) Focus on the rest of her caseload.

(99) Farah is a troubled teenager struggling academically and socially. She belongs to a financially unstable family and is a victim of negligent parenting. She acts out in class and exhibits aggressive behavior. Last week, she argued with her teacher and tore up an assignment. Which of the following terms can be used to refer to the troubles behind Farah's behavior?

(A) Setting event.

(B) Triggering event.

(C) Setting and triggering event.

(D) Isolated event.

(100) Which of the following correctly defines *parens patriae*?

(A) It is a legal term that describes people of a community contacting each other and establishing relationships amongst themselves.

(B) It is a legal term that refers to the state taking on a person's welfare or care needs to provide them with a legal guardian.

(C) It is a legal term stipulating that communication between social workers and their clients is protected, in line with ethics and the law.

(D) It is a legal term that refers to the equal distribution of social rights and resources among all community members.

(101) Seventeen-year-old Anna is struggling academically and socially. Her family is financially unstable, and she is a victim of negligent parenting. She indulges in negative behavior and acts out in class. Her behavior is generally aggressive and hostile. Last Tuesday, the physical education teacher reprimanded her and instructed her to participate actively. Rather than following instructions, Anna argued with the instructor and created a scene before her peers. Which of the following refers to the incident involving Anna's teacher?

(A) Isolated event.

(B) Associated event.

(C) Antecedent.

(D) Setting event.

(102) Adam assessed that his client, Eve, needed therapy to deal with her issues and reform her life. During therapy, Adam focuses on specific events in Eve's past or present relationships. He further explores the factors currently influencing her feelings, thoughts, actions, and relationships. What is this form of therapy known as?

(A) Cognitive behavioral therapy.

(B) Psychodynamic therapy.

(C) Dialectical behavior therapy.

(D) Humanistic or experiential therapy.

(103) According to her initial assessments, Susan's client struggles with mental and emotional health challenges. Which of the following signs does not indicate the presence of a mental illness?

(A) Presence of high anxiety, worry, and excessive paranoia.

(B) Excessive mood swings.

(C) Normal sleeping patterns and usual eating habits.

(D) Withdrawal from social activities.

(104) Michael's client expressed emotional distress. Upon analysis, further symptoms included anxiety, violent nightmares associated with physical responses, and memories and flashbacks of traumatic events. Which of the following mental health conditions has similar symptoms?

(A) Post-traumatic stress disorder (PTSD).

(B) Obsessive-compulsive disorder (OCD).

(C) Generalized anxiety disorder (GAD).

(D) Depression and mood disorders.

(105) Ethan's client, Deepak, is homeless and in extremely poor condition. Deepak delayed submitting his assistance application for three years. Which of the following could be the reason behind Deepak's delayed submission?

(A) He felt fear and mistrust of the consequences of applying.

(B) The legal resources were not available in any state in the US.

(C) No state in America supports immigration laws.

(D) US states do not allow immigrants to access resources to apply for assistance.

(106) Adam is an experienced social worker practicing in Utah. He is working with a middle-aged homeless woman who is being rehabilitated and seeking financial independence. Adam has gathered all the required information to manage the case. Which of the following should be the next stage?

(A) Stage 3: Intervention.

(B) Stage 3: Planning.

(C) Stage 4: Intervention.

(D) Stage 4: Planning.

(107) Mark is working on a case involving domestic abuse and inadequate guardianship. He is working with the mother to determine limits and consequences to ensure their plan's effectiveness. He informs the mother of her options, which include selecting an alternative guardian for the children and taking legal action against her abusive husband. The consequences of deviation from the decided limits include revocation of custody of the children. Which of the following intervention techniques is Mark implementing?

(A) Role-play techniques.

(B) Role modeling technique.

(C) Limit setting technique.

(D) Harm reduction technique.

(108) Susan's client, Jessica, suffers from anxiety and stress. Jessica is a mother of three who recently lost her father. Susan wants Jessica to express her emotions to help reduce the magnitude of her destructive and harmful behavior. Susan will design an intervention technique that allows Jessica to adopt a decision-making persona distinct from her self-imposed limitations. Which of the following techniques would best suit Jessica?

(A) Harm reduction techniques.

(B) Role model techniques.

(C) Role-play techniques.

(D) Limit setting techniques.

(109) Jasmine wants to teach her client specific behaviors by modeling and using imitation rather than giving verbal instructions. Which of the following implementation techniques should Jasmine adopt?

(A) Role modeling techniques.

(B) Role-play techniques.

(C) Self-care and coping methods.

(D) Self-monitoring techniques.

(110) Ethan's client is a 17-year-old meth addict. Ethan wants to help the teenager now instead of waiting for him to reach sobriety first. Which of the following intervention techniques should Ethan opt for?

(A) Self-monitoring techniques.

(B) Self-care and coping methods.

(C) Harm reduction techniques.

(D) Role-playing techniques.

(111) Daniel has been working on safe ride programs, outreach and support programs, and programs for mental wellness to support individuals recovering from substance abuse. How are these programs classified?

(A) Self-care and coping programs.

(B) Harm reduction programs.

(C) Self-monitoring programs.

(D) Conflict resolution programs.

(112) Bethany's client, Jessica, suffers from anxiety and stress. Jessica is an immigrant who recently lost her mother. Bethany opts to help Jessica with self-care and coping methods. Which of the following key components should Bethany include in Jessica's treatment plan?

(A) Physical, emotional, mental, religious, cultural, interpersonal, and spiritual.

(B) Physical, emotional, religious, cultural, psychological, and spiritual.

(C) Physical, emotional, psychological, religious, cultural, and relational.

(D) Physical, emotional, psychological, professional, relational, and spiritual.

(113) Alexa's client suffers from anxiety and stress. She opts to help her with self-care and coping methods. Which of the following exercises would help her client with self-care?

(A) The client should not prioritize herself.

(B) The client should be self-reliant and avoid asking for help.

(C) The client should prioritize her needs over those of others.

(D) The client should not set goals or strive for achievements to avoid disappointment.

(114) Martha has been a social worker for over two decades. She has been handling child abuse cases for most of her career. She has adopted exercises to cope with the stressors that come with the job. Which of the following exercises should she avoid?

(A) Express resentful feelings in unhealthy ways.

(B) Find activities that distract her from the stressors.

(C) Look for a channel to release built-up emotions.

(D) Meditate.

(115) Carter's task is to address conflict between two groups in an Illinois community. The conflict relates to gun violence and gun ownership. Group A wants to limit gun use, buying, and selling. Group B supports gun ownership for self-defense and self-preservation. Carter convinces Group A to allow Group B to exercise their constitutional right to avoid escalation. Which of the following strategies did Carter exercise?

(A) Avoidance.

(B) Compromising.

(C) Accommodating.

(D) Collaborating.

(116) Michael's client indulges in acts of self-abuse and self-harm. This includes unhealthy eating habits and occasional substance abuse. Michael teaches her self-monitoring techniques to ensure she develops skills to independently increase positive and healthy behaviors. Which of the following would not be effective as a self-monitoring technique?

(A) To avoid socialization.

(B) To promote socialization.

(C) To increase independence.

(D) To set a timeline to achieve the goal.

(117) Which of the following strategies is not included in the conflict-resolution technique?

(A) Avoidance.

(B) Accommodating.

(C) Collaborating.

(D) Delaying.

(118) Sarah's 16-year-old client was found unresponsive in a forest with slight bruises and a minor fracture. Initial assessment indicated the teen had escaped a kidnapping. Once the teen was conscious, Sarah assured her she was safe and had a choice in all experiences and actions from that point forward. According to the designated protocols associated with trauma-related cases, what should Sarah's next step be?

(A) Collaborate with the teen and ensure she is involved in all steps moving forward.

(B) Discharge the client.

(C) Find and inform the teen's friends.

(D) Empower the teen to make her own decisions.

(119) Killian's client struggles to control his anger. He is a 28-year-old male who is married with two children. The client finds it hard to control his anger when things do not meet his expectations. He wants to correct his behavior. Killian suggests several anger management strategies. Which of the following would not be effective as an anger management technique?

(A) To think before speaking.

(B) To exercise or pursue other physical activities to release tension.

(C) To hold on to feelings of negativity to identify the cause of the problem.

(D) To ask for help.

(120) Jacob is helping a client manage anger issues. He suggests the client use relaxation techniques to dispel anger. Which of the following might be helpful to the client?

(A) Use dark humor.

(B) Listen to music.

(C) Make sarcastic remarks.

(D) Harbor anger and ill feelings.

(121) Abe's client is dissatisfied with his social relationships. The client wants a short-term way to resolve his issue. Abe suggests incorporating specific tasks, and he collaborates with the client to set specific goals. They will mutually assess further courses of action if needed. Which of the following strategies meets the needs of Abe and his client?

(A) Task-centered approaches.

(B) Contracts and goal-setting techniques.

(C) Partializing techniques.

(D) Psychoeducational approaches.

(122) Virginia's client is suffering from underlying emotional trauma. After an initial assessment, Virginia decides that her client requires an intervention approach that incorporates a balance of education and clinical influences. Which of the following approaches should Virginia pursue?

(A) Partializing techniques.

(B) Stress management techniques.

(C) Task-centered approaches.

(D) Psychoeducational approaches.

(123) Ms. Stewart's client needs cognitive intervention to address their psychological issues. She wants to analyze their thoughts, experiences, memories, and senses to find a solution that best suits her. Which of the following measures is necessary before Ms. Stewart can begin cognitive intervention?

(A) Develop a close bond with the client.

(B) Establish a clear idea of the issues to be addressed.

(C) Develop a personal relationship with the client.

(D) Exercise behavioral intervention.

(124) Jeff is an experienced social worker. His client suffers from behavioral disorders and requires behavioral intervention. Jeff introduces certain activities to the client to instill behaviors associated with effective behavioral therapy. Which of the following behaviors are not associated with behavioral intervention?

(A) Follow a regular, daily routine.

(B) Take breaks to decompress.

(C) Use negative reinforcements to avoid negative behavior.

(D) Make use of positive reinforcements.

(125) Frankie designed an intervention and treatment plan for a troubled teenager named Ally. It involves her entire support system, including her parents and friends. The intervention plan entails Ally acknowledging her strengths and actively making decisions during the treatment. Which of the following intervention strategies did Frankie apply?

(A) Behavioral intervention strategies.

(B) Cognitive intervention strategies.

(C) Crisis intervention strategies.

(D) Strength-based and empowerment strategies.

(126) Which of the following techniques entails the social worker collaborating with the client to create a written agreement outlining their starting place, specific goals, and intended outcomes?

(A) Partializing techniques.

(B) Contracting and goal-setting techniques.

(C) Goal-centered techniques.

(D) Goal-specific techniques.

(127) Amelia has been an active social worker in Oklahoma for two years. Last month, an F3 tornado touched down near the town where she practices. Two people died, and several others were injured. Amelia intervened to help the people of the community. Once she assessed the impact of the crisis on her client and the trauma caused, what was her next step?

(A) Discharge the client.

(B) Assist the client with whatever they need.

(C) Create an intervention plan.

(D) Decrease her caseload.

(128) Zen is an experienced social worker practicing in Montauk. His client is a middle-aged homeless woman suffering from low self-esteem. The client's goals are rehabilitation and accomplishing financial independence. Zen has gathered all the required information to manage her case. Which of the following strategies should Zen use to help his client?

(A) Task-centered practice.

(B) Crisis intervention model.

(C) Group work technique.

(D) Family therapy intervention.

(129) There was a school shooting in a town in Texas. There were no fatalities, but several students were injured and deeply traumatized by the incident. After assessing the situation, a social worker created an intervention strategy incorporating group work techniques. Which of the following should be avoided in the strategy adopted by the social worker?

(A) Every student should feel validated.

(B) Each individual should be given a chance to express themselves.

(C) Every student should feel heard.

(D) Group expectations should not be set at the beginning.

(130) Blake is working on an abuse and neglect case. It is a nuclear family of three, where the parents are separated but not divorced. In the past, the father verbally and physically abused the child's mother and psychologically abused the child. The child is now a teenager who exhibits signs of aggression and unruly behavior. Blake became involved when the child's teacher reported his behavior in school and among his peers. Which of the following therapies should Blake exercise to help the family?

(A) Narrative therapy.

(B) Cognitive behavioral therapy.

(C) Transgenerational therapy.

(D) Crisis intervention model.

(131) Xander's client struggles to control his anger when his expectations are unmet. Xander set small, realistic goals for his client to help resolve his issues. Why did Xander choose this approach?

(A) Small goals are easily achievable and increase the client's self-esteem. Large goals seem intimidating and might result in regression during the treatment program.

(B) Large goals are easily achievable and increase the client's self-esteem. Small goals seem intimidating and might result in regression during the treatment program.

(C) Small goals are hard to achieve and increase the client's self-esteem. Large goals are easy to achieve and might result in regression during the treatment program.

(D) Large goals are hard to achieve and increase the client's self-esteem. Small goals are easy to achieve and might result in regression during the treatment program.

(132) Frankie designed an intervention and treatment plan for a troubled teenager named Ally. She has been acting out in school and exhibiting aggressive behavior in class. Frankie provided a rationale to Ally. What does that entail?

(A) The plan helps Ally understand why she does not need intervention to develop healthy behavior and can recover independently.

(B) The plan helps Ally acknowledge her strengths to develop healthy behavior independently.

(C) The plan helps Ally understand why she needs intervention to develop healthy behaviors.

(D) The plan helps Ally understand the issues associated with intervention and treatment strategies.

(133) Zack has been working on safe ride programs, outreach and support programs, and mental wellness programs to support individuals recovering from substance abuse. He wants to motivate them to reach their goals and develop skills to prevent relapse after recovery. Which of the following motivational strategies would be ineffective?

(A) Create a system of accountability.

(B) Create a measure of progress to apprise clients of their goals and expectations.

(C) Develop a system that would prevent clients from correlating previous actions with new habits and routines.

(D) Use a planner to outline goals and deadlines.

(134) Jake's client is a 21-year-old meth addict. The client was reported to the authorities by a college administrator due to his absence and poor academic performance. The client is unwilling to cooperate or participate in treatment and assessment plans. Which of the following measures can Jake take to help the young adult?

(A) Discharge the client.

(B) Stay calm and make the client feel heard.

(C) Avoid setting professional boundaries and form a personal bond with the client.

(D) Force the client to cooperate through aggressive measures.

(135) Which of the following techniques entails a planned approach incorporating small steps and actions to acquire desired goals?

(A) Task-centered approaches.

(B) Partializing techniques.

(C) Contracting and goal-setting techniques.

(D) Psychoeducational approaches.

(136) Abe's client, Hughie, is dissatisfied with social relations. Hughie wants a short-term way to resolve his issue. Abe created and discussed the intervention plan with Hughie, who provided feedback. Which of the following measures should Abe exercise while receiving feedback?

(A) Active listening.

(B) Competition.

(C) Ignorance.

(D) Avoidance.

(137) Peter received a school report regarding abuse and neglect. Tessa, a 14-year-old girl, had missed three days of classes and returned to school with bruises on her arms and cheek. He met with her to enquire about the injuries and assess whether she needed intervention. She said she missed school because she was not feeling well and had a bad fall down the stairs. Peter did not believe her story. Which of the following factors could have helped Peter make that assessment?

(A) Feedback.

(B) Inconsistent verbal communication.

(C) Verbal communication.

(D) Inconsistent nonverbal communication.

(138) Alicia's client is a 14-year-old autistic boy who successfully completed cognitive therapy to address specific behaviors. He is capable of taking care of himself independently but requires assistance for certain activities. Which of the following facilities should her client be placed in?

(A) Acute rehab unit.

(B) Skilled nursing facility.

(C) Independent living home.

(D) Inpatient rehab program.

(139) Judith designed an intervention and treatment plan for a troubled teenager named Alex. It involved Alex's entire support system. Alex has been acting out and getting into extremely violent fights. Judith assessed that Alex needs to be placed in a group home. Which of the following factors do not determine which kind of home she should be placed in?

(A) The reason and duration of her placement.

(B) Intensity of services needed.

(C) Severity of addiction.

(D) Competency and physical capacity of the client.

(140) Paul helped his client implement anger management techniques. Once therapy was completed, he decided to discharge the client. Which of the following measures should he execute while discharging the client?

(A) Connect with him on social media.

(B) Arrange for aftercare and follow-up services.

(C) Never contact the client again.

(D) Allow the client to determine next steps.

(141) Chris discharged his client a month ago but periodically checks on him to ensure he stays on track without intervention and treatment. What is this known as?

(A) Self-care.

(B) Aftercare.

(C) Aftercare and follow-up.

(D) Follow-up.

(142) Mr. White is working on 26 cases, most of which are child abuse cases. He is effectively managing them. Which of the following is NOT a social work responsibility of Mr. White?

(A) Cultural discrimination.

(B) Community care.

(C) Social well-being.

(D) Mental well-being.

(143) Lucas is a social worker, and Hailey is a case manager. They are collaborating to help an eight-year-old be accommodated by a legal guardian or placed into foster care. Social workers and case workers have several joint responsibilities. Which of the following is NOT a joint responsibility of Lucas and Hailey?

(A) Ensure self-care-driven assistance.

(B) Advocate for housing and legal services.

(C) Job coach to help connect to potential employers.

(D) Ensure the psychological well-being of the client.

(144) Gabriel and Louis are devising an intervention plan for community development. Their target is a small community in Montauk with poor infrastructural and economic resources. Which of the following is not associated with community resources and involvement?

(A) Nutrition programs.

(B) Psychoeducational programs.

(C) Respite care programs or services.

(D) Home care facilities and programs.

(145) Which of the following is not a likely outcome of psychoeducational approaches?

(A) Improved quality of life.

(B) Improved social understanding.

(C) Social isolation.

(D) Positive engagement of the client in their rehabilitation plan.

(146) Indiana is a skilled professional. She has been working with an NGO for five years. She has not taken any workshops in the last two years because she felt they were unnecessary. She is hoping to be shortlisted for a promotion. Which of the following ethical values did Indiana not focus on during her tenure?

(A) Help individuals and communities address their social needs.

(B) Respect the intrinsic dignity of the people she helps.

(C) Practice and develop her skill base to enhance her professional experience.

(D) Understand and realize the importance of building human relationships.

(147) Sarah aspires to become a social worker after graduating high school. She wants to start working in Nevada immediately. Which of the following scenarios represents a situation where she can work as a social worker?

(A) Her high school degree is sufficient to allow her to work in an accredited social work program.

(B) There is no need for formal education to start working in social work.

(C) A license and formal education are required to work as a professional social worker.

(D) There is no need for a license to work for a social welfare program.

(148) Hannah primarily works with clients suffering from substance abuse. One of her colleagues, Allen, deals with trauma survivors. Hannah believes Allen can help her with her client's unique needs. Which ethical responsibility does Hannah uphold by referring her client to Allen?

(A) Uphold her professional integrity and evaluation.

(B) Deal with administration and commitments.

(C) Respect a client's right to self-determination.

(D) Pursue collaborative consultation when appropriate.

(149) Hannah's client indicates that he is unsatisfied with her performance and wants to stop working with her. Hannah tells him that doing so will have legal consequences. Is Hannah correct?

(A) Hannah is correct. Clients cannot fire social workers unless both parties agree to part ways.

(B) Hannah cannot stop the client from terminating her services as long as the termination falls within the agency's guidelines.

(C) Hannah is mistaken. Clients have the authority to terminate services at any time for any reason.

(D) Clients can only terminate services once their treatment plan is completed.

(150) Sarah has been a social worker for several years. Her client, Mike, was recently released from prison. The court believes he needs intervention because he engages in violent acts due to substance abuse. Despite his situation, what right does Mike have?

(A) He can dictate his own treatment plan.

(B) He has the right to look for an alternative option.

(C) His treatment plan can only be determined by his social worker.

(D) He has the right to self-determination, which allows him to accept or decline services unless he is deemed mentally unfit.

(151) Mark has a client named Lisa. Lisa trusts Mark and confides in him. Mark discovers that Lisa's brother is his old roommate. What ethical concern does this raise?

(A) Mark would be biased when listening to Lisa's situation.

(B) The potential for a dual relationship since Mark and Lisa are bonded now.

(C) Mark may cut off the relationship with Lisa.

(D) Mark may cut off the relationship with Lisa's brother.

(152) Jessica is a seasoned social worker. She has been guiding and teaching new social workers for three years. Her role primarily involves providing information to social workers and supervising their performance. Which supervision category does Jessica's role fall under?

(A) Clinical supervisor.

(B) Supportive supervisor.

(C) Educational supervisor.

(D) Administrative supervisor.

(153) Maria is empathetic and listens actively to her clients. She has been helping Alex resolve severe emotional trauma. Alex asks Maria about her own experience with trauma. What should Maria do?

(A) Share her own experience to help Alex see how he can deal with trauma.

(B) Focus on the client and his problem.

(C) Avoid sharing personal details.

(D) Know her professional limitations.

(154) Anna believes her client is potentially dangerous. She wants to address this concern ethically. Which of the following bills might be relevant to Anna's problem?

(A) Boni Frederick Bill, Kentucky – SB59.

(B) Social Worker Safety Bill, West Virginia – SB2566.

(C) Teri Zenner Social Work Safety Act – H1490.

(D) Act to Promote Public Health Through Workplace Safety for Social Workers – H3864.

(155) Camille gives her client her personal contact information and asks them to contact her whenever they feel down. Is this a violation?

(A) Yes, it violates ethical and legal boundaries.

(B) No, offering clients personal contact information for additional support is appropriate.

(C) It is appropriate only if the client insists on having the contact information.

(D) It depends on whether the client is a minor or an adult.

(156) Emily is a competent social worker surveying people to determine if they have ever experienced homelessness. One of the participants seemed to be uncomfortable when asked the question. What should Emily consider in this situation?

(A) She should encourage the participant to answer and participate in the survey.

(B) She should reassure the participant that all her information will remain confidential and that she can skip the question if she likes.

(C) She should call the interview off and move on to the next person.

(D) She should strip her name from the list.

(157) Zoey is conducting research for a project that will benefit the community. She will have to involve the city hall in the research. Which of the following research groups does this scenario fall under?

(A) Control group.

(B) Action research.

(C) Community-based participatory research.

(D) Longitudinal study.

(158) Annabelle works with clients who struggle with severe mental disorders. One of her clients acts out during a session, begins to raise her voice, and knocks a notebook off the table. How should Annabelle handle the situation?

(A) Terminate the session and call in for help.

(B) Try to overpower the client using the same tactics the client uses.

(C) Debate with the client and raise her voice to control the situation if necessary.

(D) Use verbal de-escalation techniques to bring the situation under control.

(159) Alexander's client has a history of verbal and physical violence. What measurement is essential for Alexander to take?

(A) Develop safety procedures for office and home visits.

(B) Provide everything the staff might need.

(C) Implement alarm systems that alert staff members to escalations.

(D) Encourage a safe climate when meeting with the client.

(160) Olivia's client suffers from depression and has mentioned suicide. How should Olivia deal with this situation while protecting her client's confidentiality?

(A) Share all reports of her sessions with colleagues so everyone is on the same page.

(B) Keep all of the information strictly confidential.

(C) Immediately share only relevant information with her supervisor and colleagues.

(D) Refrain from discussing client information with the supervisor.

(161) Anderson maintains detailed client records. He is hospitalized for three days and will miss an important session with Ginger, who suffers from depression. Another colleague steps in to cover Ginger's session. How does Anderson's record-keeping help in this situation?

(A) It will help the colleague understand how to deal with Anderson's client.

(B) It will provide the colleague with clear information about Ginger's case.

(C) It helps Anderson keep track of progress.

(D) It helps Ginger to recall what she has already discussed.

(162) Michelle works for a non-profit organization that provides counseling to support families in need. She notices that a hierarchal structure is followed, where the stakeholders at the top of the pyramid are responsible for determining the roles of everyone within the organization. Which organizational aspect is reflected here?

(A) Consensus models.

(B) Bureaucracy.

(C) Organizational cultures.

(D) For-profit organizations.

(163) Lisa's clients struggle with substance abuse and addiction. She has a strong rapport with them. She has been feeling overwhelmed by her caseload for the past few weeks. What action should her agency take?

(A) Offer administrative tasks to help Lisa learn new skills to manage her workload.

(B) Reduce case complexity to help Lisa.

(C) Encourage her to address issues compassionately.

(D) Provide her with administrative and emotional support and encourage self-care.

(164) Sally works as a social worker for clients dealing with PTSD. She is facing a divorce. How should the social work organization support her?

(A) Encourage her to take some time off.

(B) Encourage her to make professional short-term goals and take breaks once the goals are achieved.

(C) Provide her with additional administrative tasks to keep her busy.

(D) Increase her caseload to keep her focus on work.

(165) Which of the following is not a good example of how organizations should care for their social workers?

(A) Ensure that all complaints reach the individual in charge.

(B) Allow for clear and concise communication across the organization.

(C) Provide emotional support only for those dealing with VIP clients.

(D) Keep caseloads to a manageable level.

(166) Jane works with a diverse group of clients. She notices that instead of practical support, her client Antonio seeks sympathy. What should Jane do when dealing with this case?

(A) Jane should implement a more sympathetic approach to accommodate Antonio's expectations.

(B) Jane should encourage Antonio to seek help from friends and family who share his cultural background.

(C) Jane should only focus on providing practical solutions to help Antonio reshape his thought process.

(D) Jane should have an open conversation with Antonio to understand his needs and motivations.

(167) Rachel strongly advocates for all her clients. She has been helping Eric with his addiction issues for a year. Eric expresses his need to overcome his addiction but also highlights that he does not have the support network to do so. She recognizes that Eric needs to build a robust support system. What role can Rachel play in this?

(A) Facilitator.

(B) Problem solver.

(C) Advocate.

(D) Mediator.

(168) Sierra is new to the field of social work. Which of the following is not something she should worry about when promoting a safe working environment as a social worker?

(A) Ensure good communication.

(B) Listen to supervisors, professional peers, and other associates.

(C) Recognize and appreciate hard work.

(D) Enjoy the job and find fun in what she does.

(169) Sam is a new social who struggles with time management. What strategy will help him complete client paperwork and turn in reports without delays?

(A) Reflect on how he can improve his routine to give more time.

(B) Make a to-do list of tasks that must be completed according to priority.

(C) Designate one day each week when he focuses on paperwork and only takes calls or replies to emails if absolutely necessary.

(D) Set goals each day and achieve them.

(170) In the field of social work, there are many record-keeping principles that social workers should adhere to. Which of the following is not one of them?

(A) Accountability.

(B) Transparency.

(C) Integrity.

(D) Compliance.

Test 2: Answers & Explanations

(1) (C) Challenges related to her physical appearance.

The question does not indicate any cognitive or mental challenges. It only mentions her compromised physical appearance, which may create difficulties as a 32-year-old.

(2) (B) Older child stage.

Since Jamie is in fifth grade, he likely falls in the older child stage category, which ranges from seven to twelve. This is when children develop opinions, show personality, and develop their thinking process.

(3) (C) Albert Bandura's social learning theory.

Albert Bandura theorizes that children develop behaviors through experiences they encounter at an early age. Children mostly model their behaviors by mimicking their parents, teachers, siblings, or the individuals that surround them.

(4) (C) Amanda sees that her parents become happy when they drink orange juice, so she brings them a glass of orange juice to elicit a happy response.

According to Albert Bandura's Social Learning Theory, children seek approval, so they behave in ways that they think will yield approval.

(5) (B) The first 18 months significantly impact a child's cognitive and mental abilities. It is important to be diligent from infancy.

The first few years are essential for the brain's development. A child develops habits during this stage.

(6) (A) Camilla's primary caregiver has been her nanny since infancy. The attachment she feels toward her nanny is not something she learned.

Camilla's nanny was her primary caregiver for many years, which explains her attachment. Bowlby's theory indicates that Camilla's tendency to shift her attachment to her nanny is a biologically derived instinct, not something she was taught.

(7) (C) Hailey suffered from maternal deprivation during the initial years of her life, which resulted in lifelong bitterness.

According to Bowlby, if a child suffers from maternal deprivation during the first five years of their upbringing, the effects can be permanent. They can result in depression, over-aggressiveness, and lower intelligence.

(8) (C) She will gradually re-engage with those around her and show anger or resentment toward her mother upon her return.

After protest and despair, Bowlby's third stage is detachment. In this stage, Hannah will eventually re-engage with people around her but will appear distant and disinterested in her mother upon her return.

(9) (A) They recognize their favorite toys and activities.

This point does not align with the mental correlations described in the theory. This might be part of the child's overall development, but it does not relate to their self-worth or other correlations.

(10) (B) Henry will protest and show distress over his mother's absence.

At around three years of age, children are usually in what is termed as the "preoperational stage" according to Piaget's theory of cognitive development. Furthermore, children have developed a strong attachment to their primary caregivers by this age.

(11) (A) Lack of consistent and responsible caregivers during her early life

According to Erikson's theory, Jane suffered from the trust versus mistrust stage during infancy. This resulted in a lack of trust in others.

(12) (B) He will lack self-esteem and confidence due to a lack of control over his choices.

Erickson's second stage focuses on autonomy vs. shame and doubt. During this stage, a child must be given autonomy to make small decisions. This aids in the development of self-esteem and confidence.

(13) (B) Sarah lacked exposure to peer interaction during her early years.

According to Erikson's theory, a child is in their initiative versus guilt stage from ages three to five. During this stage, if they do not interact freely with children their age, they will not be able to form connections or interact well with their peers.

(14) (B) Brian may struggle due to feelings of self-doubt and inferiority.

Brian is in Erickson's industry vs. inferiority stage of development. A lack of acknowledgment and encouragement for his small achievements at this age may lead to feelings of self-doubt and inferiority.

(15) (C) Identity vs. role confusion stage.

This stage occurs between the ages of twelve to eighteen years. This is when a child has the potential to develop a sense of self. Erikson identifies fidelity as a critical period for a child's growth and development.

(16) (A) Mark has been unable to make connections in healthy ways, which has resulted in feelings of isolation and a lifelong struggle with loneliness.

This is explained by Erickson's sixth stage, intimacy vs. isolation. This stage occurs from 18 to 40 years old. Mark has not developed loving relationships with others during this stage and thus suffers from long-term feelings of isolation and unhealthy close relationships.

(17) (C) He never established close relationships or a sense of nurturing, which makes him think he has a meaningless life.

Jack is in the generativity vs. stagnation stage, where an adult deepens relationships with loved ones and finds ways to make a lasting impact. Because Jack has not created any lasting bonds or impacts, he feels that his life does not hold meaning.

(18) (B) She was happy about how she had led her life.

According to Erikson's theory, Marline is in the integrity vs. despair phase. During this time, individuals reflect upon whether their lives were meaningful and fulfilling.

(19) (B) During a child's first year, they put energy into behaviors that bring the most pleasure.

This is consistent with Freud's oral stage, which occurs between birth and one year of age.

(20) (B) A child's intelligence grows with age.

Jean Piaget's theory is related to cognitive development, in which he theorizes that intelligence evolves (as opposed to being a fixed trait).

(21) (C) The sensorimotor stage.

The sensorimotor stage is the first stage, where object permanence is the focus. This is how children learn that objects exist even without being able to directly identify them.

(22) (C) Focus on symbolism and teach students that things can have multiple meanings.

This is the second stage in Jean Piaget's theory, which focuses on symbolic thought. This is called the preoperational stage.

(23) (B) Rational choice theory

The rational choice theory states that individuals use their own rational thoughts to make choices based on their own self-interest.

(24) (B) His understanding of remote, local cultures and their customs.

The PIE theory suggests that Carl is influenced heavily by the environment he was brought up in. He will likely use that to understand the local culture in remote areas.

(25) (C) An understanding of the infant's nonverbal language through crying.

Even if adults do not understand "baby language," they still find ways to understand a baby's needs by observing how they cry.

(26) (C) Practice the habit of looking both ways before crossing together.

Young children respond the best to clear rules and boundaries. Therefore, teaching them safety protocols from a young age helps support their growing independence.

(27) (B) Between ages seven to twelve.

This is the age group where children are eager to learn. Discussing topics like illicit drugs and other substances is most helpful during this time.

(28) (C) Openly communicate and negotiate boundaries with Antonio and allow him to exercise his preferences within limits.

Mutual respect and negotiation of boundaries should be prioritized between parents and children between the ages of 13 to 17.

(29) (C) Lisa should maintain a balance between her professional and personal life and avoid over-exerting herself.

Instead of earning as much as she can or climbing the corporate ladder, Lisa should maintain a balance between her professional and personal life, avoid over-exerting herself, and focus on learning about herself.

(30) (B) Mark should seek immediate medical advice and get regular checkups.

During middle age, adults should take care of their bodies and pay attention to any health risks that develop.

(31) (C) Encourage her mother to engage in cognitive activities, hobbies, and social interactions.

Encouraging her mother to stay active will help with her overall health.

(32) (B) She should increase her food intake to a minimum of 1,200 calories/day.

Food is one of the most basic needs for a healthy life. She must consume at least 1,200 calories/day even if she is trying to lose weight.

(33) (A) Sleep is critical for maintaining overall well-being and cognitive function

Humans need a minimum of six to nine hours of sleep. This allows them to process information clearly and perform daily tasks. Lack of sleep causes the brain to be foggy.

(34) (B) Mental health.

Focusing on all aspects of one's health is essential. However, in this case, Brandon needs to focus on his mental health so he can deal with stress and feeling overwhelmed.

(35) (C) Emotional intelligence plays a huge role in influencing emotional well-being.

Emotional intelligence means recognizing one's emotions. If Camille recognizes how to deal with and manage her emotions, she will be able to cope with stress better and communicate more effectively.

(36) (C) Her self-esteem is influenced by the negative and positive feedback she receives from different sources.

Both the negative and positive comments impacted how Hannah viewed herself. The comments highlight the importance of self-image, which is influenced by both internal thoughts and external feedback.

(37) (A) The baby will develop a close attachment to her grandmother and find a sense of security in her.

Parenting skills play a tremendous role in overall health and wellness. In the absence of a mother, the primary caregiver can play the same parenting role so the baby develops a sense of security and healthy feelings of love.

(38) (B) The close feeling he has during infancy will help him build self-confidence and cope with new challenges as he grows older.

The bonds created during infancy will be ultimately applied to the world. As a child grows older, the bonds created during infancy help them gain self-confidence and self-assurance.

(39) (D) Keep her parenting style rigid when her child is not listening.

Flexible parenting is essential. A parent should know and understand their limitations and change their parenting style when necessary.

(40) (A) Fosters healthy relationships.

The bonds created in infancy help to foster healthy relationships during adulthood.

(41) (C) Young adults seek independence and a sense of self. This drives Rosetta's decision to move.

Young adults develop a sense of self and become their own person. Rosetta decided to move out while keeping close ties with her family.

(42) (C) She is adjusting to an "empty nest" after her children move out and start their own families and careers.

The family life cycle theory describes various stages through which a family might go. The stages include marriage, having children, becoming grandparents and so on. One of the stages is the "empty nest" stage, which occurs after children leave the home and parents have to adjust to living without them. In this stage, parents find new roles in the family and often focus more on their relationships, careers, or hobbies.

(43) (C) Emotional stability or adaptability.

Her husband uses drugs to stabilize his emotions and control his feelings.

(44) (D) Seek professional counseling for Katie and themselves.

A divorce can severely affect a child's mental health. This is why counseling is essential in these scenarios. Therapy helps individuals learn to communicate their thoughts, feelings, and emotions and gain a healthier perspective.

(45) (C) Seek support from family members and healthcare professionals and take breaks to recharge.

Caring for a loved one with a health challenge is taxing. Self-care must be prioritized. Ignoring one's well-being can lead to burnout, which incapacitates the caretaker.

(46) (C) She may exhibit emotional and behavioral changes.

Transitioning from a family home to an institution full of strangers can be stressful, particularly for a child. Lisa will likely behave differently and experience different emotions.

(47) (A) Financial difficulties due to job loss and downsizing

The Johnsons are facing a difficult time in their life as a result of job loss and cutting down on expenses.

(48) (B) Denial.

Amy is in a state of denial. She is blocking out everything that makes her think about her divorce. Being in denial means pushing events or circumstances aside to avoid dealing with the emotional impact.

(49) (B) He turns his negative energy into a positive activity to avoid thinking about the difficulties at his job.

Sublimation is channeling negative emotions and thoughts into something constructive and productive.

(50) (B) Repression.

Repression is a mechanism used to cope with trauma. It is used to subdue upsetting memories to avoid dealing with them.

(51) (C) Rationalization.

Hailey uses rationalization to explain her unacceptable behavior with her parents and in general.

(52) (C) Episodic stress.

John is dealing with episodic stress due to his chaotic lifestyle and juggling many responsibilities.

(53) (C) Positive stress.

Positive stress helps individuals feel better and accomplished.

(54) (D) Complex trauma because he cannot resume his typical activities.

Complex trauma often involves difficulty in getting back to everyday life. Jake has been avoiding driving. This indicates long-lasting effects that go beyond the traumatic event he experienced.

(55) (C) Her childhood experience of witnessing violent acts led her to this stage.

Her experience witnessing domestic abuse as a child led her to struggle with depression and anxiety and engage in risky behaviors to cope.

(56) (C) The influence a loving family upbringing has on healthy coping mechanisms and communication skills.

Elliot's decision to communicate openly rather than negatively indicates that he has had a healthy upbringing where communication was favored over hostility.

(57) (D) Safety

The primary goal of trauma-informed care is to ensure that individuals are physically and emotionally safe.

(58) (D) The child is not adequately supervised at home.

Cameron is unable to manage all of his priorities. As a result, his son is not attended to when the nanny is absent.

(59) (C) Potential negative impact on mental health due to excessive criticism and comparison.

James is constantly compared to his sister, who is more talented academically. Such comparisons can cause a decrease in self-esteem, self-confidence, and other emotional distress.

(60) (C) A caretaker does not provide sufficient basic needs for the child, like food and clothing.

Not providing enough food or clothing is a form of neglect, not abuse. Abuse includes physical, mental, emotional, and parental substance abuse.

(61) (C) She is caring toward her staff.

Sophie is not considered to be caring toward her staff. She behaves unacceptably when she is dissatisfied with their performance.

(62) (A) Bandura's social learning theory.

According to Bandura's social learning theory, children learn by observing and imitating adults.

(63) (D) The Wormwoods provide structured and consistent routines for Matilda's daily activities.

Risky parenting refers to behavior such as not providing adequate necessities and prioritizing other needs and wants over one's child. Providing structure and consistent routines for a daughter is not an example of risky parenting. It indicates that the Wormwoods act in her best interest.

(64) (C) Charles behaves as if nothing happened, blames Hannah for his behavior, and attempts to manipulate her into thinking she is the perpetrator of abuse.

This is the reconciliation phase, where the abuser attempts to use tactics and act as if nothing happened.

(65) (D) The mascot.

Jennifer uses humor as a coping mechanism to deal with the chaos in her home. She tries to create comfort by balancing out the stressors with humor.

(66) (C) The repeating cycle reflects what he suffered as a child.

David's behavior shows us what he experienced as a child when he witnessed his father's abnormal behavior. This scenario highlights how childhood experiences can influence and shape an individual's behavior and choices later in life.

(67) (B) Behavioral.

Charlie's engagement with drug abusers, lack of control over his anger, and denial of substance use when confronted are indicative of behavioral signs of addiction. Behavioral signs often include changes in actions, habits, and associations.

(68) (D) Cultural diversity and inclusion.

Myra's advocacy for equal treatment and access to opportunities for all individuals relies on dignity and respect. This aligns with the concept of cultural diversity and inclusion, which emphasizes that individuals with diverse backgrounds should be valued, respected, and given equal opportunities.

(69) (B) His ancestral beliefs, culture, and tradition.

Antonio's behavior reflects his ancestral beliefs and culture when he meets other students in America. His belief system plays a significant role in shaping his attitude when he interacts with students in a new culture.

(70) (B) Her efforts to study Chinese culture and tradition.

The question presents Maria's action of studying Chinese culture to connect with a potential client from China. This indicates her efforts to understand and appreciate the client's background.

(71) (D) Accreditation.

Accreditation is referred to as recognition of a certification or an educational institute. A state's social work board must also approve and accept that certification. In this case, the Minnesota Board of Social Work needs to accept Abel's certification. It will allow him to legally practice and dispense his services to the community.

(72) (C) Lack of accessibility.

Accessibility is the ability to access and receive available services. In this case, social workers could not reach the people in need of services due to a lack of accessibility.

(73) (B) Advocacy.

Intervening on someone else's behalf to represent, support, or protect them against any kind of injustice is referred to as advocacy. Jim advocated for structural changes in the community to ensure that everyone had unimpeded access to contraception. He represented Michelle and fought on her behalf to ensure she achieved equal opportunity and equal access before the law of Arizona and to protect her from racial discrimination.

(74) (C) The number of individuals or groups that Susan is responsible for within a certain period of time.

A social worker's caseload is the number of individuals or groups they are responsible for within a certain period of time. Susan is responsible for 29 individuals and will manage their cases until they no longer require services. Her caseload is 29.

(75) (A) Case management.

Case management entails reviewing the available processes, protocols, and services and coordinating their allocation per a client's needs.

(76) (A) A set of rules outlining the protocols a social worker must abide by and the procedures a social worker has to follow in the case of an ethical dilemma.

The code of ethics is a code of conduct for all social workers. They are ethically bound to practice the tenets of the code of ethics in the field. It is a set of rules outlining the proper way a social worker is supposed to behave, the practices they need to avoid, and the procedures they are supposed to follow in the case of an ethical dilemma.

(77) (C) Codependency.

This case illustrates an unhealthy relationship between Agatha and her husband. Agatha has taken on most of the marital and family responsibilities and indulges in her husband's self-harming habits. This is classic codependency, as Agatha prioritizes her husband's needs over hers.

(78) (B) Community development.

Community development occurs when social workers interact with community members to aid society's overall growth and development. The social workers assess and analyze the community's needs and then develop resources to meet those needs. Moreover, community development entails the promotion of networking within the community as well.

(79) (A) Confidentiality.

Confidentiality is part of the code of ethics a social worker must follow. It entails protecting a client's private information unless the client explicitly waives it. In this case, disclosing private information was unnecessary and against the client's wishes. Therefore, it is referred to as a breach of confidentiality.

(80) (D) Continued education.

Continued education is the education one pursues even after obtaining a social work degree and entering the practical field of social work.

(81) (C) Ethical practice dilemma.

Ethical dilemmas refer to scenarios where there is a conflict in core values. Walker is a social worker and is bound by the code of ethics. Social workers must maintain a professional distance from their clients and cannot develop personal relationships with them. Accepting the connection request would overlap their personal and professional lives, which creates an ethical dilemma.

(82) (B) Confidentiality.

Core social work values are service, social justice, the dignity and worth of the person, integrity, the importance of human relationships, and competence. Confidentiality is not part of the professional framework of the social work field.

(83) (D) Global assessment of functioning.

The global assessment of functioning is a scale of zero to one hundred. It assesses how likely a person is to inflict self-harm, how likely they are to harm someone else, their ability to care for themselves, and their ability to do so while facing other issues.

(84) (B) Indirect practice.

Indirect practice is social work that is non-face-to-face. In the given case, the social worker only executes tasks that do not include or involve face-to-face interaction with community members or their clients.

(85) (C) Functional assessment

Functional assessment entails assessing how capable individuals are of taking care of themselves. The assessment of that particular ability is known as a functional assessment. Global assessment entails the assessment of other abilities as well.

(86) (C) He forgot to ensure accountability.

A social worker has to ensure that the program they enforce is effective.

(87) (A) Implied consent is a verbal or nonverbal agreement implying the individual's consent to treatment. In contrast, informed consent entails clearly informing the individual of all information they require to make an informed decision.

The fundamental difference between implied and informed consent is that informed consent is based on information provided by the social worker, and implied consent is based on nonverbal or verbal communication implying consent.

(88) (B) When Frankie wants to discuss case details with her family members.

Frankie's desire to discuss private information with personal connections or relations is not a valid reason to disclose information discussed during privileged communication.

(89) (A) To form an intervention plan.

An intervention plan can only be formed if the social worker has all the required information to determine whether the client requires assistance from a professional social worker. Intervention plans also entail assessments determining validity in intervening.

(90) (D) Interviewing or counseling techniques.

Interviews are an integral part of assessments carried out by social workers to determine whether intervening is valid. Social workers must apply these techniques while interviewing or counseling an individual.

(91) (A) Biological assessment.

The biological assessment entails questions regarding the individual's genetics, mental and physical health, and age and development.

(92) (B) Social assessment.

Social assessment entails questions about the individual's past and present relationships with family, friends, and acquaintances. The social assessment also includes questions related to the spiritual and religious affiliations of the individual, social support, and work-related stressors.

(93) (D) Biological and psychological assessments.

Psychological assessments are associated with an individual's mental state, thoughts, feelings, and emotions. Biological assessments are associated with an individual's physical health, age, development, and other genetic factors.

(94) (A) It will allow Ms. Bailey to analyze any early indicators of abuse or negligence and highlight any emerging patterns raising concern.

Ms. Bailey will use the data to help the family and serve them in the best way possible. The information will be used to analyze their case and look for any signs of domestic abuse or child negligence.

(95) (C) Mental health issues of the parent.

These questions are associated with the mental capabilities of the parent. They enquire about the parent's cognitive abilities and their thoughts and emotions regarding domestic matters and their children.

(96) (D) Assess whether the client is ready to change and open to help from a social worker.

The client must be actively involved in the assessment process to ensure their concerns and needs are met. One such involvement entails the assessment of their will to change and accept help from an outsider.

(97) (B) These questions allow Parker and the client to set goals for the treatment plan.

Client involvement is vital for case assessment and case management. Each intervention plan can be effective if goals and expected outcomes are set. The listed questions gauge the involvement and expectations of the client.

(98) (C) Plan the intervention.

Personal relations are against the code of ethics in social work. Once the assessment indicates the need for intervention, the next step should entail planning that intervention.

(99) (A) Setting event.

A setting event makes the problem behavior more likely to occur. Such events influence negative behavior. The instability of Sarah's family causes her to act out and is therefore referred to as a setting event.

(100) (B) It is a legal term that refers to the state taking on a person's welfare or care needs to provide them with a legal guardian.

Parens patriae is a legal term used to refer to the state ensuring the needs and welfare of individuals by providing a legal guardian in the absence of a safe alternative.

(101) (C) Antecedent.

Antecedents are events or factors that directly precede problematic behavior.

(102) (B) Psychodynamic therapy.

Psychodynamic therapy highlights specific life events that impact an individual's feelings, thoughts, actions, and relationships.

(103) (C) Normal sleeping patterns and usual eating habits.

Regular sleeping patterns and typical eating habits do not indicate mental or emotional illness.

(104) (A) Post-traumatic stress disorder (PTSD).

These symptoms indicate the presence of post-traumatic stress disorder. GAD characterizes uncontrollable nervousness, and OCD is associated with experiencing repeated impulses.

(105) (A) He felt fear and mistrust of the consequences of applying.

It is common for immigrants not to apply for assistance. Some of the most typical reasons include fear and mistrust of the consequences of applying, cultural boundaries, lack of transportation, and administrative burdens.

(106) (B) Stage 3: Planning.

The process of treatment and intervention has multiple stages. The first two stages of engagement and assessment entail gathering information about the client and assessing their case and need for intervention. The third stage involves planning the intervention.

(107) (C) Limit setting technique.

This technique further entails avoiding a power struggle with the client by making all decisions mutually.

(108) (C) Role-play techniques.

Role-play techniques are effective when they allow clients to express genuine and raw emotions without self-imposed limitations. Such a technique allows Jessica to think beyond the limitations of her current circumstances and help improve her self-perception and awareness.

(109) (A) Role modeling techniques.

Role modeling techniques will allow Jasmine to help her client by using modeling behaviors and imitation instead of specific verbal instructions.

(110) (C) Harm reduction techniques.

The harm reduction technique is critical in helping an addict in the active addiction stage. Unlike other techniques, the harm reduction technique does not involve waiting for the addict to achieve a certain degree of sobriety independently before becoming eligible to access professional support.

(111) (B) Harm reduction programs.

Harm reduction programs provide support to addicts and substance abusers without judgment. They develop healthy relationship-building.

(112) (D) Physical, emotional, psychological, professional, relational, and spiritual

Self-care methods are associated with these six key components.

(113) (C) The client should prioritize her needs over those of others.

Self-care methods include maintaining friendships and other relationships, prioritizing one's own needs over those of others, setting goals and aiming for achievements, and asking for help when needed.

(114) (A) Express resentful feelings in unhealthy ways.

Social workers are heavily affected by their cases. They must find healthy ways to release pent-up emotions and resentful feelings.

(115) (C) Accommodating.

Carter adopted the strategy of accommodation. Group A conceded to the demands of Group B, which showed a lack of assertiveness on their side. Collaboration would have entailed a solution benefiting both parties. A compromise would have entailed both parties coming together to find a middle ground where each party gained something.

(116) (A) To avoid socialization.

Self-monitoring techniques entail the social worker working with the client to identify harmful behavior and collaborating on ways to reduce and limit that behavior. It includes increasing independence and promoting socialization.

(117) (D) Delaying.

Conflict resolution methods include five key strategies: avoidance, competition, accommodation, collaboration, and compromise.

(118) (A) Collaborate with the teen and ensure she is involved in all steps moving forward.

The trauma-informed care method's principles include choice, collaboration, developing trust, and empowering the victim. Sarah has already made the teen feel at ease. The next step is collaboration.

(119) (C) To hold on to feelings of negativity to identify the cause of the problem.

A key strategy of anger management is forgiveness. Holding onto negative feelings and harboring anger will hamper the client's progress. Identifying the issue is important but should be done without harboring ill feelings.

(120) (B) Listen to music.

A key strategy of anger management is using relaxing techniques to dispel anger. They include writing in a journal, listening to music, meditating, and practicing yoga. Using dark humor and sarcastic remarks and harboring ill feelings will trigger anger episodes rather than dispelling them.

(121) (A) Task-centered approaches.

Task-centered approaches are a short-term way to resolve issues. They entail the social worker collaborating with the client to set certain goals and specific tasks.

(122) (D) Psychoeducational approaches.

A psychoeducational approach incorporates a balance of education and clinical influences to deal with issues related to underlying emotional trauma.

(123) (B) Establish a clear idea of the issues to be addressed.

Ms. Stewart needs to establish a clear idea of the issues that need to be addressed before analyzing the cognitive issues of the client. It will help Ms. Stewart create a comprehensive plan to help her client in the best possible way.

(124) (C) Use negative reinforcements to avoid negative behavior.

Behavioral intervention instills certain behaviors in the client to address their physical health. These behaviors include sticking to a daily routine, using reminders to stay on track, taking small breaks to decompress, and incorporating positive reinforcements.

(125) (D) Strength-based and empowerment strategies.

Strength-based and empowerment strategies of intervention engage the client and their support systems to ensure they feel like an active part of the solution. These strategies apprise clients of their strengths and empower them to take control of their lives.

(126) (B) Contracting and goal-setting techniques.

The contracting and goal-setting technique involves collaboration between the social worker and the client to create a written agreement outlining where they started, their specific goals, and how they expect to end up.

(127) (C) Create an intervention plan.

When a crisis occurs, social workers actively intervene to help those affected. Once the nature of the trauma has been determined, they assess the client and step in to assist them. The next course of action is to develop an intervention plan and help the client recover or cope with the trauma.

(128) (A) Task-centered practice.

A task-centered approach will help the client break down her goal into smaller tasks and milestones. This makes them easier to achieve. Moreover, fulfilling smaller tasks will improve the client's self-esteem.

(129) (D) Group expectations should not be set at the beginning.

All forms of group therapy entail everyone feeling heard, being given the chance to express their thoughts and feelings, and feeling validated. Moreover, setting group expectations at the beginning of the treatment is essential for group therapy to be effective.

(130) (C) Transgenerational therapy.

Transgenerational therapy can help resolve intergenerational trauma associated with abuse and neglect. It uses past issues or conflicts to foreshadow future issues. This type of therapy allows the solutions of past issues to be used to resolve problems in the future.

(131) (A) Small goals are easily achievable and increase the client's self-esteem. Large goals seem intimidating and might result in regression during the treatment program.

Small goals are realistic and assure the client that they are succeeding during the intervention and treatment process. If goals are too large, they become unattainable and lead to the client losing hope of recovery.

(132) (C) The plan helps Ally understand why she needs intervention to develop healthy behaviors.

Receiving rationale from social workers helps the clients understand why they need intervention. It increases the effectiveness of intervention programs, and clients are motivated to complete tasks independently.

(133) (C) Develop a system that would prevent clients from correlating previous actions with new habits and routines.

If clients want to progress, they must have a system that correlates past actions and habits with new habits and routines. It will apprise the client of their progress and show them how far they have come.

(134) (B) Stay calm and make the client feel heard.

Social workers often encounter individuals who are unwilling to ask for or accept help. Jake must remain calm and inform the client that he is there to help.

(135) (B) Partializing techniques.

Partializing techniques entail a planned approach incorporating small steps and actions to acquire desired goals.

(136) (A) Active listening.

When a social worker receives feedback from a client, they should actively listen to their suggestions and observe to assess their needs and requirements.

(137) (D) Inconsistent nonverbal communication.

Inconsistent nonverbal communication implies a difference in what one says and facial expressions. Social workers use this to tell if someone is lying. In this case, Tessa's bruises were more severe than a fall would have warranted.

(138) (C) Independent living home.

Placement is an essential step in a treatment plan. Each individual must be placed in a facility according to their needs.

(139) (C) Severity of addiction.

The case concerns a troubled teenager with unruly behavior and does not involve substance abuse or addictions.

(140) (B) Arrange for aftercare and follow-up services.

When a social worker discharges a client after treatment, they create a discharge plan. That plan outlines the aftercare of the client and any follow-up services they might require.

(141) (D) Follow-up.

Aftercare and follow-up are essential after a client is discharged from the care and services of a social worker. Aftercare entails rendering services after treatment. Follow-up entails checking up on their health after they have been discharged.

(142) (A) Cultural discrimination.

Social workers act according to a code of ethics. The code prohibits social workers from discriminating against any individual in the community based on religion, race, color, or ethnicity. Their responsibilities include taking care of the community, providing counseling, and ensuring the mental and physical well-being of the client.

(143) (D) Ensure the psychological well-being of the client.

Ensuring the psychological well-being of a client is the responsibility of a social worker, not a case manager. A case manager ensures the availability of technical and financial resources required to help the client. Joint services of a social worker and a case manager include advocacy, brokerage, coordination, and support.

(144) (B) Psychoeducational programs.

Community resources and involvement include programs affecting a group of people and an entire community. Such programs include healthy living programs, housing programs, transportation facilities, employment opportunities, and senior centers.

(145) (C) Social isolation.

Psychoeducational approaches ensure that an individual suffering from emotional trauma does not relapse after treatment. These approaches improve quality of life and social understanding and ensure clients actively engage in their treatment plans.

(146) (C) Practice and develop her skill base to enhance her professional experience.

One of the core ethical values is to continue developing skills to enhance one's competence and understanding. Indiana did not focus on this core ethical value.

(147) (C) A license and formal education are required to work as a professional social worker.

Proper education and licensure are required to practice social work. Every state has different requirements, but a bachelor's degree and license are the standard.

(148) (D) Pursue collaborative consultation when appropriate.

Hannah demonstrates her ethical responsibility to her client and colleague by referring her to a specialist who can better help address her needs.

(149) (B) Hannah cannot stop the client from terminating her services as long as the termination falls within the agency's guidelines.

Clients have the right to terminate services as long as the termination falls within the policy guidelines.

(150) (D) He has the right to self-determination, which allows him to accept or decline services unless he is deemed mentally unfit.

Mike's prison record does not negate, his right to accept or decline treatment according to the Civil Rights Act.

(151) (B) The potential for a dual relationship since Mark and Lisa are bonded now.

This falls under the category of boundary issues and multiple relationships for ethical concerns.

(152) (C) Educational supervisors.

Jessica's role is to provide information and promote learning as a supervisor.

(153) (C) Avoid sharing personal details

Maria should not share any details about her own experiences or personal life.

(154) (D) Act to Promote Public Health Through Workplace Safety for Social Workers – H3864.

The bill focuses on workplace safety for social workers, which is relevant to Anna's concern.

(155) (A) Yes, it violates ethical and legal boundaries.

Providing clients with personal contact information is considered a red flag behavior.

(156) (B) She should reassure the participant that all her information will remain confidential and that she can skip the question if she likes.

This reflects an ethical approach and ensures the participant's well-being while collecting data for the study.

(157) (C) Community-based participatory research.

This approach utilizes the collaboration of stakeholders and implements effective change to achieve goals.

(158) (D) Use verbal de-escalation techniques to bring the situation under control.

Verbal de-escalation is a communication skill that social workers utilize when handling tense situations and preventing violence.

(159) (C) Implement alarm systems that alert staff members to escalations.

A client with a violent history can be a threat. It is essential to implement systems that alert staff members if a situation becomes dangerous.

(160) (C) Immediately share only relevant information with her supervisor and colleagues.

The principle of confidentiality does not hold absolute when there is a risk of harm. Workers should share information to ensure the well-being of their clients without divulging unnecessary details.

(161) (B) It will provide the colleague with clear information about Ginger's case.

The record will help the colleague fill Anderson's position diligently and address Ginger's needs effectively.

(162) (B) Bureaucracy.

Bureaucracy is a hierarchal structure where a specific group makes decisions, and there is a clear division of roles for everyone involved.

(163) (D) Provide her with administrative and emotional support and encourage self-care.

This will help Lisa manage the emotional toll her work takes on her.

(164) (A) Encourage her to take some time off.

Taking time off will help Sally address her emotional well-being. Her own emotional health must be strengthened before she can help others.

(165) (C) Provide emotional support only for those dealing with VIP clients.

Emotional support should offered to everyone within the organization.

(166) (D) Jane should have an open conversation with Antonio to understand his needs and motivations.

Jane should focus on having an open discussion with Antonio, address his needs, and tailor them according to his requirements and cultural context.

(167) (B) Problem solver.

Rachel will primarily act as a problem solver. She will help Eric identify loopholes, find practical solutions, and create a support system.

(168) (D) Enjoy the job and find fun in what she does.

Enjoying the job is for personal satisfaction and achieving personal goals, but it is not critical in creating a positive and safe work environment.

(169) (C) Designate one day each week when he focuses on paperwork and only takes calls or replies to emails if absolutely necessary.

Although all the strategies mentioned are great for time management, for Sam's particular case, it is essential to set a day aside when he only focuses on filing paperwork and reports.

(170) (D) Compliance.

Compliance is not one of the eight principles that social workers need to adhere to when keeping records.

Test 3: Questions

(1) There are multiple popular theories on human development. One theory states that children most often learn through observation of their parents, caregivers, and common adults in their lives. The theory states that children then mimic what they observed, using adult behavior as a base model for how they should act, react, and behave. This is known as which of the following theories?

(A) Piaget's cognitive development theory.

(B) Erikson's psychosocial development theory.

(C) Bandura's social learning theory.

(D) Bowlby's attachment theory.

(2) The achieved education, training, and certification required to enter a professional field and practice in that profession in an active capacity is known as what?

(A) Continued education.

(B) Accreditation.

(C) Critical thinking.

(D) Eligibility criteria.

(3) Which of these stages is defined as the completion of treatment goals and the dismissal from the program?

(A) Assessment.

(B) Planning.

(C) Intervention.

(D) Termination.

(4) What is the formal term when a program or professional certification is deemed adequate in terms of the knowledge base it provides to its participants and such credentials are formally acknowledged?

(A) Accreditation.

(B) Benchmark.

(C) Advocacy.

(D) Certification.

(5) A young child is sitting on the floor playing with another child in the block center at his preschool. The teacher announces that it is time to clean up for snack time. Peers around the room begin to clean up their centers when the other child starts to scream that he does not want to clean up and begins to kick and throw the blocks. The following week, when it is time to clean up and go home for the day, the child who witnessed his peer's outburst repeats the behavior he observed, screams that he does not want to go home, and kicks and throws the toys that he had been playing with.

This is an example of which of the following theories?

(A) Bandura's social learning theory.

(B) Freud's psychosexual development theory.

(C) Erikson's psychosocial development theory.

(D) Piaget's cognitive development theory.

(6) Which process contains all of the following steps: assessment and review of the skills developed when undergoing a program; review and comparison of any interventions, treatments, or service programs and the progress achieved by participants over set periods of time; determination of whether additional resources should be given to a specific program or multiple programs; use of a program's met objectives and the accomplishments achieved by participants in order to determine the success and effectiveness of that program; and assurance that accountability requirements are being met are all steps in what process?

(A) Assurance that liability is applied for poorly developed programs.

(B) Decision of where funding should be allocated.

(C) Determination of the effectiveness of programs.

(D) Assurance of a program's inclusion in community involvement.

(7) What phase of the intervention process focuses on examination of the client on several different levels in order to make conclusions about the issues they may have and the needs that possibly need to be met, as well as helping highlight any other important points that should be addressed?

(A) Engagement.

(B) Assessment.

(C) Planning.

(D) Intervention.

(8) Which of the six core values of social work is defined as the binding commitment to help individuals and communities identify and address social needs?

(A) Social justice.

(B) Competence.

(C) Service.

(D) Integrity.

(9) In Erikson's eight stages of development, at what stage does Erikson theorize that a child is at their most vulnerable point, meaning the point at which they must rely on caregivers or parents for the entirety of their basic human needs in addition to having their needs for affection, connection, and attachment met?

(A) Intimacy vs. Isolation.

(B) Trust vs. Mistrust.

(C) Generativity vs. Stagnation.

(D) Integrity vs. Despair.

(10) Harry notices his younger brother Toby struggles with reading. Harry speaks with his parents, and the three of them then discuss it with the school. In the end, Toby begins to receive extra help with his reading and comprehension at school. What is the action Harry committed known as?

(A) Bravado.

(B) Concern.

(C) Codependence.

(D) Advocating.

(11) During what phase of the intervention process are goals made and methods with which to meet such goals outlined and organized?

(A) Planning.

(B) Evaluation.

(C) Engagement.

(D) Intervention.

(12) What do confidentiality, privacy, and access to services mean to a client?

(A) They are a client's privilege.

(B) They are the protections afforded to clients.

(C) They are the client's rights.

(D) They are therapy assurances.

(13) Social learning theory explains that children learn through mimicry of behaviors, reactions, and social responses. Such mimicry is based mostly on the visual, verbal, and physical actions or reactions of a child's primary parent or caregiver, secondary caregivers, siblings, peers, and favorite TV characters. Which of the following people developed the social learning theory?

(A) Albert Bandura.

(B) Erik Erikson.

(C) Sigmund Freud.

(D) Jean Piaget.

(14) Kelly conducts a session with a client she has seen a few times now. As they discuss the issues and goals that have been set, Kelly makes an active effort to express her understanding and respect. What Kelly is doing is known as what?

(A) Empathy.

(B) Reflection.

(C) Prompting.

(D) Interpretation.

(15) What intervention technique uses a clear process in which actions have direct consequences?

(A) Role modeling.

(B) Self-monitoring.

(C) Limit setting.

(D) Anger management.

(16) What legal rights allow clients and patients to decline treatment or services offered to them?

(A) Right to informed consent.

(B) Right to refuse services.

(C) Right to terminate services.

(D) Right to obtain medical records.

(17) Alex is almost a year old, and sucking his thumb brings him pleasure and comfort. Based on which of the following theories could this lead to the development of an oral fixation in Alex's adolescent or adult years as a means of finding pleasure and comfort in order to help alleviate the stressors in his adult life?

(A) Massumi's theory of sexuality.

(B) Bowlby's attachment theory.

(C) Piaget's cognitive development theory.

(D) Freud's psychosexual development theory.

(18) Erin is a social worker. She has a new client who is an alcoholic. As they explore the different treatment options, the client expresses their desire to take part in an outpatient program. Erin reviews several programs before the decision is made to use a 12-step program that has shown great success and fits the client's needs ideally. What is it called when a social worker, such as Erin, chooses the best possible way to address an issue and help a client?

(A) Direct practice.

(B) Best practice.

(C) Accreditation.

(D) Mentorship.

(19) What technique in therapy has clients model behaviors after others using a three-step system that includes behavior, possibilities, and inspiration?

(A) Partializing technique.

(B) Self-monitoring technique.

(C) Limit setting technique.

(D) Role modeling technique.

(20) What is the technical term for a supervisory role that directs teaching, models behavior, and evaluates the mastery of defined behaviors?

(A) Creative supervision.

(B) Collaborative supervision.

(C) Alternative supervision.

(D) Directive supervision.

(21) As a baby, bonding with a parent or caregiver in a profound way will help facilitate healthy, lifelong bonds with other people and create a sense of security in which the child grows and develops. What theory is this?

(A) Attachment theory.

(B) Rational theory.

(C) Social learning theory.

(D) Psychosocial development theory.

(22) Through the establishment of a trusting and respectful relationship with her social worker, Autumn has been actively involved in the development of her intervention plan, has set goals, followed along with the steps of her 12-step program, and made positive decisions in her life in order to achieve sobriety, gain overall health and wellness, and learn how to stay sober when she eventually exits the treatment program. What type of method is used to create this relationship between Autumn and her social worker?

(A) Empathetic method.

(B) Engagement method.

(C) Rapport-building method.

(D) Reframing method.

(23) What is the therapeutic approach that utilizes stress reduction, maintains health and well-being, and fosters lifelong tool building?

(A) Limit-setting techniques.

(B) Self-care and coping methods.

(C) Harm-reduction techniques.

(D) Self-monitoring techniques.

(24) Rebecka is a social worker who is dealing with her antagonistic client, Jason. What is the best thing for Rebecka to do in this situation?

(A) Tell Jason he has a bad attitude and that it is making their interaction unmanageable.

(B) Tolerate Jason's antagonistic behavior while trying not to upset him further.

(C) Tell Jason that his attitude will not be tolerated and that if he cannot adjust his behavior, she will have to end the session early and try again another day when he can conduct himself more appropriately.

(D) Tell Jason that she understands how he is feeling and ask to discuss his feelings further.

(25) Every day, Anna makes breakfast then cleans up the house and does laundry. At lunchtime, she says, “Lunchtime,” before she places her toddler-aged boys in their highchairs to eat. Then, she cleans up from the children’s morning play. Her kitchen, dining room, and living room make one great room that allows Anna to keep an eye on her children while she cleans and they eat.

Today, when Anna called out, “Lunchtime,” she walked into the living room to find her toddlers putting away their own toys. Which of the learning methods below correctly theorizes why her children would behave in this manner?

(A) Cognitive learning.

(B) Psychosocial learning.

(C) Social learning.

(D) Attachment learning.

(26) Tessa has four family client cases, nine alcoholism client cases, three drug addict client cases, one client who is a case of trauma, and four cases of clients with mental health disorders. What do all of these cases make up for Tessa?

(A) Case management.

(B) Functional assessment.

(C) Caseload.

(D) Network.

(27) What is the first strategy of conflict resolution?

(A) Competing.

(B) Accommodating.

(C) Avoidance.

(D) Compromise.

(28) An important part of a social worker's job is to keep accurate and up-to-date files on each of their clients. Such files should include the initial assessment, intervention plans, goals set, meeting or session notes, progress, and other similar information and updates. All of this collated information is the result of what social work task?

(A) Intervention planning.

(B) Record keeping.

(C) Discharge evaluation.

(D) Reevaluation.

(29) A newborn baby, who is later called Ava, is abandoned within hours of her birth. Ava is placed into the foster system, but due to a heart condition, she is never adopted. The location in which this occurs is filled beyond capacity with abandoned babies. Ava spends a great deal of her time in a crib alone. In the beginning, she cries when she is hungry, needs a diaper change, or seeks the comfort and affection that a mother would typically give. At nine months old she no longer cries when she is alone in her crib. In fact, if she is being held for any other reason than to be fed or changed, she cries until she is placed back in her bed and left alone. This continues until Ava is five years old, when she is finally adopted. Ava does not make attachments with her adoptive parents. She becomes aggressive, and hits or bites any time either of her parents tries to show her affection. How does John Bowlby's attachment theory explain this behavior?

(A) Ava suffered from inadequate attachment bonding in her first five years of life. As a result, she does not have the ability to develop healthy attachments to her adoptive parents and she rejects touch.

(B) Ava was abused while in foster care, so she does not want people to touch her. She is only defending herself in an age-appropriate manner because she is being forced to do things that make her uncomfortable.

(C) Ava is a healthy and well-adjusted child. These are normal reactions that all adoptive parents have to go through when they adopt a child from foster care.

(D) Ava misses her birth mother. She is traumatized by the memories of abandonment, suffers from her displacement in foster care, and experiences common behavioral outbursts that are related to the trauma she has been through.

(30) What type of assessment looks at an individual's biology, psychology, social life and interactions, physical and mental health history, and other relevant information?

(A) Psychosocial assessment.

(B) Cognitive assessment.

(C) Behavioral assessment.

(D) Biopsychosocial assessment.

(31) What is the third strategy of conflict resolution?

(A) Compromise.

(B) Accommodation.

(C) Competition.

(D) Collaboration.

(32) What model of supervision is defined as a role that puts the final decision in the hands of the client, which is done through the suggestion of various alternative solutions, kept to a limited number of choices so as not to overwhelm them, while also allowing them to have choices and take charge of how things will go?

(A) Alternative supervision.

(B) Collaborative supervision.

(C) Nondirective supervision.

(D) Creative supervision.

(33) Which of the options best explains why a child would experience lifelong side effects that can include affectionless psychopathy, reckless behavior, impulsivity, delinquency, and hyper aggression?

(A) Social deprivation.

(B) Maternal deprivation.

(C) Cognitive deprivation.

(D) Sensory deprivation.

(34) Michael prides himself on maintaining professional boundaries. When a case came in that involved a close acquaintance, he passed the case off to a colleague so there would be no conflict of interest. In addition, Michael makes sure to keep client appointments and work duties within the confines of work hours. The maintenance of such boundaries between himself, as a social worker, and clients is just a small part of how he works within the moral limits of what type of conduct?

(A) Advocacy.

(B) Evidence-based practice.

(C) Just cause.

(D) Code of ethics.

(35) What is the fifth strategy of conflict resolution?

(A) Competition.

(B) Accommodation.

(C) Compromise.

(D) Collaboration.

(36) An employee whose responsibility is to supervise and coordinate directly with the administrative and clerical staff is known as what type of supervisor?

(A) Clinical.

(B) Administrative.

(C) Supportive.

(D) Educational.

(37) According to Erikson, the period between birth and 18 months is the most crucial time in a child's fundamental development. He explains that during this time, babies develop a foundation for all future development by bonding with the mother or primary caregivers. These bonds provide for a baby's basic needs, foster trust, give them confidence, and make them feel safe. This creates a healthy and lasting foundation for the child's future development. What is this stage in Erikson's theory known as?

(A) Trust vs. Mistrust.

(B) Generativity vs. Stagnation.

(C) Intimacy vs. Isolation.

(D) Ego Integrity vs. Despair.

(38) What is the formal term for a perspective that includes self-awareness, intellectual pliability, and comprehensive knowledge that gives an array of views from varying points?

(A) Diversity perspective.

(B) Feminist perspective.

(C) Generalist perspective.

(D) Strength perspective.

(39) There are ten strategies for anger management. What is the second strategy?

(A) Calm down.

(B) Identify the cause.

(C) Relaxation practices.

(D) Control your anger.

(40) What supervisory position is defined as a supervisor who oversees the education, training, and initial placement of social workers in an academic setting?

(A) Educational supervisor.

(B) Clinical supervisor.

(C) Supportive supervisor.

(D) Administrative supervisor.

(41) Which form of health refers to one's ability to mentally cope with life stressors such as home life, personal life, work life, and social life?

(A) Emotional health.

(B) Spiritual health.

(C) Physical health.

(D) Mental health.

(42) What is an unhealthy relationship in which emotional reliances or psychological reliances are developed?

(A) Networking.

(B) Codependency.

(C) Mentorship.

(D) Supervision.

(43) There are ten strategies for anger management. What is the fourth strategy?

(A) Relaxation practices.

(B) Control anger.

(C) Take a timeout.

(D) Forgiveness.

(44) What supervisory method is characterized by a supervisor who actively participates with clients as a means to establish a shared relationship?

(A) Nondirect supervision.

(B) Alternative supervision.

(C) Direct supervision.

(D) Collaborative supervision.

(45) Anna is 25 years old and has lived on her own for several years now. Every evening when she leaves work, she threads keys between her fingers as a safety precaution as she walks to the parking garage. She does the same when she returns home. Once inside, she locks her door and sets her home security system. Anna does not feel she is paranoid; she just does not believe that people are wholly trustworthy. Therefore, she feels the need to always be prepared. According to Erikson, during which stage of development did Anna most likely experience difficulty?

(A) Trust vs. Mistrust.

(B) Intimacy vs. Isolation.

(C) Generativity vs. Stagnation.

(D) Industry vs. Inferiority.

(46) What perspective looks into women, their roles and interactions, and the effects of gender inequalities?

(A) Feminist perspective.

(B) Strength perspective.

(C) Ecological perspective.

(D) Diversity perspective.

(47) What is the sixth strategy for anger management?

(A) Relaxation practices.

(B) Take responsibility.

(C) Take a timeout.

(D) Control your anger.

(48) What is the supervisory method in which the supervisor stays removed from the day-to-day details unless it is absolutely necessary, which allows individuals to make decisions for themselves and reach their own solutions when possible?

(A) Creative supervision.

(B) Directive supervision.

(C) Collaborative supervision.

(D) Nondirective supervision.

(49) Which form of health refers to being in control of one's behaviors, feelings, and thoughts?

(A) Spiritual health.

(B) Mental health.

(C) Emotional health.

(D) Social health.

(50) The town of Seaside has spent the last year focused on community improvements and expansion of the resources available to residents. It has added a community center and a senior center; implemented community-wide after-school programs; and held community get-togethers where local businesses and organizations can advertise services, offer outreach, and share information while community members are given the chance to socialize. What are these examples of?

(A) Community development.

(B) Continued education.

(C) Advocacy.

(D) Direct practices.

(51) Of the ten strategies for anger management, what it the eighth strategy?

(A) Control your anger.

(B) Forgiveness.

(C) Relaxation practices.

(D) Utilize humor.

(52) A client has been thoroughly assessed, and it is determined that they are of sound mind and should be allowed to make their own decisions regarding their health and welfare. What is this mental status formally known as?

(A) Consent.

(B) Inhibitions.

(C) Competency.

(D) Tenancies.

(53) Robert is 42. He works in a fairly successful career, has a nice home, paid off his car, and would say that he functions sufficiently in his life. However, when he spoke with his therapist recently, he divulged that he lacks confidence in himself and in his abilities to do his job. His bosses have never complained, and he has been promoted twice, but he still feels somehow his performance is not what it should be. Based on Erikson's theory of development, in which stage did Robert most likely experience difficulties that would have resulted in him feeling this way as an adult?

(A) Autonomy vs. Shame.

(B) Identity vs. Confusion.

(C) Generativity vs. Stagnation.

(D) Integrity vs. Despair.

(54) What formal term in social work refers to the social functioning of an individual and how that relates to their physical and mental health as well as the issues they deal with?

(A) Diversity perspective.

(B) Person-in-environment perspective.

(C) Diversity perspective.

(D) Feminist perspective.

(55) Of the ten steps to manage anger, what is the tenth and final step?

(A) Calm down.

(B) Relaxation practices.

(C) Utilize humor.

(D) Control your anger.

(56) A social worker has a duty to the public to investigate when a possible threat arises. What is this safety obligation to the public formally known as?

(A) Protection of the public.

(B) Public outreach.

(C) Community representation.

(D) Crisis intervention.

(57) Marina has always had a very doting mother. She is now 28 years old, and her mother still does her laundry every week and cleans the house they share. In a recent conversation with her friends, Marina came to the realization that it is very odd to still have her mother doing these things for her. She would like to talk to her mother about learning to do these things on her own; however, the idea of a discussion with her mother on the idea of becoming more independent makes her feel very reluctant. Marina does not want to upset her mother. Based on Erikson's theory of development, in which stage did Marina most likely experience difficulty in order to have given up such independence for this long and feel guilty over her desire for more independence now?

(A) Identity vs. Inferiority.

(B) Initiative vs. Guilt.

(C) Intimacy vs. Isolation.

(D) Industry vs. Inferiority.

(58) William refers to each of his clients as "the client" when he takes notes or adds notes to each individual's file. Additionally, his files are kept in a locked cabinet. The only people who see those files are William and his supervisor. The only exceptions are if someone is suspected of having the potential to hurt someone (including themself) or William applies for services for a client that require specific details, in which case he has the client's consent to share necessary information. What is it called when a person's private information is protected from being openly shared, such as in this scenario?

(A) Informed consent.

(B) Diagnosis.

(C) Confidentiality.

(D) Consent.

(59) What therapeutic technique focuses on a written plan to set and meet goals?

(A) Task-centered.

(B) Partializing.

(C) Contracting and goal setting.

(D) Psychoeducational.

(60) Wendy is responsible for overseeing the day-to-day operations at the therapy clinic. What is the formal name for this type of supervisor role?

(A) Administrative supervisor.

(B) Educational supervisor.

(C) Support supervisor.

(D) Clinical supervisor.

(61) In which of Piaget's four stages of development do children learn through sight, smell, sound, touch, and taste?

(A) Sensorimotor stage.

(B) Formal operational stage.

(C) Preoperational stage.

(D) Concrete operational stage.

(62) When an assessment is conducted, information such as a client's name, age, date of birth, gender, and marital status are which type of information?

(A) Biological information.

(B) Historical information.

(C) Socioeconomic information.

(D) Basic information.

(63) What therapeutic model is characterized by a short-term problem-solving approach?

(A) Limit setting.

(B) Stress management.

(C) Task-centered.

(D) Anger management.

(64) What is the key boundary in social work that puts the client's needs as the priority?

(A) Dual relationship.

(B) Client focus.

(C) Self-disclosure.

(D) Self-care.

(65) In Erikson's psychosocial development theory, what stage occurs between 18 months and 3 years of age and is described as the stage in which a child begins to achieve personal control, which includes potty training and making simple choices like milk or water, and begins to gain a sense of independence?

(A) Identity vs. Role Confusion.

(B) Trust vs. Mistrust.

(C) Initiative vs. Guilt.

(D) Autonomy vs. Shame.

(66) In her spare time, Mary is one of the chairpersons of a prestigious art school. The rest of the time she is the agency supervisor for a local adoption agency. Her agency has just entered into an adoption agreement with a young woman. As the agency reviews the file, it turns out that the woman in question has just received a scholarship for the art school that Mary chairs for.

Since Mary has important decision-making authority and influence over the young woman's art education as well as her continued future scholarship approval for each semester of art school, she feels that it is inappropriate to directly supervise the young woman's adoption case. As such, Mary appoints another social worker as special supervisor over the young woman's case in order to eliminate such an ethical and moral disruption.

In this scenario, why does Mary see the need to make this choice?

(A) Best practice.

(B) Cultural competence.

(C) Generalist practice.

(D) Conflict of interest.

(67) What group therapy approach involves individuals who work together to promote a shared cause or interest?

(A) Advocacy groups.

(B) Educational groups.

(C) Mutual aid groups.

(D) Group counseling.

(68) Anna is a social worker who leads a weekly substance abuse meeting in her community. While Anna is happy to empathize with group members, state general details related to a situation, and connect with group members on a professional level, she is careful not to disclose her own experiences or details about her life. What is the discussion of personal information about a professional known as?

(A) Self-reflection.

(B) Competence.

(C) Self-disclosure.

(D) Dual relationships.

(69) Maintenance of healthy interpersonal relationships is important to which type of health?

(A) Social health.

(B) Mental health.

(C) Emotional health.

(D) Spiritual health.

(70) What is it called when a social worker or counselor meets with a client and they establish the initial issue that needs to be addressed?

(A) Definitive diagnosis.

(B) Planned intervention.

(C) The presenting problem.

(D) Attainable goals.

(71) What therapeutic group method is characterized by an informal support group that gathers to share, help, and support one another?

(A) Counseling group.

(B) Advocacy group.

(C) Mutual aid group.

(D) Crisis management group.

(72) What type of relationships are most often frowned upon between social workers and their clients?

(A) Professional relationships.

(B) Existential relationships.

(C) Codependent relationships.

(D) Dual relationships.

(73) In Piaget's cognitive development theory, in which stage does logical thought develop in children?

(A) Sensorimotor stage.

(B) Preoperational stage.

(C) Concrete operational stage.

(D) Formal operational stage.

(74) What is the description that is generated based on an individual's initial appearance and behaviors known as?

(A) Hypothetical description.

(B) General description.

(C) Clinical description.

(D) Detailed description.

(75) What therapeutic group approach is specifically characterized by a professional using a psychiatric approach to therapy or counseling?

(A) Entomology.

(B) Psychotherapy.

(C) Sociology.

(D) Psychology.

(76) What does it mean to work within your competence?

(A) To know your field of profession.

(B) To work with what you know and understand.

(C) To stay mentally fit for yourself and your job.

(D) To be aware of your professional limits and know when to ask for help.

(77) In Erikson's psychosocial theory, which stage occurs between three and five years of age and is characterized by a child's development of a feeling of purpose in themself through peer play, further exploration of their environment, and gaining a further sense of independence and control in their world?

(A) Initiative vs. Guilt.

(B) Industry vs. Inferiority.

(C) Identity vs. Role Confusion.

(D) Intimacy vs. Isolation.

(78) The Brighten Institute of Social Services requires, in addition to the minimum licensing requirements of 60 hours of annual training for each social worker, that any social worker employed by their company complete 40 hours of family counseling education, 40 hours of substance abuse and recovery training, and 40 hours of trauma-informed care training. What is all 120 hours of annual education and training known as?

(A) Continued education requirements.

(B) Eligibility criteria.

(C) Informed consent requirements.

(D) Informed consent.

(79) What form of family therapy is characterized by breaking down the family's hierarchy in order to understand and restructure the family dynamics?

(A) Transgenerational family therapy.

(B) Strategic family therapy.

(C) Narrative family therapy.

(D) Structural family therapy.

(80) Because social work involves the creation of close relationships with individuals, establishment of trust, and working through some people's most vulnerable moments, it is particularly important to ensure what?

(A) Interpersonal relationships.

(B) Codependencies.

(C) Professional boundaries.

(D) Self-determination.

(81) In what stage in Piaget's cognitive development theory do children develop symbolic thought?

(A) Sensorimotor stage.

(B) Preoperational stage.

(C) Concrete operational stage.

(D) Formal operational stage.

(82) What is the first step in the creation of an intervention plan?

(A) Choose a problem behavior that is earmarked for change.

(B) Collect data to measure the behavior.

(C) Create a functional behavioral assessment.

(D) Teach the new alternative behavior.

(83) Which family therapy method is solution-based in its approach to solve and resolve issues?

(A) Systemic family therapy.

(B) Narrative family therapy.

(C) Transgenerational therapy.

(D) Strategic family therapy.

(84) Victor is a county social worker. He gives out his personal number to female clients, invites them over to his home for dinner, communicates with them, follows them on social media, and even introduces them to family and friends when he brings them along to family gatherings. Such behaviors are known by what term?

(A) Conscious behaviors.

(B) Ethical behaviors.

(C) Red flag behaviors.

(D) Unconscious behaviors.

(85) The development of abstract thinking occurs during which stage of Piaget's cognitive development theory?

(A) Formal operational stage.

(B) Concrete operational stage.

(C) Preoperational stage.

(D) Sensorimotor stage.

(86) A commitment to service, social justice, dignity and worth of the person, integrity, competence, and the importance of human relationships are known as what in the world of social work?

(A) Culture competencies.

(B) Core values.

(C) Code of ethics.

(D) Codependency.

(87) What type of social work is defined as helping an individual develop better social relationships and adjust existing ones?

(A) Social work research.

(B) Social casework.

(C) Social group work.

(D) Social welfare.

(88) What type of social work research is characterized by the study of communities in order to create programs to meet their needs?

(A) Action research.

(B) Community-based participatory research.

(C) Double-blind studies.

(D) Field studies.

(89) What is the fourth stage of Erikson's psychosocial development theory, which is focused on self-competency, occurs between 5 and 12 years of age, and is characterized by learning how to set and meet goals and the expectation to do more in school?

(A) Generativity vs. Stagnation.

(B) Autonomy vs. Shame.

(C) Ego Integrity vs. Despair.

(D) Industry vs. Inferiority.

(90) What is the third step in the creation of an intervention plan?

(A) Create a behavioral plan.

(B) Collect data to measure the behavior.

(C) Determine the function of the behavioral problem.

(D) Choose a problem behavior that is earmarked for change.

(91) Formal and informal allocation and distribution of resources are typically the responsibility of which individuals?

(A) Site supervisors.

(B) Clients.

(C) Social workers.

(D) Public relations officers.

(92) What type of social work research uses the collaborations of stakeholders involved to set and reach goals?

(A) Focus group data collection.

(B) Community-based participatory research.

(C) Double-blind research studies.

(D) Longitudinal research studies.

(93) Which type of health refers to an individual's emotions and feelings about having a purpose in life, and has had a significant impact on their moral and ethical values?

(A) Spiritual health.

(B) Physical health.

(C) Social health.

(D) Emotional health.

(94) What is the fifth step in the creation of an intervention plan?

(A) Create a behavioral plan.

(B) Collect data to measure the behavior.

(C) Choose a problem behavior that is earmarked for change.

(D) Teach the new alternative behavior.

(95) What condition is the medication Xanax typically used to treat?

(A) Depression.

(B) Overstimulation.

(C) Hyperactivity.

(D) Anxiety.

(96) What technical term is used to refer to the use of an identically composed group to compare against your experimental group in order to examine and measure the effects of the experiment and the outcome of a study?

(A) Mixed methods.

(B) Control group.

(C) Field study.

(D) Focus group.

(97) What is an individual's personal perspective in regard to how they look at themself known as?

(A) Body image.

(B) Personal goals.

(C) Self-image.

(D) Self-determination.

(98) Mario makes informed decisions about each of his cases when he examines the key factors in each case file before he reviews the personal details, histories, and traumas experienced by a given client. His ability to gather and comb through all of the information to get a clear picture of each case using reason and knowledge is known as what?

(A) Indirect practice.

(B) Eligibility criteria.

(C) Direct practice.

(D) Critical thinking.

(99) A schizophrenic is brought into the hospital having a severe psychotic episode. What medication is the hospital most likely to immediately give the patient to calm them down so health care providers can assess injuries?

(A) Haldol.

(B) Ativan.

(C) Adderall.

(D) Prozac.

(100) What type of research study involves the subject and the researcher being unaware of who receives the placebo and who receives the treatment in the study?

(A) Field study.

(B) Double-blind study.

(C) Pilot study.

(D) Longitudinal study.

(101) What is the most common way to avoid pain, seek pleasure, cope with cravings, stimulate response learning, and cater to impulsivity?

(A) Substance abuse.

(B) Mental health disorder.

(C) Out-of-home placement.

(D) Psychotropics.

(102) What role do effective communication and skills play in cultural consideration?

(A) Training and certification.

(B) Organizational support.

(C) Skills development.

(D) Awareness and knowledge.

(103) A bipolar patient comes to her therapist's office in a state of bipolar mania. The doctor admits the patient and uses what medication to stabilize the patient's mood?

(A) Concerta.

(B) Lithium.

(C) Paxil.

(D) Cymbalta.

(104) What type of research study collects raw information, usually outside a formal research setting?

(A) Pilot study.

(B) Longitudinal study.

(C) Double-blind study.

(D) Field study.

(105) What classification is given to emotional or psychological issues that affect the health of an individual?

(A) Spiritual health.

(B) Mental health.

(C) Social health.

(D) Physical health.

(106) What is the technical term for the preliminary divulgence of information in the five key practices of therapy?

(A) Commitment to action.

(B) Initial disclosure.

(C) Evaluation and termination.

(D) Counseling intervention.

(107) A client in their early 20s displays signs of psychosis and fades in and out of touch with reality. These symptoms are most likely a sign of what issue?

(A) Obsessive-compulsive disorder.

(B) Depression.

(C) Schizophrenia.

(D) Dysmorphia.

(108) Once a month, Karen's bosses put together an activity for all the employees to participate in together in order to foster healthy professional relationships. What are these activities known as?

(A) Peer reviews.

(B) Progress reports.

(C) Staff meetings.

(D) Team building.

(109) Jessica has been incredibly successful in her life. At 22, she has a successful career in the fashion industry, she's purchased her first home, and she's been promoted several times, which has allowed her to become a designer. This is Jessica's dream job. She thrives on achievement of tasks to the absolute best of her abilities. She has never allowed herself to feel inferior or like she hasn't worked her way to where she is now. Based on Erikson's psychosocial development theory, during which stage did Jessica flourish in order to be such a task-oriented and self-assured individual now?

(A) Industry vs. Inferiority.

(B) Trust vs. Mistrust.

(C) Autonomy vs. Doubt.

(D) Identity vs. Confusion.

(110) Rodrigo grew up in the community in which he now serves as a social worker. As such, he feels it has given him insight into how the culture in the area works, how individuals build their self-identities, how family dynamics work, and how best to provide outreach. In this scenario, Rodrigo's understanding is known as what?

(A) Cultural competence.

(B) Functional assessment.

(C) Critical thinking.

(D) Field of practice.

(111) What disorder is typically characterized by emotional distress, anxiety, flashbacks, and nightmares?

(A) Schizophrenia.

(B) Obsessive-compulsive disorder.

(C) Generalized anxiety disorder.

(D) Post-traumatic stress disorder.

(112) A teacher at Lily's school is terribly upset by the fact that her dad rides dirt bikes and takes Lily with him on the weekends. The teacher is so concerned that she contacts the school social worker and asks her to review the case for child endangerment. The teacher's request for a social worker to check on a child for their safety is known by which technical term?

(A) Crisis check.

(B) Standard check.

(C) Welfare check.

(D) Follow-up check.

(113) In Erikson's psychosocial development theory, which stage occurs when a child is between the ages of 12 and 18 and focuses on a teen's development of a sense of identity, typically done through healthy encouragement, positive reinforcement, the individual having feelings of self-control, and the individual developing a sense of self?

(A) Intimacy vs. Isolation.

(B) Trust vs. Mistrust.

(C) Identity vs. Role Confusion.

(D) Industry vs. Inferiority.

(114) Which of the following terms refers to the death rate of a given group of people over a certain period of time?

(A) Morbidity rate.

(B) Infusion rate.

(C) Mortality rate.

(D) Induction rate.

(115) What disorder is typically characterized by the current and ongoing occurrence of panic?

(A) Generalized anxiety disorder.

(B) Attention deficit disorder.

(C) Obsessive-compulsive disorder.

(D) Panic disorder.

(116) Danielle, like all of the social workers in her office, has her own filing cabinet that locks. In accordance with their facility's policies, social workers are required to lock up all case files at the end of the day unless they are taking work home with them, in which case those specific files are allowed to go home with the social worker while the rest remain locked in their cabinet. Protection of files in this way is most likely done for which of the following reasons?

(A) Case management.

(B) Confidentiality.

(C) Organization.

(D) Temperance.

(117) What is the theory that people make decisions based on their own self-interests?

(A) Rational choice theory.

(B) Choice at random theory.

(C) Structure of choice theory.

(D) Classic choice theory.

(118) If a condition returns periodically over time, how is it classified?

(A) Acute.

(B) Chronic.

(C) Benign.

(D) Malignant.

(119) What disorder is typically characterized by the compulsive need to do or repeat a specific action?

(A) Post-traumatic stress disorder.

(B) Autism spectrum disorder.

(C) Obsessive-compulsive disorder.

(D) Attention-deficit hyperactivity disorder.

(120) Haley has noticed that her coworker Steve spends extended periods of time in his office when he has meetings with female clients. In these meetings, his door is always kept shut. The company's office policy requires staff members who are the opposite sex of their client to leave their office doors open when they conduct meetings. Steve's office door being closed with female clients bothers Haley, and this week, two female clients of Steve's have withdrawn from the program. What is the most logical step Haley should take in regard to her concern about this issue?

(A) Confront Steve and tell him how this makes her feel.

(B) Speak with her direct supervisor and bring the issue to their attention.

(C) Schedule an appointment with the office's branch manager to discuss the issue.

(D) Mind her own business and leave Steve and his clients alone.

(121) Arianna is three months old. She responds well to the things she can see; she often startles when she is touched before she actually sees the person who touches her; she prefers to be in contact with her mother or at least have her in sight; and she does not respond to sounds, people's speech, or startling noises. Based on this information, what type of health does she most likely have an issue with?

(A) Emotional health.

(B) Social health.

(C) Mental health.

(D) Physical health.

(122) Oliver has been having nightmares for weeks. He flinches every time a match is struck or a lighter is lit, and he has not been able to light a fire in his fireplace or outdoor burn pit since he was trapped a few weeks before in a fire at his company's warehouse. As the weeks go by, Oliver's nightmares continue to get worse and his paranoia in regard to fire grows. Finally, Oliver takes the advice of family members and friends and schedules an emergency appointment with a well-known therapist, who tells him he is suffering from PTSD. Putting a label to the symptoms is known as what?

(A) Accreditation.

(B) Malfeasance.

(C) Diagnosis.

(D) Networking.

(123) What mental health issue most commonly causes individuals to experience significant feelings of loss or sadness?

(A) Depression and mood disorders.

(B) Hypersensitivity disorders.

(C) Eating disorders and body dysmorphia.

(D) Anxiety disorders.

(124) Everly oversees four social workers. As part of her job, she is responsible to review cases at least once a month in order to make sure that clients make progress and that social workers assigned to their cases properly assess and meet their needs. What is Everly's role within the organization?

(A) Subordinate.

(B) Supervisor.

(C) Manager.

(D) Director.

(125) In Erikson's psychosocial development theory, what stage occurs between the ages of 18 and 40, which is defined as the time in which individuals develop a belief in love through intimate connections and the healthy growth and development of relationships?

(A) Intimacy vs. Isolation.

(B) Trust vs. Mistrust.

(C) Generativity vs. Stagnation.

(D) Initiative vs. Guilt.

(126) Erica was involved in a severe car accident. She received several bruises on her face, neck, and arms. What is the medical term for bruises?

(A) Abrasions.

(B) Abscess.

(C) Fracture.

(D) Contusions.

(127) Kayla has been overly obsessed with her weight since she hit puberty. She weighs herself every morning before she dresses, counts her calories every day, and cuts calories if she gains more than two pounds. She maintains the absolute lowest weight that doctors recommend for her height. What is this type of unhealthy food and weight relationship most likely a sign of?

(A) Stress disorder.

(B) Anxiety disorder.

(C) Eating disorder.

(D) Depressive disorder.

(128) Tori keeps business cards that she can give out to each new client with her contact information. This information includes her office phone number, her exclusive work cell phone number, and her work email address. She insists on giving out only the contact information contained on her business card. What is Tori establishing between herself and her clients?

(A) Professional boundaries.

(B) Personal relationships.

(C) Unhealthy bonding.

(D) Personal boundaries.

(129) Danny is six years old. He often has uncontrollable tantrums, a difficult time changing between activities, and episodes in which he seems so hyper that he cannot focus. What type of health is Danny most likely experiencing an issue with?

(A) Cognitive health.

(B) Behavioral health.

(C) Emotional health.

(D) Physical health.

(130) Margery is a social worker. She meets with each of her clients at the office or in their home. She does her best to put clients at ease while she maintains a professional and ethical relationship with each of them. Conducting in-person, face-to-face interviews, meetings, and follow-ups is known as what?

(A) Indirect practice.

(B) Community development.

(C) Evidence-based practice.

(D) Direct practice.

(131) Kelly and her social worker discuss the issues that Kelly would like to fix. Those issues include anger management, modern parenting, and self-confidence. These three goals will be broken down into tasks that Kelly must meet in order to exit the program. What type of therapy practice is this known as?

(A) Solution-focused therapy.

(B) Task-centered practice.

(C) Problem-solving practice.

(D) Narrative therapy.

(132) What is the ninth strategy in the anger management technique?

(A) Control your anger.

(B) Forgiveness.

(C) Exercise.

(D) Relaxation practices.

(133) What is the framework that social workers utilize in order to better understand an individual's or group's broader social, political, and economic context and how this affects their overall health and well-being?

(A) Strength perspective.

(B) Ecological perspective.

(C) Person-in-environment perspective.

(D) Feminist perspective.

(134) Anna is a new mom. She participates in baby-wearing throughout the day, which keeps her newborn wrapped against her chest. The only times when Anna is not baby-wearing are when she breastfeeds, when the baby is in its car seat for car journeys, when the baby is being held by others, or when the two are co-sleeping during naps or at bedtime. Which type of relationship is this likely to facilitate between Anna and her baby?

(A) Stress and anxiety.

(B) Independence and self-soothing.

(C) Attachment disorders and an inability to express emotions.

(D) Bonding and security.

(135) What protection training is typically taught to mental health and community professionals?

(A) Nonviolent self-defense.

(B) Deflective self-defense.

(C) Reactive self-defense.

(D) Passive self-defense.

(136) What is the seventh strategy in the anger management technique?

(A) Calm down.

(B) Control your anger.

(C) Forgiveness.

(D) Take a timeout.

(137) The law puts into place special protections for those who cannot protect themselves. What are such laws known as?

(A) *Guardian ad litem.*

(B) *Parens patriae.*

(C) *De lega lata.*

(D) *In loco parentis.*

(138) During what age range do men and women typically begin to develop health issues that they may experience for the remainder of their lives, and women experience menopause?

(A) During middle age, which is between the ages of 36 and 64.

(B) During elder age, which is anyone 80 years or older.

(C) As older adults, between the ages of 65 and 79.

(D) As young adults, which is between the ages of 18 and 35 years old.

(139) What techniques are used when a situation is dangerous and an individual needs to be calmed and talked down before violence erupts?

(A) Intervention and resolution techniques.

(B) Verbal de-escalation techniques.

(C) Nonverbal self-defense techniques.

(D) Crisis intervention techniques.

(140) There are ten strategies for anger management. What is the fifth strategy?

(A) Think before you speak.

(B) Exercise.

(C) Identify the cause.

(D) Take responsibility.

(141) Harrison focuses on the development of strong connections with his clients as a means of to help them make decisions, interact in the treatments or services being utilized, and participate actively in the process. To make connections like this, the social worker should do what?

(A) Engage the client.

(B) Comfort the client.

(C) Prompt the client.

(D) Summarize for the client.

(142) Ernest is getting older. As he ages, his hearing begins to fail, his eyesight weakens and he must rely on glasses, and he no longer gets around as easily as he once did. These changes are all part of what phase in life?

(A) Growth and development.

(B) Aging and degeneration.

(C) Incubation and formation.

(D) Infancy and growth.

(143) What procedure is used to ensure social worker and client well-being during visits or transportation?

(A) Treatment plans.

(B) Intervention plans.

(C) Safety plans.

(D) Discharge plans.

(144) There are ten strategies for anger management. What is the third strategy?

(A) Relaxation practices.

(B) Calm down.

(C) Identify the cause.

(D) Exercise.

(145) As a social worker, Ashley communicates with clients via phone, email, postal mail, and in person. These communications are noted in the client's files as to the dates, times, and durations of such communications. Ashley also typically takes notes to later utilize if important information is discussed. Part or all of those communications may need to be added to a client's file. What are communications such as this protected under?

(A) Social worker/client confidentiality.

(B) Privileged communications.

(C) Code of ethics.

(D) Confidentiality.

(146) What is the irreversible increase in size of any organism until cell growth reaches its peak and the process through which any organism gains mental and psychological growth called?

(A) Growth and development.

(B) Discharge and follow-up.

(C) Assessment and intervention.

(D) Regression and disengagement.

(147) What type of assessment is used to evaluate the likeliness of an individual to commit a violent act?

(A) Initial assessment.

(B) Needs assessment.

(C) Crisis assessment.

(D) Risk assessment.

(148) There are ten strategies for anger management. What is the first strategy in the anger management technique?

(A) Exercise.

(B) Think before you speak.

(C) Explore solutions.

(D) Calm down.

(149) Taylor builds mutual respect and understanding for each of her clients when she listens to what they have to say, actively engages with responses that contribute to the discussion, and assists in solving issues. What is this approach known as?

(A) Passive listening.

(B) Rapport-building.

(C) Active listening.

(D) Summarization.

(150) During which age range do adults typically experience a natural decline in their physical abilities and memory skills, though at a gradual speed, and may begin to need more assistance even as they still maintain their independence?

(A) At age 80 or older.

(B) Between the ages of 36 and 64.

(C) Between the ages of 65 and 79.

(D) After age 60.

(151) What is it called when a mini research study is done on an idea or project in order to predict the success of a large-scale experiment?

(A) Double-blind study.

(B) Longitudinal study.

(C) Comprehensive study.

(D) Pilot study.

(152) What is the fourth strategy of conflict resolution?

(A) Collaboration.

(B) Avoidance.

(C) Competition.

(D) Accommodation.

(153) What is the first step in the decision of whether if an individual or group needs help or an intervention?

(A) Interview.

(B) Assessment.

(C) Treatment.

(D) Planning.

(154) According to Freud's psychosexual theory of development, there is a period of time when children use their mouth as the key source from which they derive pleasure, learn, and explore their world. What is the name of this stage?

(A) Oral stage.

(B) Phallic stage.

(C) Latency stage.

(D) Genital phase.

(155) What is a small group, similar in demographic to the larger one being researched, that is interviewed in order to predict the outcome of a change to the larger group?

(A) Control group.

(B) Social group.

(C) Focus group.

(D) Mixed group.

(156) What is the second strategy of conflict resolution?

(A) Collaboration.

(B) Accommodation.

(C) Competition

(D) Avoidance.

(157) Hamilton Community College uses a blind application process to ensure that each applicant is given an equal opportunity when they apply for admittance to the college or for one of the college's many scholarship opportunities. The board is given the applicant's application information without any identifiable information, students' averaged GPA over the course of their high school career, and their admittance exam scores. This information allows the application and scholarship boards to factor in only the academic criteria of each applicant and not be influenced by any gender, race, ethnicity, or unconscious bias that may occur by having such information. What reason and result would the college have or like to achieve by conducting their scholarship and admittance processes this way?

(A) Social justice.

(B) Equal rights.

(C) Unbiased appraisal.

(D) Equal opportunity.

(158) During which age group do individuals begin to experience a more significant decline in health, face more significant health issues, and develop memory decline in a time when it takes them longer to learn and absorb new things?

(A) 36 to 64 years old.

(B) 80 years or older.

(C) 18 to 35 years old.

(D) 65 to 79 years old.

(159) What is the method of using multiple research types to gather information formally called?

(A) Engagement methods.

(B) Mixed methods.

(C) Divisive methods.

(D) Entertainment methods.

(160) What is the therapeutic technique that utilizes new-skill building, positive behavior approach, and increased independence through socializing?

(A) Self-care and coping technique.

(B) Conflict resolution technique.

(C) Self-monitoring technique.

(D) Harm-reduction technique.

(161) What is the counseling or therapy method that directly brings awareness to a client about conflicts in their verbal and nonverbal communications when dealing with an issue or variety of issues?

(A) Engagement method.

(B) Confrontation method.

(C) Reflection method.

(D) Summarizing method.

(162) Matilda is nearly 85 years old. She sits on her porch each evening to watch the neighborhood kids ride their bikes and play in the cul-de-sac. Being so contented for her age is associated with which stage of Erikson's psychosocial development theory?

(A) Ego Integrity vs. Despair.

(B) Generativity vs. Stagnation.

(C) Intimacy vs. Isolation.

(D) Identity vs. Role Confusion.

(163) What research study is conducted over a set time frame using repetition?

(A) Longitudinal study.

(B) Pilot study.

(C) Field study.

(D) Action study.

(164) What is a common technique used in the treatment of substance abuse?

(A) Self-care and coping.

(B) Harm reduction.

(C) Conflict resolution.

(D) Anger management.

(165) There are three sobriety programs in the city of Mena. Haley, a social worker for the city, collects data in regard to each program. This includes the number of individuals who have been admitted into each program, the number of individuals who have dropped out of the program after starting, the number of individuals who have successfully completed the sobriety programs, and the number of individuals who have relapsed after completing each program.

Additionally, of those who have relapsed, Haley also pulls data in order to find out whether they entered the same rehab program again or whether they tried a different rehab program the next time, and whether one program worker was better than another for those who did change programs after a relapse. Haley most likely needs to collect all of this information in order to determine what?

(A) To decide which program uses the best practice method.

(B) To rate the programs for the city's community outreach and resources brochure.

(C) To determine the effectiveness of each sobriety program and how well they have been able to help those who enter each of their programs.

(D) To determine the accreditation of the sobriety programs.

(166) What are food, water, shelter, sleep, and human interaction all considered to the human body?

(A) Luxuries.

(B) Economic commodities.

(C) Privileges of community involvement.

(D) Basic human needs.

(167) William is a social worker whose client Alyssa arrived agitated, jumpy, and very skittish. What is the best thing for William to do in this situation?

(A) Tell Alyssa she seems very out of sorts and that she is not cooperating with their session by having such reactive behavior.

(B) Tolerate Alyssa's terrified behavior while trying not to upset her further.

(C) Tell Alyssa that her behavior is highly reactive and that if she cannot pull herself together, he will be forced to end the session early and try again another day when she is more composed.

(D) Tell Alyssa that he understands how she is feeling and ask to discuss her feelings further.

(168) What is an effective tool that counselors and therapists often utilize in which clients use personas as a means to express strong emotions, limit the impact of destructive emotions, improve self-perception, and bring better awareness?

(A) Harm-reduction technique.

(B) Trauma-informed care method.

(C) Role-play technique.

(D) Self-monitoring technique.

(169) The homeless population has a greater risk of health issues, a lack of health care accessibility, a limited ability to meet basic human needs, and a higher morbidity and mortality rate, which means that the homeless belong to which population?

(A) Dispersed population.

(B) Vulnerable population.

(C) Influential population.

(D) Ethnic population.

(170) What form of health care refers to the proper care of the human body through the balance of physical activity and nutrition, among other things?

(A) Physical health.

(B) Mental health.

(C) Emotional health.

(D) Spiritual health.

Test 3: Answers and Explanations

(1) (C) Bandura's social learning theory.

Bandura's social learning theory proposes that children learn, grow, and develop through mimicry of the behaviors and responses of the behavioral interactions they observe around them. These mimicked behaviors can come from their mothers and fathers, close family members, caregivers, teachers, and other people they commonly come in contact with.

These behaviors can also be affected by their favorite characters on TV, the friends they have, and the peers who attend school with them. The modeled behaviors can include how children conduct themselves, the attitudes they express and how they express them, and how they react emotionally. Of course, behavior and development are also influenced by a child's experiences. It is important to understand that such modeled behaviors would not be limited to gender specifics or conform to social norms.

(2) (B) Accreditation.

Accreditation is when an individual is recognized in an official capacity as having acquired the qualifications to perform a specific activity or profession. Such an achievement is typically gained through completion of specific education or training. Once the education or training is completed, the individual must then be examined and approved for sufficient practical knowledge, and that knowledge is then certified as sufficient or above necessary capacity.

(3) (D) Termination.

The termination of a client from a treatment program occurs when the client has successfully reached all of their set goals, has been thoroughly reassessed and deemed to have dealt with the issues that brought them there in the first place, and is now ready to re-enter the world as a whole and well-balanced individual.

(4) (A) Accreditation.

Accreditation is the formal acknowledgement that an educational or training program provides a standard level of education or training to its participants and is deemed sufficient to provide at least the minimum knowledge base, upon completion, which is needed to enter that field of work.

(5) (A) Bandura's social learning theory.

In the example given, a child observes his peer having a tantrum when it is time to clean up and then later repeats that same behavior. This is an example of Bandura's social learning theory, in which he theorized that children mimic others and learn through observation of sights and sounds, which they later repeat when they find themselves in a similar situation or emotional setting.

(6) (C) Determination of the effectiveness of programs.

Determination of a program's efficiency is the process of ensuring that programs are accountable for their actions and treatment choices, meet their objectives, achieve accomplishments, measure progress over a set period of time, and assess and review program skills development. This is used to decide whether further resources are needed and can be allocated to a program.

(7) (B) Assessment.

Assessments are the detailed information that is collected on an individual as part of the intervention process.

(8) (C) Service.

Service as a social worker is characterized by a commitment to help individuals, couples, families, groups, and communities identify their needs, decide how to meet those needs, utilize resources that can assist in resolution of those needs, and assist in having those needs met and resolving the issues.

(9) (B) Trust vs. Mistrust.

Erikson theorized that a crucial time in a child's development is between birth and roughly 18 months. He claimed that during this stage of growth and development a child can learn to trust their parents or caregivers based on whether they meet their basic needs like food, shelter, and warmth, but also on whether they provide comfort, develop healthy attachments, and create a sense of security. He also noted that failure to meet those needs could result in development of mistrust for the parents, caregivers, or other adults in the child's life.

(10) (D) Advocating.

Advocating refers to a person or group that comes in to assist on the behalf of another individual or group for the purpose of defense, representation, or support of that individual or group. Harry advocates for his brother's needed assistance and support so he can learn to read better and not struggle.

(11) (A) Planning.

During the planning phase of the intervention process, issues have been detected, goals to resolve the issues are set, and plans are devised to meet those goals and resolve the issues at hand.

(12) (C) They are the client's rights.

Confidentiality, privacy, and access to services are only a few of the rights afforded to clients.

(13) (A) Albert Bandura.

Albert Bandura took a different perspective on human behavior than most theorists when he published his social learning theory in 1977. He differed from his colleagues, who felt that conditioning, punishment, and reinforcement directly correlated with how children are taught and learn. Rather, Bandura felt that learning was the direct result of the things that children observe and then copy. He expanded this idea by stating that not only do children learn by visual observation, but also by auditory observation. The Bandura social learning theory concluded that children learn through the things they see on TV and the things they witness in their homes, day cares, schools, and out in the world. They also learn by what they hear in these same environments and how they hear parents, peers, care providers, and other trusted adults in their lives speak, respond, and react.

(14) (A) Empathy.

Kelly expresses empathy toward her client as she actively listens to what the client says. To do this, she expresses understanding and respect toward the client and their experience or feelings in regard to the issue or situation.

(15) (C) Limit setting.

The limit setting technique offers individuals an array of personal choices and consequences. It is a streamlined process that can be used at almost any age. The principle is that the client and social worker decide a set of limits and a set of consequences. It is important that these limits and expectations be unquestionably clear. Ensure that you state exactly what the choices are and what the consequences for noncompliance will be. Ensure that you follow through. If the client does not follow through with the agreed-upon limits, be sure that the consequences are clearly enforced and that you are consistent with each occurrence. Remind individuals that these are the consequences for their choice but avoid lectures and over explaining. Ensure that you avoid power struggles when clients push back against the limits. In a power struggle, both parties will lose, so avoidance of such instances is crucial.

(16) (B) Right to refuse services.

Every client or patient has the right to refuse services or treatment options that are offered to them.

(17) (D) Freud's psychosexual development theory.

Learning to eliminate distress through pleasure is theorized in Sigmund Freud's psychosexual development theory. Thumb sucking, the example that is given in this question, falls under Freud's oral stage. The oral stage is developed in children from birth to their first year of life. Freud states that infants find pleasure and comfort through things such as breast feeding, bottle feeding, or sucking on a pacifier or even their own fingers. In infancy, the child may use these pleasures and comforts to soothe a hungry belly or comfort themself.

As we grow and mature, the means we use to alleviate discomfort and restore pleasure change. However, Freud claimed we still use those tools we developed in the beginning of life, which can lead adults to develop oral fixations such as chewing gum, smoking, or even simply kissing a lot as a means to lower stress, dissolve distress, and reward us with the pleasure response we seek.

(18) (B) Best practice.

Best practice is the technique used to address, cope, or deal with a given situation by applying the best possible methods to resolve the issue in the best interests of the client.

(19) (D) Role modeling technique.

The role modeling technique teaches clients learned behaviors by modeling those behaviors without the trial and error of doing it themselves. The role modeling technique uses imitation as its focus rather than verbal directions that specifically instruct the client on what to do. The role model framework outlines three functions of the role model. The first is to actually model the behavior, the second is to show the client what is possible, and the third is to inspire the client.

(20) (D) Directive supervision.

Directive supervision is defined as the role a supervisor plays when they direct and inform, model behaviors, and evaluate defined behaviors.

(21) (A) Attachment theory.

Attachment theory states that the bond that is created between a baby and mother or primary caregiver is driven by a biological desire that is present at birth. The bonding that occurs causes the infant to learn and grow with a sense of safety and security. This bond lays the foundation for the healthy bonds and relationships that the baby will have as they grow into a child, adolescent, and eventually an adult.

Beyond the attachment that is formed and the fostering of future relationships, attachment bonding also helps a child see the world as a safe place to explore and develop. Attachment theory states that the majority of an individual's development foundations, sense of security, and sense that it is safe to venture out and explore the world can all be associated with the first bonds they made as a baby when those bonds are created in a healthy way.

(22) (A) Empathetic method.

Autumn and her social worker have developed a trusting and respectful relationship in which Autumn feels safe in making decisions, supported in her efforts, and driven to meet her goals. This relationship is known as an empathetic relationship.

(23) (B) Self-care and coping methods.

Self-care and coping are considered key skills needed to survive. Self-care and coping methods help individuals through engagement in activities that reduce stress and maintain health in both a short-term and lifelong capacity, which fosters a healthy sense of well-being. Some of the things an individual can do that constitute self-care are have friends and maintain those relationships, exercise regularly, maintain a healthy diet, be able to ask for help and accept that help when it is offered, be able to prioritize yourself and your needs over those of other people, and set goals or other achievements as a means to keep moving forward and work toward something of purpose.

(24) (D) Tell Jason that she understands how he is feeling and ask to discuss his feelings further.

Rebecka should acknowledge Jason's antagonistic and irritable behavior and ask him to talk more about how he is feeling and why he might be feeling this way. To address the situation in this manner will allow Rebecka to help Jason defuse the situation while she brings his attention to what causes him to feel this way. Then, he can focus on possible ways to resolve the issue causing his agitation.

(25) (C) Social learning.

Albert Bandura theorized that children learn best when they listen to and watch the world around them and then mimic the behaviors that they see and hear. In the example situation, Anna would tell her children it was lunchtime and they would be put in their highchairs to eat their lunches. While they ate, they were able to watch their mother clean up their toys. The children, therefore, learned to associate the word "lunchtime" with eating, but they also associated it with their toys being picked up.

(26) (C) Caseload.

A caseload is the numerical number of clients a social worker is responsible for. For clients in their caseload, social workers are responsible for management of client assessments, implementation of intervention plans, and arrangement of services. It is also their job to follow the progress of the client as they receive services or treatment, assess any further needs, and discharge clients when such services or treatments are no longer needed.

(27) (C) Avoidance.

The first strategy of conflict resolution is avoidance. When they use this strategy, an individual will remove himself from the conflict as a means to eliminate the confrontation and dissolve the tension. Avoidance does not resolve conflict; it only delays the discussion and neutralizes the conflict in that moment. Avoidance is a short-term solution to a problem that will need a more elaborate solution in the end.

(28) (B) Record keeping.

Record keeping is the administrative and clerical task of maintenance of accurate current, past, and future information on a given client. This information should be organized, detailed, and properly documented while they are in your care.

(29) (A) Ava suffered from inadequate attachment bonding in her first five years of life. As a result, she does not have the ability to develop healthy attachments to her adoptive parents and she rejects touch.

John Bowlby's attachment theory suggests that an infant's ability to bond with the mother or primary caregiver in the first months of life until they are at least two years old, but preferably five, plays a key role in a child's development. This development allows them to make attachments to their parent or caregiver, as well as other trusted individuals. It further creates a feeling of safety and security about the world around them so that they feel secure enough to explore this world as they grow.

(30) (D) Biopsychosocial assessment.

A biopsychosocial assessment gathers a great deal of information about an individual, their home life, work life, social life, biology, health history, and other valid information to compile a thorough and comprehensive picture before further decisions in regard to the client or their needs can be made.

(31) (B) Accommodation.

The third strategy of conflict resolution is known as accommodation. This strategy typically involves one individual or group having to concede to the demands of the other. There is a lack of assertiveness on the giving party's side, and while it may seem like this would solve the conflict, it most often results in feelings of being wronged, which leads to further conflict. This is because one individual or party feels like they have given too much, while the other individual or party gets everything they want.

(32) (A) Alternative supervision.

Alternative supervision is defined as a role that suggests various alternative solutions to the client, kept to a limited number of choices so as not to overwhelm them, while also allowing them to have choices and take charge of how things will go.

(33) (B) Maternal deprivation.

Maternal deprivation is experienced by an infant or child who is separated from the mother or primary caregiver within the first five years of their life. Because of that separation, the child will develop attachment, behavioral, cognitive, and social issues from lacking that bond.

(34) (D) Code of ethics.

The code of ethics is a set of rules and standards that social workers are ethically bound to follow when the practice in the field. The code outlines the proper way in which social workers are to conduct themselves, behaviors that will not be tolerated, and the procedures to be followed should an ethical dilemma occur.

(35) (C) Compromise.

The fifth and final strategy for conflict resolution is compromise. This involves the individuals or parties coming together to establish what they each want. They then split the difference or find a middle ground where they each gain something. In these instances, neither party walks away with everything they wanted. Compromise is considered to be one of the fairest ways to resolve a conflict.

(36) (B) Administrative.

An administrative supervisor is an individual who is directly responsible for coordination and supervision of administrative staff, clerical staff, support staff, and the work-related activities they conduct.

(37) (A) Trust vs. Mistrust.

In Erik Erikson's psychosocial development theory, the first stage occurs between birth and 18 months of age. It is called the Trust vs. Mistrust stage because if a healthy bond is developed between the infant and mother or primary caregiver, the infant will develop feelings of trust, safety, and security. However, not having this bond can cause feelings of mistrust, insecurity, and a suspicion of the world. In either case, these experiences will set the foundation for future development.

(38) (A) Diversity perspective.

Diversity perspective is defined as a level of self-awareness, cognitive flexibility, and expansive knowledge that allows individuals to gain perspective through the viewpoint of others.

(39) (A) Calm down.

The second strategy for anger management is to calm down so that you can express your frustrations or anger in a calm and healthy way.

(40) (A) Educational supervisor.

An educational supervisor is an individual appointed strictly to support and provide leadership to staff and their educational activities.

(41) (D) Mental health.

Mental health specifically refers to an individual's ability to mentally cope with life stressors. Poor mental health can cause physical and emotional unhealthiness if left unchecked.

(42) (B) Codependency.

Codependency is an unhealthy emotional or psychological attachment or relationship that occurs between individuals. Codependencies often occur in relationships where one partner is a substance abuser.

(43) (C) Take a timeout.

The fourth strategy in the anger management technique is to take a timeout. This means to remove yourself for a short period in order to reduce your stress, help you deal with the feelings you are having, and come back to the situation with your anger in check.

(44) (D) Collaborative supervision.

Collaborative supervision is the role in which a supervisor establishes a sharing relationship in order to collectively make decisions, consider problems, and create effective solutions that work for everyone.

(45) (A) Trust vs. Mistrust.

According to Erikson's theory of psychosocial development, the Trust vs. Mistrust stage begins at birth and continues to 18 months of age. Erikson considers this stage to be fundamental, as it is when infants form bonds through having their basic needs met. These bonds foster trust and give the baby confidence through being fed, warm, safe, and nurtured. His theory states that when these bonds are fostered in a healthy way, the infant associates the feelings of safety and security that develop during this time with the outside world and develops a healthy trust in the world around them. On the other hand, infants who do not make these connections and bonds or develop this healthy view of trust will instead put little faith in others and often be untrusting.

(46) (A) Feminist perspective.

The feminist perspective seeks to understand and analyze gender inequalities and survey the social roles, experiences, and interests of women.

(47) (B) Take responsibility.

The sixth strategy in the anger management technique is known as the ‘sticking with “I” statements’ strategy. This strategy helps the individual to not blame or criticize others for the individual’s own reactions, and emphasizes that the individual take responsibility for their own anger.

(48) (D) Nondirective supervision.

Nondirective supervision refers to a hands-off supervisory role that allows the client to be more involved in choosing the direction and solutions that work best for them. The supervisor gets actively involved only when it is necessary.

(49) (C) Emotional health.

Emotional health and wellness refer to being in control of how you behave, feel, and think. A lack of emotional health management can affect other areas of your life, especially your mental health.

(50) (A) Community development.

Community development is the process in which an individual or group assesses a community’s needs, develops resources to help meet those needs, and promotes networking within the community. These things are all done as a means to aid the community’s overall growth and development.

(51) (D) Utilize humor.

The eighth strategy for anger management is to utilize humor as a tool for the reduction and expulsion of tension. Being able to lighten the mood and laugh dispels anger and hurt feelings. It is important to remember to use positive humor rather than sarcasm in these situations, as the latter can breed anger and make situations worse by causing others to feel hurt.

(52) (C) Competency.

Competency is an individual’s mental ability to understand the things that are going on and actively participate in their role and decisions pertaining to their situation.

(53) (A) Autonomy vs. Shame.

Erikson described the second stage of development in his psychosocial development theory as Autonomy vs. Shame. At this stage, children start to make choices for themselves. This may be choices such as what T-shirt they'll wear, milk or orange juice at breakfast, or what to have as a snack in the afternoon. These choices help children develop a sense that they can accomplish certain things themselves and give them the will to want to make those choices. Accomplishment of these small tasks and the ability to make these small choices give children the confidence to keep going and do more. Erikson's theory suggests that children who are not allowed to make choices or for whatever reason do not develop during this stage will develop doubts in their abilities as they progress and age.

(54) (B) Person-in-environment perspective.

The person-in-environment perspective is a principle in social work that illuminates the importance of comprehending individuals, their behaviors, and the environmental factors that affect how individuals act and conduct themselves.

(55) (D) Control your anger.

The tenth and final strategy for anger management is the ability to control your anger and the knowledge of when and willingness to ask for help. Sometimes anger issues seem incredibly out of control and too big to handle alone. When this is the case, it is important to seek help.

(56) (A) Protection of the public.

Protection of the public is a social worker's ability to investigate situations, carry out assessments, collect necessary information to evaluate a situation, and offer assistance and services in the event that a qualifying situation or environment is discovered. They have the right to step in and take action if policies, plans, and actions are not conducted and if the situation persists in a way that endangers self, others, or the public.

(57) (B) Initiative vs. Guilt.

Based on Erikson's psychosocial development theory, Marina would have had developmental difficulties during her Initiative vs. Guilt stage of development. Typically, during this stage, an individual would learn how to initiate a task or a plan; however, when that development does not occur, individuals usually end up burdened with guilt about their efforts to be independent.

(58) (C) Confidentiality.

William protects his client's information in accordance with the idea of confidentiality. Confidentiality is defined as the ethical principle of protecting private information. Confidentiality can be waived by the person in question if they agree to share their information. It can further be released without consent if it is being done for the safety of that person or others (such as in cases of a suicidal individual or those who plan to harm others), or for professional disclosure when it specifically applies to arrangement for services or treatment to be provided.

(59) (C) Contracting and goal setting.

Contracting and goal setting techniques are based on the social worker and client coming together to put a written agreement into place that will act as a guide or road map from where they are starting to where they would ultimately like to end up. Such goals may include challenges that must be overcome or specific goals in the individual's life that need to be achieved. It must be done in a way that allows the individual to accept responsibility, take charge in regard to the improvements or achievements they attempt to reach, and actively participate in reaching those goals.

(60) (D) Clinical supervisor.

A clinical supervisor is typically someone who is responsible for overseeing operations and activities in a clinical setting.

(61) (A) Sensorimotor stage.

The sensorimotor stage of Piaget's cognitive development theory is defined as the stage that occurs between birth and two years of age. During this time, Piaget's theory states that children begin to understand the concept of object permanence through the use of their five senses.

(62) (D) Basic information.

In reference to the collection of information for social work assessments, information that includes but is not limited to the individual's name, date of birth, age, gender, marital status, ethnicity, spoken language, current employment, income, living situation, and community network are all part of that individual's basic information that a social worker will collect.

(63) (C) Task-centered.

The task-centered approach or model is designed to be a short-term way to approach problem solving. Typically, social workers will first identify target problems with their client, collaborate in setting goals for that problem or problems, develop a task-centered action plan, and execute it. They will then evaluate the results when that task action plan has been fulfilled and assess any remaining needs that the client may have.

(64) (B) Client focus.

Client focus means that the intervention, planning, services, and treatments afforded to the client are done so based on the client's needs, decisions, and goals.

(65) (D) Autonomy vs. Shame.

The second stage in Erikson's psychosocial development theory is Autonomy vs. Shame. In this stage, children begin to learn personal control and independence. Erikson theorizes that making simple choices, such as their outfit or snack, development of a sense of independency, and potty training, are key to foster healthy growth in this phase.

(66) (D) Conflict of interest.

Mary chooses to remove herself as supervisor of the woman's adoption case because there is a conflict of interest between her professional interest as an agency supervisor and her private interest as the chairperson of the art school. This conflict is created because it is possible that her thoughts or feelings about the young woman in regard to adoption placement and her authority over the young women's scholarship could affect one another. This could affect the decisions that are made in each situation in regard to the response, care, or other choices Mary makes for the young woman.

(67) (A) Advocacy groups.

Advocacy groups are characterized as individuals who work together to promote a shared cause or interest. This advocacy can be for self-interest or in the interest of others. This can focus on self-empowerment or attempt to promote social change.

(68) (C) Self-disclosure.

Self-disclosure is when a professional divulges their personal information and happenings in their personal lives with clients.

(69) (A) Social health.

Social health refers to an individual's ability to maintain healthy interpersonal relationships with individuals. These relationships can be with coworkers, friends, family, romantic partners, or anyone else you interact with on a regular basis.

(70) (C) The presenting problem.

A presenting problem is the issue for which the individual needs help. The social worker and client will meet to establish the client's description of the issue, a short history of the issue, how long the issue has been going on, any previous ways they attempted to fix the issue, whether a social worker has been involved before, and whether the client is considered high risk (such as a danger to themself or others).

(71) (C) Mutual aid group.

A mutual aid group is specifically composed of those with a shared experience or condition. Such groups are informal and designed to support one another, share information, and help each other. A facilitator may be someone who shares the experience or condition or a professional who helps bring such individuals together.

(72) (D) Dual relationships.

A dual relationship refers to a professional, such as a social worker, who, in addition to their professional relationship, also develops a personal relationship with a client. Such relationships create a conflict of interest and a most often a breach in ethics.

(73) (C) Concrete operational stage.

In the concrete operational stage of Piaget's cognitive development theory, which occurs between the ages of 7 and 11, children begin to put sequences of events together and organize their feelings and thoughts. These steps are the development of logical thinking.

(74) (B) General description.

A general description is a description of the client, which includes appearance, attitude, and how the individual acted and reacted during the interview.

(75) (B) Psychotherapy.

Psychotherapy can be facilitated by a professional in a group setting to deal with psychosocial issues. This uses a set psychiatric approach to the therapy or counseling sessions.

(76) (D) To be aware of your professional limits and know when to ask for help.

To work within your competence means that you need to know and respect your knowledge base and the limits of that knowledge, be willing to ask for help from professional colleagues and those who are more informed in certain areas, and accept the advice or information you are being given.

(77) (A) Initiative vs. Guilt.

Erikson's Initiative vs. Guilt stage occurs during the time children generally attend preschool, between three and five years of age. Erikson surmised that the choices they are able to make more freely in preschool and their social interaction with peers allow them to further explore their environment, gain more self-control, and more independently see what they are capable of.

(78) (A) Continued education requirements.

The Brighton Institute of Social Services' education requirements are known as continued education requirements. This refers to the education that an individual will have to continue to pursue after they have obtained their initial degree and certification and entered the practical and professional world. In order to continue to practice in that profession and keep current any required certification and licensing, the board for that field has set requirements. Additionally, some agencies and organizations like the Brighton Institute of Social Service require additional continued education in order to continue to work for that entity. Some agencies or organizations require this addition in order to maintain staff standards, maintain a higher state of accreditation, or otherwise maintain that their staff and facilities are at an above par standard.

(79) (D) Structural family therapy.

Structural family therapy refers to development of an understanding of how a particular family is structured, how the individual family members interact with one another, and how the family works. It involves breaking down the family's hierarchy, relationships, and the various boundaries within the family. Once those things are understood, therapy can begin to help restructure the family in a positive way that will benefit all members all as a whole.

(80) (C) Professional boundaries.

In social work, it is extremely important to maintain professional boundaries to ensure that the social worker can perform their duties effectively, prevent the development of unhealthy bonds with clients, and help ensure that the client can be discharged from the system with the best chance of success.

(81) (B) Preoperational stage.

In the preoperational stage of Piaget's cognitive development theory, which occurs between the ages of 2 and 7, children learn to understand symbolism, where one thing might have an abstract meaning. Symbolic thought is the focus of this stage.

(82) (A) Choose a problem behavior that is earmarked for change.

The first step in the creation of an intervention plan is to choose a problem behavior that needs to be addressed and changed. If there are multiple issues to address, choose the biggest issue first.

(83) (D) Strategic family therapy.

Strategic family therapy examines family members and any defined patterns of interaction that exist. This form of therapy is solution-based, the idea being to identify problems within the family that are solvable and set goals and create strategies to help family members achieve those goals. Ultimately, the aim is to help the individual family members think strategically in order to meet their goals, and develop plans and solutions for future problems.

(84) (C) Red flag behaviors.

Red flag behaviors are things that a social worker or other professional commits that indicate or lead to unethical relationships with clients.

(85) (A) Formal operational stage.

During the formal operational stage of Piaget's cognitive development theory, which occurs at age 12 and up, children experience more drastic development of character traits and develop abstract thinking.

(86) (B) Core values.

The social work professional framework dictates that a commitment to service, social justice, dignity and worth of the person, integrity, competence, and the importance of human relationships are the core values of social work.

(87) (B) Social casework.

Social casework is defined as helping individuals create better social relationships and adjust existing ones in order to ensure a healthy and balanced social relationship network.

(88) (A) Action research.

Action research is defined as research in the field of social work in which a community is studied and its needs assessed in order to develop a program to meet those needs.

(89) (D) Industry vs. Inferiority.

The fourth stage of Erikson's psychological development theory revolves around a child gaining self-competency. This stage is experienced when a child is between the ages of 5 and 12 years old. Typically, this is when children are in elementary and middle school. Self-competency is gained when a child is expected to work hard, is assigned more work and has to set goals to finish it, is held accountable for these tasks, and has a set idea that they need to succeed.

(90) (C) Determine the function of the behavioral problem.

The third step in the creation of an intervention plan is to figure out the reason for the behavioral problem. Knowledge the reason can assist in the plan for how to treat and resolve it.

(91) (C) Social workers.

Social workers are typically responsible for the allocation of resources.

(92) (B) Community-based participatory research.

Community-based participatory research is the collaboration of all stakeholders across the board to identify issues, research and design changes, implement effective change, and achieve goals. This also calls for the community and professionals to be involved and to contribute the skills and perspectives needed.

(93) (A) Spiritual health.

Spiritual health refers to an individual's feelings and emotions about having a purpose in life. It has a major impact on how an individual shapes their ethical principles and moral values. It can also be a system of spirituality, faith, or a belief in a higher power.

(94) (A) Create a behavioral plan.

The fifth step in the creation of an intervention plan is to create a behavioral plan. The behavioral plan is designed to address the root cause of the behavior and address the issue in general.

(95) (D) Anxiety.

Anxiety is the feeling of worry, concern, apprehension, or unease in correlation with current or upcoming events. Xanax is one agent used to treat anxiety.

(96) (B) Control group.

A control group is used when an experiment is being conducted. Two groups that are identical in composition are used to conduct the experiment. The first group is the control and is essentially unchanged by the experiment; the other group is given the treatment. The control group is then used to compare the effects of the treatment.

(97) (C) Self-image.

Self-image refers to how individuals view themselves personally. This image is learned and developed over time. It is also something that is influenced, at least in part, by the views of our parents, friends, family, peers, coworkers, superiors, and anyone else with a significant role in our environment. Self-image can be either positive or negative and is typically based on the positive or negative feedback and opinions in our environment. In order develop and maintain a positive self-image, individuals can do a self-image inventory, make a list of their positive qualities, and ask romantic partners to list their positive body attributes, while they avoid the need to compare themself to others. Furthermore, development of self-love, use of positive affirmations, setting reasonable personal goals, and reflection on personal growth and achievements over time are all great ways to improve or maintain the self-image.

(98) (D) Critical thinking.

Mario uses the process known as critical thinking. During this process, a social worker must challenge underlying assumptions; consider all viewpoints; and use reason, judgment, and knowledge in order to make informed, objective, and intellectually based decisions on each case.

(99) (A) Haldol.

Haldol is a prescription medication. It rebalances dopamine in the brain, which improves thinking, mood, and behavior. It is a proven way to treat schizophrenia.

(100) (B) Double-blind study.

A double-blind study is a research study where both the subject and the researcher do not know whether the subject received a placebo or the treatment. This is done to ensure that the treatment and care are the same across the board and prevent unconscious bias from affecting the study.

(101) (A) Substance abuse.

There are five key reasons individuals seek out and abuse alcohol and drugs. Those reasons are to avoid pain, get pleasure, get a fix for a craving, as a part of a habit, or out of impulsive behavior.

(102) (C) Skills development.

Effective communication and possessed skills are the key factors in skills development as it applies to cultural considerations in the creation of an intervention plan.

(103) (B) Lithium.

Lithium is a proven treatment for bipolar disorder and is a mood stabilizer that decreases the severity of a manic episode. When used as prescribed, it can also decrease how often manic episodes occur.

(104) (D) Field study.

A field study is the collection of raw data or information outside a lab or formal research setting.

(105) (B) Mental health.

Mental health refers to the mental, emotional, and psychological health of an individual.

(106) (B) Initial disclosure.

Initial disclosure is the first of the five key stages in the practice of therapy.

(107) (C) Schizophrenia.

Schizophrenia is a disorder characterized by an individual who experiences a psychosis that causes them to lose touch with reality. Typically, children who develop this do not show signs until their late teens or early 20s. The disorder is characterized by hallucinations, delusions, and disorders in regard to an individual's thinking or behavior.

(108) (D) Team building.

Team-building activities are designed to allow employees to get to know their professional peers better, resolve conflict, and facilitate the growth of stronger and more cohesive relationships.

(109) (A) Industry vs. Inferiority.

Based on Erikson's psychosocial development theory, individuals who grow and develop adequately during this phase typically become well-adjusted individuals who are task-oriented and driven to succeed in all they do.

(110) (A) Culture competence.

Rodrigo's perspective and understanding from this viewpoint is known as his cultural competence. Cultural competence is one of many core responsibilities of social work. Social workers have a responsibility to understand how a person's culture affects their personal identity, and to study and understand the diversity of cultures and ethnicities.

(111) (D) Post-traumatic stress disorder.

Post-traumatic stress disorder, or PTSD, has long-lasting effects that can include emotional distress, anxiety, memories and flashbacks, and nightmares that cause physical responses due to their severity. With this illness, behaviors can include acting out violently, being abusive, or injuring others.

(112) (C) Welfare check.

A welfare check is typically carried out when allegations of neglect or abuse are made and the individual feels that there isn't imminent threat of harm or death. Typically, social workers need a little bit of background information about why the person who makes the complaint feels that there are concerns or how their allegations are supported.

(113) (C) Identity vs. Role Confusion.

Erik Erikson described the fifth stage of his psychosocial development theory as the stage of Identity vs. Role Confusion. During this stage, children have reached their teen years, in which a heavy amount of independent growth and development occur. During this time, teens typically develop identities of their own that are separate from their parents and families. They gain a sense of self through the development of their feelings and the formation of a more comprehensive independence (such as when the teen goes out with friends, works, and drives). The teenager will take more control in their lives through decision-making and will become more responsible for their environment. These things all play into their ability to build a sense of self through encouragement and reinforcement. This encouragement and positive reinforcement come from parents, teachers, peers, employers, and other people of influence in their lives.

(114) (C) Mortality rate.

A mortality rate is the rate of death as it relates to a time period and group of people.

(115) (D) Panic disorder.

A panic disorder is characterized by an individual's experience of multiple occurrences of panic attacks that continue over time.

(116) (B) Confidentiality.

Confidentiality is defined as an individual's right to have their personal and medical information kept private between themself and those involved with their direct care. Therefore, Danielle's facility policy ensures that client information is put away in a safe location so that other professionals in the building do not have access to it unless they are supposed to and no one who visits the office may happen upon that information by accident.

(117) (A) Rational choice theory.

The rational choice theory suggests that when put into a difficult position, an individual will always put their self-interests and personal needs before those of others.

(118) (B) Chronic.

If a condition is recurrent over time, then the issue becomes known as a chronic issue.

(119) (C) Obsessive-compulsive disorder.

One of the common symptoms of obsessive-compulsive disorder is the impulse or compulsion to repeat a behavior.

(120) (B) Speak with her direct supervisor and bring the issue to their attention.

Haley should speak with her direct supervisor and make them aware of the situation. The issue may have gone unnoticed up until this point, or it may have already been addressed. Since Steve is breaking an office policy that is designed to protect employees and ensure that clients feel safe in the office environment and with their social worker, it is important that it be addressed, especially if clients are leaving because they are being made to feel uncomfortable or unsafe.

(121) (D) Physical health.

Based on the information in the passage, Arianna's issues are related to her physical health. Physical health is defined as the physical wellness of a body that is properly cared for and requires a balance in physical activity, nutrition, and mental wellness.

The passage notes her lack of physical responses to noise stimuli, her preference to have things in her sight, and her lack of ability to notice when she is being approached until she is physically touched. A logical conclusion to this situation would be that Arianna is experiencing some form of interference or loss in her hearing.

(122) (C) Diagnosis.

The therapist was able to collect information from Oliver, which included his symptoms and the root cause of all the things he has gone through over the last several weeks, in order to diagnose the issue he is experiencing. A diagnosis is the professional identification of a condition based on an individual's or group's symptoms or assessment.

(123) (A) Depression and mood disorders.

Depression and other mood disorders typically cause persistent emotions and feelings related to sadness and a loss of interest. These are significant enough to interrupt the individual's ability to interact with their peers or family and cause difficulty functioning at work or school.

(124) (B) Supervisor.

Everly is a supervisor at her facility and oversees or supervises four employees. Her job is to ensure that the social workers she has been assigned to supervise are completing their work properly and efficiently and that clients assigned to them are having their needs met and are being accurately assessed. She also must ensure that those social workers are able to access services for their clients. If they are not able to do this, they must be able to approach Everly and see if she can find resources to address needs if there are not current systems in place to address certain issues.

(125) (A) Intimacy vs. Isolation.

The sixth stage of Erik Erikson's psychosocial development theory is Intimacy vs. Isolation. This stage occurs between early and middle adulthood and is the time in individual growth and development when a true belief in love with other people can flourish. This is because people develop romantic relationships and nurture intimacies.

(126) (D) Contusions.

Contusion is the medical term used in reference to bruises.

(127) (C) Eating disorder.

Kayla is most likely suffering from an eating disorder, which is defined as being overly occupied with a specific body type. Those who suffer from such disorders focus a great deal on weight, weight loss, unsafe eating habits, and dieting habits. The most common eating disorders include anorexia nervosa, bulimia nervosa, and binge eating disorder. Such disorders can cause life-threatening complications if not treated.

(128) (A) Professional boundaries.

When she offers only her work office number, work cell number, and work email address, Tori ensures that clients can reach her only by professional means through her office-related communications. Doing so sets boundaries between herself and clients.

(129) (B) Behavioral health.

Behavioral health refers to how mental health, resilience, and well-being are related to physical expression or behaviors.

(130) (D) Direct practice.

Margery performs her social work duties using the direct practice method. Direct practice means that Margery performs her duties in a face-to-face capacity, meeting with clients in person.

(131) (B) Task-centered practice.

Task-centered practice is the therapy technique that focuses on the problem that an individual wants to overcome and breaks this down into manageable tasks to meet. This helps the individual gain control and improve their self-view. Unless Kelly adds additional tasks to this therapy method once she has completed those three initial tasks and as long as she is doing well, she will graduate from the program.

(132) (D) Relaxation practices.

The ninth strategy in the anger management technique is to use relaxation practices as a way to dispel anger. To practice relaxation, an individual may listen to music, use a journal to write down feelings and get them out, and practice yoga or meditation, among other things.

(133) (B) Ecological perspective.

The ecological perspective is defined as the perspective that looks at how a system (an individual, a family, or community) functions within its outside or external environment.

(134) (D) Bonding and security.

Relationships like the example of Anna and her baby show a healthy development of bonding and nurturing. It increases the baby's feelings of safety and security, reduces stress levels, and promotes the overall health and wellness of mother and baby.

(135) (A) Nonviolent self-defense.

Nonviolent self-defense is a training method that is specially tailored for mental health professionals or those working with individuals who have mental health issues who may be unaware or not in control of their mental faculties. These clients may therefore act irrationally or violently in a way that they are not in control of.

(136) (C) Forgiveness.

The seventh strategy in the anger management technique is forgiveness. To retain feelings of negativity prevents an individual from moving forward in a positive way. It is important to find ways to let go and move forward to ensure that the person does not harbor anger that will only hold them back.

(137) (B) *Parens patriae.*

Parens patriae is a legal term that is applied when the welfare or care needs of an individual are put into the hands of the state in order to provide a legal guardian for that individual. This ensures that the individual's needs and welfare are considered and taken care of when there is no one else or no safe alternative.

(138) (A) During middle age, which is between the ages of 36 and 64.

Between the ages of 36 and 64, individuals enter what is known as middle age. During this time, our bodies begin to slow down. Both in men and women, health issues may develop that can be chronic for the rest of their lives, and most women go through menopause. During this time, it is important that individuals find a balance of overall health and wellness, continue getting regular health checks with their doctors, and pay attention to how their bodies are aging in order to notice any age-associated health risks. This is also a time when people start to plan for their future as an older individual. Such plans typically include retirement and how health decisions should be handled in regard to physical and mental needs as they may need to be made with age. During this time, individuals also typically reach the career goals they set as young adults.

(139) (B) Verbal de-escalation techniques.

Verbal de-escalation techniques are used to defuse or de-escalate a situation that is potentially or actually explosive.

(140) (C) Identify the cause.

The fifth strategy in the anger management technique is to focus on identification of the cause and exploration of solutions. To do this, an individual should consider what made them angry in the first place, accept that anger is not a solution, and consider other ways the situation can be handled.

(141) (A) Engage the client.

Harrison uses the engagement method as a means to connect with his clients and help them help themselves through treatment or services. During this process, the social worker connects with the client in a trusted, respected, and professional manner in order to assist them in to make decisions, help drive to reach goals, and encourage their interaction and participation.

(142) (B) Aging and degeneration.

Our body grows new cells and makes new mental connections throughout our life-span. As we age, those cells take longer to regenerate and be replaced, while parts of our body may also begin to fail. The examples listed in the question are all signs of the degeneration that naturally occurs as the body ages in older age and elder years.

(143) (C) Safety plans.

Safety plans are the procedures and actions that are supposed to be followed when a social worker visits with or transports a client.

(144) (D) Exercise.

The third strategy of the anger management technique is to exercise because physical activity reduces stress, releases hormones that increase good feelings, and can be an outlet for anger.

(145) (B) Privileged communications.

The communication that occurs between Ashley and her clients is known as privileged communications. Privileged communications consist of communication that occurs between social workers and clients and is protected, both by ethics and law, unless a client is suspected of being about to commit self-harm or harm to others, or the client gives consent to share such information.

(146) (A) Growth and development.

Growth is defined as the growth and maturation of cells and organs until they reach maturity. Development refers to the acquisition and growth of mental and psychological knowledge. Together, growth and development refer to an individual's physical, mental, and psychological development over time.

(147) (D) Risk assessment.

A risk assessment is conducted in order to determine whether a client is potentially, likely, or actually violent or prone to violence.

(148) (B) Think before you speak.

The first strategy is to think before you speak, which means to simply take a beat, take a breath, consider your emotions, and consider if the reaction you are having is a rational one or driven by strong feelings.

(149) (C) Active listening.

Active listening is when an individual listens to what the other person says and responds to what is being said. This joint communication leads to the development of mutual understanding. Active listening is a good tool to assist to defuse situations, resolve problems, or utilize problem-solving solutions.

(150) (C) Between the ages of 65 and 79.

Older adults gradually age and experience the natural decline that occurs in regard to physical abilities and mental capacities. At this point in life, the need to find a balance between independence and any needed assistance becomes an important step for overall health, wellness, and safety. Healthy living is incredibly important in order to maintain mental and physical capacities for as long as possible. Seeing doctors regularly is also important during this stage. Continued social connections and friendships and a support system when losing older friends and relatives is important during this time. People should also keep up with the interests and activities that engage them.

(151) (D) Pilot study.

A pilot study is when a new idea or project is tested on a small scale in order to help analyze the effectiveness of a project, its cost, the community response, any possible drawbacks, overall performance, and likelihood of success on a large scale before such a project is launched to full capacity.

(152) (A) Collaboration.

The fourth strategy in conflict resolution is known as collaboration. Collaboration works because both parties actively participate to find a solution and work together to create a shared solution that works for everyone involved.

(153) (B) Assessment.

An assessment is the first step that a social worker will take to decide whether an individual, couple, family, group, or community needs assistance, help, or an intervention. Typically, a quick assessment is first conducted to determine whether there is an imminent threat to self or others or if the issue in question is in any way unhealthy or unsafe. Once the initial assessment is carried out, more comprehensive assessments and planning can then be done.

(154) (A) Oral stage.

This stage is called the oral stage. According to Freud, infants from birth through their first year of life activate their pleasure center when they suck and taste, as they do when they nurse or take a bottle. They explore other things in their environment when they put them in their mouth.

(155) (C) Focus group.

A focus group is a small group, similar in demographic to the one being used for a research study, that is composed in order to answer research-associated questions to gauge answers and give reactions that show how the research group will most likely and similarly react.

(156) (C) Competition.

The second strategy of conflict resolution is known as competition. This is when an individual enters into a conflict with the idea that they are going to win. This type of conflict resolution decreases cooperation and usually results in everyone losing out on finding a solution. Competing ultimately creates more conflict and generally results in a worse situation than what was initially there.

(157) (A) Social justice.

The Hamilton Community College conducts their application and scholarship applications and awards this way in order to create unbiased social justice in their entrance program. Social justice is defined as the equal distribution of social rights and resources to all members of a community.

(158) (B) 80 years or older.

Once an individual reaches 80, they are classified as elderly. During this stage of life, individuals experience more significant health issues and typically are on the decline. It takes longer for an individual's brain to learn and absorb new information, and memory loss becomes an issue. Individuals near the end of their lives, and sometimes acceptance of this fact can be difficult. Maintenance of as much independence as physically and mentally possible, engagement in social activities, proper nutrition, staying active, and maintenance of lower stress levels are all important to the overall health and wellness of the individual. At this point in an individual's life, ensuring that end-of-life decisions have been made, being checked on regularly by friends or family if they live alone, and ensuring that their living arrangements are safe are key to elder living.

(159) (B) Mixed methods.

Mixed methods of research use a variety of research types mixed together in order to obtain a more comprehensive and detailed analysis.

(160) (C) Self-monitoring technique.

Self-monitoring techniques help individuals learn and develop skills that increase their use of positive and appropriate behaviors, reduce behavioral issues, increase independence, and promote socialization. Self-monitoring uses effective strategies in order to increase behaviors that are wanted and decrease behaviors that are considered negative and unwanted.

(161) (B) Confrontation method.

The confrontation method is when counselors or therapists clearly communicate to clients—as a means of bringing awareness to the client—any conflicts in their words, emotions, or actions when they address and deal with issues or situations.

(162) (A) Ego Integrity vs. Despair.

According to Erikson's psychosocial development theory, Matilda develops this sort of contentment in the eighth and final stage. Erikson's theory states that this stage is reached when an individual feels fulfilled in the life that they lead, happy with where their life is at, and content in the wisdom that they've gained over that time.

(163) (A) Longitudinal study.

A longitudinal study is research that is conducted repeatedly over a set period of time. Such studies can be done over short or long periods and focus on observation.

(164) (B) Harm reduction.

Harm reduction uses a variety of techniques and strategies in order to tackle substance abuse in a public health format. When these techniques are used, individuals are met at their level of substance abuse and then helped in their work toward sobriety. This is opposed to making them reach a specific point alone before they are given help on their journey. These techniques center on the provision of judgment-free support, respect for the individual, and connections that foster healthy relationship-building.

(165) (C) To determine the effectiveness of each sobriety program and how well they have been able to help those who enter each of their programs.

Haley has most likely gathered the data from each of the city's sobriety programs to determine the effectiveness of each program and identify whether one program is more effective than others.

(166) (D) Basic human needs.

The minimum necessities required in life are known as basic human needs. Basic human needs include food, water, shelter, sleep, and human interaction. Some also consider novelties, like the ability to have access to learning, as a necessity as well. Most typically, basic human needs refer to the things that are required to maintain healthy growth and development throughout the lifespan. On a daily basis, the human body needs a minimum of 1,200 calories in order to continue its basic functions. It also needs between 2.7 and 3.8 liters of water each day. Additionally, the human body requires adequate shelter from harsh weather. A lack of such things can cause life-threatening damage to the skin and internal organs. The human body also requires six to nine hours of sleep in a 24-hour period in order for the brain to function properly, absorb information, process information, and properly regulate the inner workings of the body. Finally, humans are not meant to be an isolated and lonely creature. Physical touch and emotional connections are required in order to maintain emotional health, mental health, and physical health.

(167) (D) Tell Alyssa that he understands how she is feeling and ask to discuss her feelings further.

William should acknowledge Alyssa's feelings of agitation and possible fear and ask her what occurred or what led her to be in such a heightened emotional state.

(168) (C) Role-play technique.

Role-play techniques can be an effective tool to express strong emotions, reduce the intensity of destructive emotions and behavior, and improve self-perception and awareness. The benefits of role play include the opportunity for the individual to adopt a decision-making persona separate from self-imposed limitations, think beyond the confines of their environment, and develop a correlation between the act that is occurring and the real-life situation. It is important to set a parameter for the role you are playing and the context in which it should be expressed. You should also ensure that there is a discussion and decompression at the end of the role play.

(169) (B) Vulnerable population.

Homeless individuals are classified as part of the vulnerable population. A vulnerable population refers to those groups of individuals who are at an increased risk for health, social, or environmental harm because of life circumstances or life conditions that ultimately leave them open to a lower quality of life.

(170) (A) Physical health.

Physical health is defined as taking care of the human body. This includes the balance of the body's nutrition and physical activity as a means to manage the physical body of an individual for the benefit of their overall health and wellness.

Test 4: Questions

(1) Job fairs, social media groups, webinars, and volunteer work are all ways in which social workers can reach out for what community purpose?

(A) Recruitment.

(B) Outreach.

(C) Networking.

(D) Awareness.

(2) David is 40 years old. He has dated a lot over the years but never felt like he met the right woman. He has been dating his girlfriend, Morgan, for the past 6 years. She does not pester him, but he does know that she would like to get married at some point. David thinks Morgan may be the one, but he is scared that he is incapable of making the commitment since this is his first serious relationship. Which stage in Erikson's psychosocial development theory would David most likely have experienced difficulties?

(A) Industry vs. Inferiority.

(B) Intimacy vs. Isolation.

(C) Autonomy vs. Shame.

(D) Ego Integrity vs. Despair.

(3) Demonstrating credibility and confidence, being open to and providing problem-solving solutions, showing empathy, and listening to professional peers are all components of what?

(A) Conflict management among professional peers.

(B) Active listening in social work.

(C) Emotional and psychoeducational training methods.

(D) Peer management and assignment distribution.

(4) How many core values are there in the field of social work?

(A) 3.

(B) 5.

(C) 8.

(D) 6.

(5) During which stage of Freud's psychosexual development theory do male and female children develop stronger attachments to the parent of the opposite sex?

(A) Phallic stage.

(B) Oral stage.

(C) Newborn stage.

(D) Genital stage.

(6) Which stage of Freud's psychosexual development theory postulates that children experience pleasure through an interest in their genitals and develop bonds with the opposite sex parent?

(A) Genital stage.

(B) Latency stage.

(C) Phallic stage.

(D) Oral stage.

(7) Social workers are required to complete additional education and training annually for what purpose?

(A) Benchmark.

(B) Recertification.

(C) Facilitation.

(D) Advocate.

(8) Programs such as child and family outreach, volunteer, job training, nutrition, and case management are all part of which of the following?

(A) Community involvement.

(B) Social services.

(C) Sobriety support.

(D) Follow-up care.

(9) What form of neglect or abuse is characterized by behaviors such as criticism, affection deprivation, isolation, or humiliation?

(A) Physical.

(B) Sexual.

(C) Psychological.

(D) Social.

(10) During which stage of Freud's psychosexual theory do children repress their desires in lieu of friendships and learning.

(A) Latency stage.

(B) Phallic stage.

(C) Oral stage.

(D) Anal stage.

(11) Among the 6 core values of social work, which is the value that reflects honesty and moral principles?

(A) Competence.

(B) Service.

(C) Integrity.

(D) Social justice.

(12) Providing technical training, connections to potential employers, and the facilitation of internships is a part of which of the following?

(A) Advocacy.

(B) Brokerage.

(C) Coordination.

(D) Job coaching.

(13) What is the term for the use of empirical evidence to ensure that the processes involved in assessments, interventions, and treatments of individuals are solid, reliable, and effective regarding indicated purpose?

(A) Direct practice.

(B) Evidence-based practice.

(C) Field of practice.

(D) Generalist practice.

(14) During which stage of Freud's psychosexual development theory do children derive pleasure by developing social and intellectual skills through repressing their sexual interests?

(A) Phallic stage.

(B) Anal stage.

(C) Oral stage.

(D) Latency stage.

(15) Among the 6 core values of social work, which refers to helping, assisting, or working for the benefit of others?

(A) Integrity.

(B) Competence.

(C) Dignity and worth of the person.

(D) Service.

(16) Which term encompasses resources that assist with housing programs, legal services, free clinics, and family reunification?

(A) Coordination.

(B) Advocacy.

(C) Brokerage.

(D) Support.

(17) What is the fourth step in intervention planning?

(A) Choose a problem behavior that is earmarked for change.

(B) Teach the new alternative behavior.

(C) Create a functional behavioral assessment.

(D) Create a behavioral plan.

(18) For the past several months, Tyler has been getting his siblings up and off to school before going to school himself. After school, he picks each of them up and takes them all home. He then does the laundry, makes dinner, helps with homework, facilitates bathing, and puts them to bed. After receiving a "final notice" in the mail this week, Tyler even learned how to go online and pay bills using his mother's bank account. Thankfully, his father appears to make monthly child support payments or Tyler would not have the money to do that. Most days, his mom is too wasted and strung out to even notice that she has kids, much less that bills need to be paid. What family role of addiction does Tyler play in this scenario?

(A) Enabler.

(B) Scapegoat.

(C) Mascot.

(D) Lost child.

(19) Which of the 6 core values of social work means being worthy of respect by others and having self-respect?

(A) Integrity.

(B) Service.

(C) Competence.

(D) Dignity and worth of the person.

(20) In the field of social work, which resource in addition to counseling is provided with regard to relationships, parenting, decision-making, and independent living?

(A) Treatment centers.

(B) Follow-ups.

(C) Classes.

(D) 12-step programs.

(21) What is the most common action a doctor would take to treat serious cases of anxiety, depression, bipolar disorder, or sleep disorder that cannot be managed alone?

(A) Medication.

(B) Therapy.

(C) Residential treatment.

(D) 12-step program.

(22) Adelaide takes her time breastfeeding her son. During these special times throughout the day, she strokes his cheek softly, sings to him, and ensures a relaxed environment. These moments when bonding is nurtured are an important time in what life stage?

(A) Adolescent stage – 13 years to 17 years.

(B) Infant stage – birth to 2 years.

(C) Toddler stage – 2 years to 4 years.

(D) Young child stage – 5 years to 7 years.

(23) What protection is afforded to clients and patients by the Health Insurance Portability and Accountability Act that entitles them to get copies of and view their medical information?

(A) Right to refuse services.

(B) Right to terminate services.

(C) Right to obtain medical records.

(D) Right to terminate services.

(24) Twelve-step programs, addiction recovery programs, sobriety support groups, and sober living are covered under which social work service?

(A) Treatment and services.

(B) Spiritual enrichment and support.

(C) Community involvement.

(D) Individual and family support.

(25) What form of therapy is characterized by a focus on building skills and changing behavior patterns to cope with emotions?

(A) Psychodynamic therapy.

(B) Cognitive behavioral therapy.

(C) Holistic therapy.

(D) Dialectical behavior therapy.

(26) According to Freud's psychosexual development theory, during which phase does a child derive pleasure from potty training?

(A) Anal stage.

(B) Latency stage.

(C) Genital stage.

(D) Phallic stage.

(27) Henry has a tightly wound and irritated client in his office today. Parker is using nonverbal cues like pulling his knees to his chest, wringing his hands, and avoiding eye contact. In order to connect with Parker, what would Henry most likely say to him first?

(A) "Parker, you're really upset today. Maybe we should meet when you're more composed."

(B) "Parker, you seem more upset than usual today. Can you tell me what you're feeling or what has upset you?"

(C) "Parker, I can't work with you if you're going to be uncooperative."

(D) "Parker, you're making this meeting tense and stressful because you're acting erratic. We'll have to cancel this meeting and reschedule when you have collected yourself."

(28) Which of the options below is not included in a discharge plan?

(A) Where the individual will be residing upon discharge.

(B) The follow-up care plan that will be put into place for the individual.

(C) Behaviors the individual would like to improve and the time frame needed.

(D) Needs and resources that will be provided for the individual to function and improve upon discharge, if any apply.

(29) If Gena works in a hospital as a social worker, Edna works in long-term care facilities as a social worker, and Patrick works in public schools as a social worker. What are these various settings known as?

(A) Caseload.

(B) Generalist practice.

(C) Best practice.

(D) Fields of practice.

(30) Maybell lives in her own home at 85 years old. She gets out of bed on her own, gets a cup of coffee, and sits on her back porch to drink it each morning. A home health aide comes every day to help Maybell bathe and dress, make her breakfast, and help her with a few house chores. Maybell makes herself a sandwich for lunch and eats it on her front porch before taking a nap there until the home health aide returns to make dinner and help her get ready for bed. Her afternoon naps seem to get longer as the days go by, and the tasks she does independently seem to take more out of her. What stage of life is Maybell experiencing?

(A) Older adult stage.

(B) Adolescent stage.

(C) Elder stage.

(D) Middle-aged stage.

(31) Even if you are a fairly passive person, as a social worker you need to be capable of assertive confrontation when dealing with some of your clients. Why is this necessary?

(A) To confront clients who are being inconsistent or uncooperative and call them out on their behaviors.

(B) To convey your understanding of the things your client is expressing.

(C) To participate in conversations with clients, share your viewpoint, and help them see other points of view.

(D) To assist clients in discussing behavioral options that are healthy and constructive to replace existing unhealthy behaviors.

(32) Periodically checking in on a client after they have been discharged from a service or treatment is known by which of the following technical terms?

(A) Assessment.

(B) Treatment plan.

(C) Discharge plan.

(D) Follow-up care.

(33) What form of therapy is characterized by focusing on the whole person and their natural instincts rather than typical therapy methods?

(A) Dialectical behavior therapy.

(B) Holistic therapy.

(C) Cognitive behavioral therapy.

(D) Psychodynamic therapy.

(34) According to Piaget's cognitive development theory, at which stage do children learn object permanence through sight, sound, smell, touch, and taste?

(A) Sensorimotor stage.

(B) Preoperational stage.

(C) Concrete operational stage.

(D) Formal operational stage.

(35) Reed is assessing a new client. He spends several hours conducting assessments to see how the client functions in their home. While doing this, he also asks questions regarding how the client manages their bills, purchases groceries, and gets around to doctor's appointments and such. What is this form of assessment known as?

(A) Risk assessments.

(B) Trauma-based assessments.

(C) Skill-based assessments.

(D) Functional assessments.

(36) Placement services typically depend on the needs of an individual. The following are taken into consideration when deciding on placement, except:

(A) The reason and duration that the individual will be sent to stay at a facility.

(B) The reason they are being sent to a facility.

(C) The individual's ability to live independently.

(D) The level of an individual's ability to complete activities of daily living.

(37) Which of the 5 key stages of the practice of therapy is used in sessions to deal with serious issues?

(A) Initial disclosure.

(B) Counseling intervention.

(C) In-depth exploration.

(D) Commitment to action.

(38) Zoe has recently grown over a foot, started puberty, and is working to build her self-identity. These development skills occur during which ages?

(A) 7 to 12 years old.

(B) 18 to 35 years old.

(C) 36 to 64 years old.

(D) 13 to 17 years old.

(39) All of the options listed below are examples of ways a social worker can improve time management, except:

(A) Make to-do lists with daily goals as well as goals to achieve throughout the week.

(B) Take frequent breaks and ensure healthy emotional and mental health respites.

(C) Schedule a set day to focus on paperwork, file updates, and correspondence.

(D) Ensure that client referrals or treatment changes are immediately established so as not to be lost in the shuffle.

(40) What is the technique in which a social worker listens to a client's feelings in a way that supports and allows them to feel understood and heard, followed by providing input and insight to the client when they have finished speaking?

(A) Active listening and feedback.

(B) Observation and assessment.

(C) Assessment and intervention.

(D) Treatment and discharge.

(41) Matt uses the problem-solving method to approach his assessments and intervention practices as a social worker. This method of work is referred to by which technical term?

(A) Best practice.

(B) Direct practice.

(C) Generalist practice.

(D) Indirect practice.

(42) During which stage of Piaget's cognitive development theory do children learn to think about concepts from a logical perspective?

(A) Concrete operational stage.

(B) Sensorimotor stage.

(C) Formal operational stage.

(D) Preoperational stage.

(43) Which of the following options is not something that facilitates a positive and safe working environment for social workers?

(A) Ensuring good communication.

(B) Enjoying the job and finding fun in what you do.

(C) Posting security guards at major entrances.

(D) Recognizing and appreciating hard work within the system.

(44) Setting goals that are within reach for a client can be an incredible motivator for which purpose?

(A) Making treatment options seem too big to manage.

(B) Creating a sense of accomplishment and encouragement.

(C) Creating a rational environment for improvement.

(D) Developing a correlation between habits and routines.

(45) What is the term for a scale that is universally recognized to measure how severe a mental illness is at a given time?

(A) Global assessment of functioning.

(B) Crisis intervention assessment.

(C) Imminent needs assessment.

(D) Intervention planning assessment.

(46) During what lifespan stage do individuals start to see signs of aging on the physical body, potentially develop new chronic health issues, and have fully developed problem-solving skills?

(A) Young adult.

(B) Middle-aged adult.

(C) Older-aged adult.

(D) Elder.

(47) In a typical organization hierarchy, who is the first person a social worker will report to?

(A) District manager.

(B) Facility supervisor.

(C) Department manager.

(D) Direct supervisor.

(48) Using a timer to start and stop an activity for a set time frame can do what for a child?

(A) Support.

(B) Entice.

(C) Motivate.

(D) Restrict.

(49) What is the technical term for the thorough, detailed, and carefully constructed study of the client in the 5 key practices of therapy?

(A) Counseling intervention.

(B) In-depth exploration.

(C) Initial disclosure.

(D) Commitment to action.

(50) According to Piaget's cognitive development theory, in which stage of development do children learn to play pretend, develop their language skills, and develop ego?

(A) Preoperational stage.

(B) Formal operational stage.

(C) Sensorimotor stage.

(D) Concrete operational stage.

(51) What is a social worker's role when a client is unable to speak on their own behalf or is too young to do so?

(A) Assess.

(B) Intervene.

(C) Support.

(D) Advocate.

(52) Nina is the spouse of an alcoholic. Which of the following groups would most likely benefit Nina and support her?

(A) Advocacy group.

(B) Educational group.

(C) Psychotherapy group.

(D) Mutual aid group.

(53) Erin conducts phone interviews to verify information regarding her subordinate's caseloads. She also does file reviews and signs off on client discharges, just to name some of her responsibilities as a social work supervisor. Erin's work is mainly conducted in-office and occasionally as part of their community outreach. What type of social work practice does Erin engage in?

(A) Generalist practice.

(B) Indirect practice.

(C) Best practice.

(D) Direct practice.

(54) Which stage of Freud's psychosexual theory postulates that pleasure is derived by a child's ability to control bodily elimination and gain independence through their ability to regulate their own bodies?

(A) Oral stage.

(B) Phallic stage.

(C) Anal stage.

(D) Genital stage.

(55) Which of the options below is not something that you would do to reduce burnout as a social worker?

(A) Set reachable, short-term goals and allow some sort of break or reward as you meet them.

(B) Limit your caseload to the number of clients that you can practically and realistically manage at one time, and work within the designated hours of your profession.

(C) Take unfinished work home with you at the end of your shift in order to work in a comfortable setting and not be in your office after hours.

(D) Ensure that you have a healthy outlet to cope with emotions regarding job stressors and that you take the time to use those outlets regularly.

(56) Peter is suffering from severe depression and experiencing excessive thoughts of self-harm. What is the best therapeutic approach for him?

(A) Cognitive behavioral therapy.

(B) Crisis intervention therapy.

(C) Narrative therapy.

(D) Solution-focused therapy.

(57) Which is the sixth and final step of intervention planning?

(A) Choose a problem behavior that is earmarked for change.

(B) Determine the function of the behavioral problem.

(C) Teach the new alternative behavior.

(D) Create a behavioral plan.

(58) Building gross motor skills, gaining some independence with self-help skills, and developing imagination through play are all part of which lifespan stage?

(A) Young children.

(B) Older children.

(C) Adolescents.

(D) Young adults.

(59) Agencies that employ social workers can oversee their best interests by doing all the following, except:

(A) Ensure that social workers continue annual professional development training through reputable sources.

(B) Keep social workers on call 24 hours a day, 7 days a week. This includes not rotating the schedule on a regular basis or having specific social workers who handle on-call cases only.

(C) Limit caseloads to ensure that social workers are not overwhelmed and under-resourced and ensure that they have sufficient time to manage each case properly.

(D) Ensure that social workers are given personal or vacation time to take breaks and seek respite from the responsibilities they hold.

(60) Quinn is attacked on her way home and brutally beaten. When she arrives at the hospital, she is incredibly skittish and does not want anyone to touch her. She also jumps at every noise she hears and motion she sees. What method of care would best serve Quinn to allow her to be examined and treated?

(A) Crisis intervention care.

(B) Trauma-informed care.

(C) Advocacy care.

(D) Best practice care.

(61) Organization policies, practices, and systems are part of which phase of cultural consideration in intervention planning?

(A) Awareness.

(B) Skills development.

(C) Organizational support.

(D) Knowledge.

(62) Which stage of Piaget's cognitive development theory accounts for the development of abstract logic and the opportunity for mature moral reasoning?

(A) Preoperational stage.

(B) Concrete operational stage.

(C) Sensorimotor stage.

(D) Formal operational stage.

(63) Organizations use which of the following to formally present their values and goals?

(A) Mission statement.

(B) Code of ethics.

(C) Organizational culture.

(D) Consensus model.

(64) James is an adult and has just graduated from college. He moves out of his parents' house and into a home of his own. After moving out, he meets Lily, and they get married. Lily and James have 2 children. When their children are in their teens and do not need them as much, Lily and James begin caring for their aging parents. Their children graduate from high school and move out to have lives of their own. Lily and James settle into life as empty nesters and begin planning for retirement. These life stages are part of what?

(A) Growth and development.

(B) The aging process.

(C) The family life cycle.

(D) Caregiving effect.

(65) Eva is severely anorexic. She has lost a tremendous amount of weight and has been admitted to the hospital for multiorgan system failure. The doctor would like to place a feeding tube to attempt to reverse her organ systems' need to shut down by getting sufficient calories into her system. Eva does not verbally tell the doctor yes. However, when the doctor comes in with the feeding tube and nutrition bag, Eva nods her head in agreement. The doctor moves forward with placing the feeding tube and starting her nutrition. Giving consent in this way is formally known by what term?

(A) Revoked consent.

(B) Implied consent.

(C) Forced consent.

(D) Informed consent.

(66) Slow but steady growth, improved reading and writing skills, ability to work through situations using conflict resolution, and awareness of some of the dangers in the world are all part of which life stage age range?

(A) 7 to 12 years.

(B) 13 to 17 years.

(C) 18 to 35 years.

(D) 4 to 6 years.

(67) Professional relationships between clients and social workers are formally known by which of the following terms?

(A) System relationships.

(B) Personal relationships.

(C) Interpersonal relationships.

(D) Professional relationships.

(68) What is the technical term for abusing a substance to avoid pain?

(A) Positive reinforcement.

(B) Incentive salience.

(C) Stimulus-response learning.

(D) Negative reinforcement.

(69) Which part of cultural consideration refers to a person's self-awareness, individual knowledge, and acknowledgement of biases?

(A) Skills development.

(B) Self-reliance.

(C) Awareness and knowledge.

(D) Organizational support.

(70) During what stage of abusive relationships does the abusive act actually occur?

(A) Stage 1: The catalyst.

(B) Stage 2: The abusive act.

(C) Stage 3: The honeymoon or aftermath.

(D) Stage 4: The calm before the storm.

(71) Professional development is defined by all the items below, except:

(A) Improvement and expansion of professional competencies.

(B) Knowing professional competency levels and limitations.

(C) Improvement and expansion of professional skill bases.

(D) Improvement and expansion in one's professional position.

(72) What is the technical term for abusing a substance to find pleasure?

(A) Positive reinforcement.

(B) Inhibitory control dysfunction.

(C) Incentive salience.

(D) Stimulus-response learning.

(73) Cortney informs her client Tessa of the treatment center rules and procedures so that Tessa can decide if she can adhere to the program requirements and guidelines before making the decision to enter the program. Once Tessa is fully apprised of the rules and guidelines of the treatment program, she agrees to adhere to the criteria and signs the forms confirming her acknowledgement. What is the technical term for Tessa receiving all the information before making the decision and confirming it in writing?

(A) Intervention planning.

(B) Informed consent.

(C) Treatment plan.

(D) Implied consent.

(74) What type of lifespan interaction occurs in cognitive, emotional, physical, and sexual forms?

(A) Development.

(B) Stage.

(C) Growth.

(D) Coherence.

(75) Accountability, transparency, accessibility, protection, compliance, and information retention are all principles of which action?

(A) Conducting assessments.

(B) Making referrals.

(C) Record-keeping.

(D) Setting intervention goals.

(76) What is the technical term for abusing a substance to feed a craving?

(A) Stimulus-response learning.

(B) Negative reinforcement.

(C) Inhibitory control dysfunction.

(D) Incentive salience.

(77) Which is the second step in intervention planning?

(A) Collect data to measure the behavior.

(B) Teach the new alternative behavior.

(C) Create a functional behavioral assessment.

(D) Choose a problem behavior that is earmarked for change.

(78) What theory is based on the idea that individuals will make choices that are in their own best interest?

(A) Impulsive reasoning.

(B) Fight or flight.

(C) Rational choice.

(D) Person-in-environment.

(79) Though organization rules and laws specific to your state or province may vary, how long are social workers usually required to maintain records on a given adult client?

(A) 1 year.

(B) 8 years.

(C) 12 years.

(D) 6 years.

(80) Returning control to the victim is the first step in addressing what type of issue?

(A) Abuse.

(B) Accident.

(C) Trauma.

(D) Alcoholism.

(81) Yolanda has written up one of her subordinates for wrongdoing in the workplace. The man has had several warnings regarding this behavior already. After a formal complaint was submitted by a client, Yolanda has no choice but to formally put a letter of reprimand in his personnel file. Yolanda has adequate reasons for writing the employee up and gave him a fair chance to correct the behavior before taking such a drastic step. What is the formal term for having a fair reason to discipline an employee?

(A) Right to work.

(B) Just cause.

(C) Fabricated cause.

(D) Employee dismissal.

(82) What theory suggests that the environment an individual grows up in and experiences plays a vital role in influencing that person's development in a social, economic, and cultural way?

(A) Person-in-environment theory.

(B) Psychosocial development theory.

(C) Attachment theory.

(D) Social learning theory.

(83) How long should records usually be retained for a client who is a minor at the time of service?

(A) The same 6 years that is required for adult clients.

(B) Until the child reaches the age of majority, after which minor files may be discarded if the child in question is no longer receiving services.

(C) Twelve years after the child's dismissal from services.

(D) Six years from the time they reach the age of majority in their state or province.

(84) Tonya goes kickboxing twice a week, attends yoga every Sunday, and runs on most nights when she is not kickboxing. Tonya works in an advocacy center for battered and abused women and children. Yoga helps her relax and decompress before she starts her next week of work, while kickboxing and running give her an outlet for her negative thoughts and emotions related to her job. This healthy and positive psychological defense mechanism that Tonya uses to cope and work through her thoughts and feelings is formally known by which of the following?

(A) Sublimation.

(B) Rationalization.

(C) Progression.

(D) Projection.

(85) As part of the divorce process, a mother is meeting with a social worker who will also meet with her soon-to-be ex-husband before the final rulings are made on the divorce. The social worker finds that the child and parent are affectionate toward one another, the mother speaks kindly and respectfully to the child even when correcting misbehaviors, and the overall home and atmosphere seem lived-in yet clean and comfortable. How would the social worker most likely label this relationship between mother and child?

(A) An enabling child caring for a parent.

(B) A healthy parent-and-child relationship.

(C) A codependent relationship between parent and child.

(D) An unhealthy parent-and-child relationship.

(86) What is the age range in which children experience the most brain growth, several growth spurts, and bonding that is vital to their overall growth and development?

(A) 4 to 6 years.

(B) 13 to 17 years.

(C) 7 to 12 years.

(D) Birth to 3 years.

(87) Which of the following reasons is not a principle in breaching confidentiality?

(A) Justifying the purpose for which confidentiality needs to be breached.

(B) Removing identifiable client information that should be released only on a need-to-know basis to those who have the right to the information.

(C) Sharing information within your own organization.

(D) Having a clear understanding of the laws in your state or province pertaining to confidentiality and ensuring compliance within those laws.

(88) Jenna's boyfriend, Bobby, broke her son's arm. Rather than leaving her boyfriend or charging him for harm, Jenna instead explains repeatedly that her 4-year-old was misbehaving excessively and that it was his own fault his arm got broken. This type of psychological defense mechanism is formally known by which of the following terms?

(A) Regression.

(B) Rationalization.

(C) Repression.

(D) Displacement.

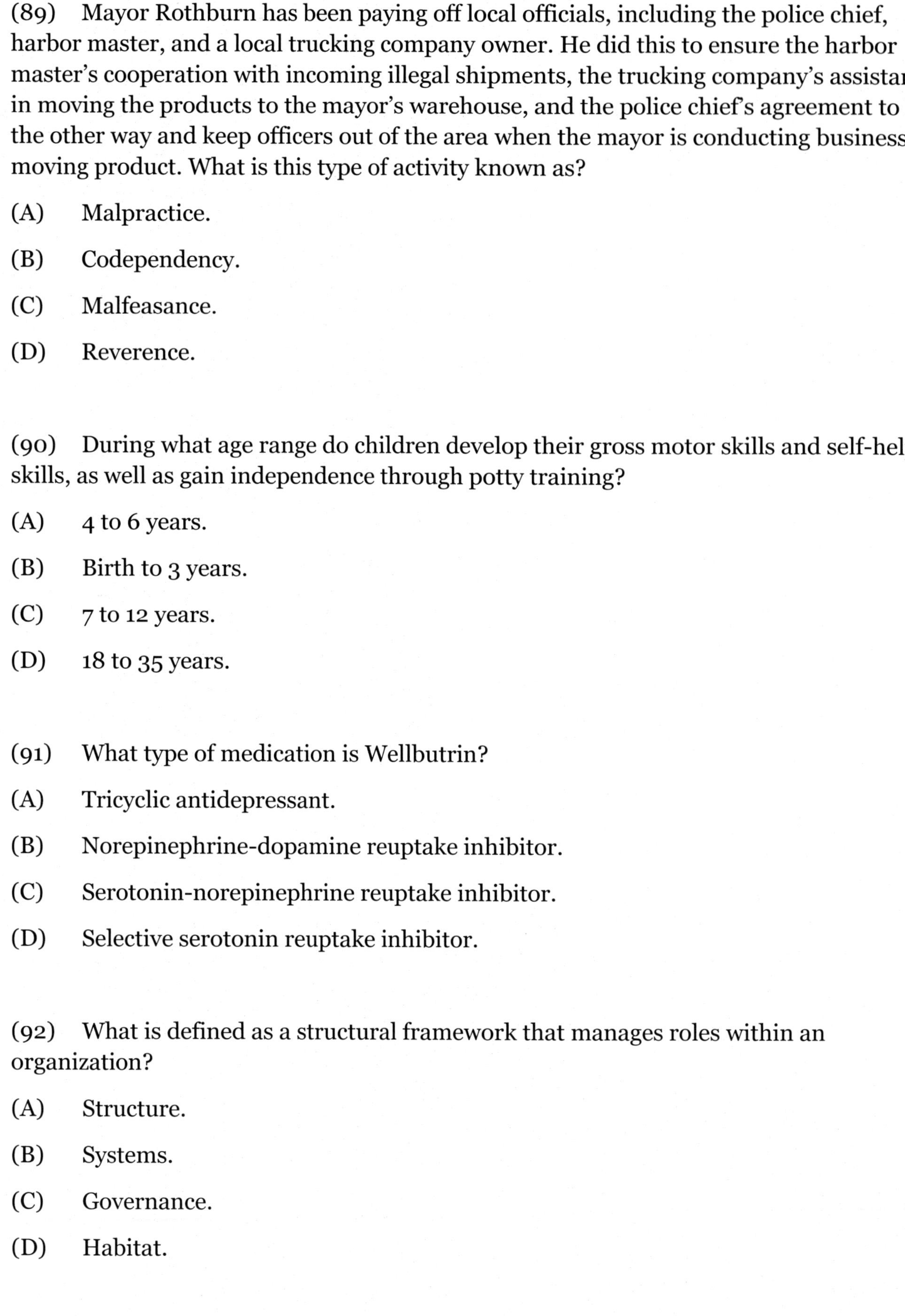

(89) Mayor Rothburn has been paying off local officials, including the police chief, harbor master, and a local trucking company owner. He did this to ensure the harbor master's cooperation with incoming illegal shipments, the trucking company's assistance in moving the products to the mayor's warehouse, and the police chief's agreement to look the other way and keep officers out of the area when the mayor is conducting business or moving product. What is this type of activity known as?

(A) Malpractice.

(B) Codependency.

(C) Malfeasance.

(D) Reverence.

(90) During what age range do children develop their gross motor skills and self-help skills, as well as gain independence through potty training?

(A) 4 to 6 years.

(B) Birth to 3 years.

(C) 7 to 12 years.

(D) 18 to 35 years.

(91) What type of medication is Wellbutrin?

(A) Tricyclic antidepressant.

(B) Norepinephrine-dopamine reuptake inhibitor.

(C) Serotonin-norepinephrine reuptake inhibitor.

(D) Selective serotonin reuptake inhibitor.

(92) What is defined as a structural framework that manages roles within an organization?

(A) Structure.

(B) Systems.

(C) Governance.

(D) Habitat.

(93) What is the formal term for the summary that is generated at the end of a comprehensive intervention assessment?

(A) Clinical summary.

(B) Initial assessment.

(C) Discharge summary.

(D) Comprehensive assessment.

(94) Lilith is 54 years old. Her children are grown and living on their own. Every morning, Lilith drives across town to help her mother dress and get ready for the day before she heads off to work. Each evening, Lilith returns to her mother's home to prepare dinner, help her mother bathe, and assist her in getting dressed for bed. When Lilith goes home at the end of each day, she makes sure that she takes any leftovers from making her mother's dinner so she does not have to cook a separate meal for herself. Since Lilith does not work weekends, she makes sure to attend a yoga class, get coffee with her girlfriends, and have free time to relax or do other things that she enjoys. This compassion, caring for her mother, and ensuring that she balances her priorities and self-care are all part of the healthy development achieved in which stage of Erikson's psychosocial development theory?

(A) Identity vs. Confusion.

(B) Generativity vs. Stagnation.

(C) Initiative vs. Guilt.

(D) Ego Integrity vs. Despair.

(95) Margaret keeps a tight schedule. Every day, she spends the first hour of the morning reviewing the case files of the clients she will be meeting with that day. For the following several hours, Margaret meets with clients before spending the remaining part of her day responding to emails and returning phone calls. Margaret feels that her approach works best because it allows her to complete most, if not all, of her daily tasks. What skill has Margaret mastered?

(A) Time management.

(B) Clerical management.

(C) Systems management.

(D) File management.

(96) Which party is responsible for ensuring resources and managing financial support within a system?

(A) Support staff.

(B) Social workers.

(C) Administrative staff.

(D) Case managers.

(97) For the last few months, Bert has been requiring his clients to pay a fee to him each time they need a referral or permission for continued services. He has collected a hefty amount of money from clients in his heavy caseload. What is this behavior known as in a professional setting such as social work or medical care?

(A) Professional bribery.

(B) Negligence.

(C) Malpractice.

(D) Ethical boundaries.

(98) Adam is in an anger management program. He attends meetings twice a week. He meets with his social worker twice a month to review his progress and ensure that he is working toward the goals that they have set together. What are these check-ins formally known as?

(A) Semimonthly assessments.

(B) Bi-weekly assessments.

(C) Twice-annual assessments.

(D) Annual assessments.

(99) As a social worker, making lists, keeping a schedule, addressing referrals immediately, setting daily goals, managing time, and setting aside a day for correspondence, filing, and documentation are all part of being what?

(A) Organized.

(B) Trained.

(C) Efficient.

(D) Motivated.

(100) What method of social work is defined as a group experience to improve overall functioning within the group?

(A) Social case work.

(B) Social work research.

(C) Social work group.

(D) Social action.

(101) When referring to a social work assessment and the in-depth information that is collected, the individual's detailed background and other assessment information is known as what?

(A) First impressions and initial assessments.

(B) General descriptions and recommendations.

(C) Basic information and presenting problems.

(D) Background and current functioning.

(102) Which age group experiences bodily changes that include significant growth spurts, puberty-based changes and the ability to reproduce, and cognitive development of skills in abstract thinking, individual value systems, and growth in personal identity?

(A) 18 to 35 years.

(B) 7 to 12 years.

(C) 13 to 17 years.

(D) 36 to 64 years.

(103) What should all social workers ensure they do to lower their risk of burnout, reduce their stress levels, and relax from the tension that comes with the job?

(A) Accept additional cases.

(B) Develop self-care and coping mechanisms.

(C) Maintain confidentiality and respect.

(D) Succeed at record-keeping and documentation.

(104) What therapeutic method utilizes past problems and how those issues were resolved to predict future occurrences and plan a resolution?

(A) Structural family therapy.

(B) Transgenerational family therapy.

(C) Systemic family therapy.

(D) Narrative family therapy.

(105) Zoe has been working as a social worker for the past 5 years. Her supervisor, Margaret, asks her to work closely with a new hire to teach the ropes of the position, share her experience, and help her along the way if she needs it. What is it called when a more experienced employee helps guide a new employee in the same position?

(A) Supervisor.

(B) Counselor.

(C) Subordinate.

(D) Mentor.

(106) When a child develops in a manner that does not conform to what is considered normal or regular, this is known by which formal term?

(A) Atypical development.

(B) Stereotypical development.

(C) Quintessential development.

(D) Representative development.

(107) Any system or organization that earns money and generates a profit is known as what type of organization?

(A) Nonprofit.

(B) Volunteer.

(C) For-profit.

(D) Barter.

(108) Which family therapy structure is characterized by assisting individuals in separating who they are from the problems they have?

(A) Narrative family therapy.

(B) Systemic family therapy.

(C) Transgenerational family therapy.

(D) Strategic family therapy.

(109) Thomas conducts a new client interview. As he completes the in-depth interview, he collects a wide array of information from multiple sources. What is the collection of data from multiple and various sources formally known as?

(A) Data confirmation.

(B) Sources of data.

(C) Historical data.

(D) Empirical data.

(110) Infants require consistent and continued care, nurturing, physical touch, sufficient nutrition, clothing, and warmth from their mother or primary caregiver in order to develop in a normal and healthy manner. What occurs when an infant cannot properly bond with their mother or caregiver?

(A) Conduct disorder.

(B) Oppositional defiant disorder.

(C) Intellectual disorder.

(D) Infant reactive attachment disorder.

(111) What is an organized group with legal responsibilities regarding government of a system or organization?

(A) Mentor program.

(B) Advisory board.

(C) Council.

(D) Board of directors.

(112) Of the 5 family therapy techniques, which is characterized by a belief system as the core of the therapy process?

(A) Strategic family therapy.

(B) Systemic family therapy.

(C) Transgenerational family therapy.

(D) Narrative family therapy.

(113) Andre saw his primary care doctor last week. During the visit, they discussed some of the issues that Andre has been experiencing for the past several months. His doctor gets in touch with a psychologist that he feels will be able to help Andre with these issues and arranges for him to have an appointment with the therapist the following week. What is the technical term for the actions taken by the primary care doctor to arrange for Andre to see the psychologist?

(A) Referral.

(B) Diagnosis.

(C) Sourcing.

(D) Discharge.

(114) Anton evaluates new clients and looks for 3 key items: their ability to access and obtain adequate water and food, access to sufficient shelter, and their ability to properly bathe and have fresh clothing. What does Anton want to ensure that his clients have immediate access to?

(A) Basic human needs.

(B) Additional novelties.

(C) Physical and mental healthcare.

(D) Reproductive needs.

(115) What organization contributes to the social work system by advising and offering opinions in a given situation?

(A) Board of directors.

(B) Interception board.

(C) Bureaucracy.

(D) Advisory board.

(116) What therapeutic group approach uses psychology, sociology, and education to provide support in a group setting?

(A) Psychotherapy.

(B) Educational.

(C) Psychoeducational.

(D) Advocacy.

(117) A systematic way of determining whether individuals, couples, families, or groups have needs that require being met or gaps in their present needs is a process formally known as what?

(A) Crisis evaluation.

(B) Benefits analysis.

(C) Discharge evaluation.

(D) Needs assessment.

(118) Based on Freud's psychosexual development theory, during what stage do individuals develop a sexual attraction to the opposite sex?

(A) Phallic stage.

(B) Genital stage.

(C) Latency stage.

(D) Anal stage.

(119) What do social workers achieve as they continue training courses, refresh themselves on professional advancements, and take additional training hours on an annual basis?

(A) Continued education.

(B) Professional certification.

(C) Professional development.

(D) Scholastic education.

(120) Which group therapy approach involves educated professionals using an accredited approach to therapy?

(A) Psychoeducational groups.

(B) Advocacy groups.

(C) Mutual aid groups.

(D) Educational groups.

(121) What social work approach focuses on the helpful resources an individual has over the problems they are dealing with?

(A) Generalist perspective.

(B) Strength perspective.

(C) Diversity perspective.

(D) Ecological perspective.

(122) Bandura's social learning theory, Bowlby's attachment theory, Erikson's psychosocial development theory, Freud's psychosexual development theory, and Piaget's cognitive development theory all play a role in explaining what?

(A) Human development.

(B) Psychological analysis.

(C) Emotional understanding.

(D) Growth through the lifespan.

(123) With few exceptions, social workers are bound to keep client information private. This binding is known as what?

(A) Ascertain.

(B) Confidentiality.

(C) Privileged.

(D) Accreditation.

(124) What therapeutic approach is characterized by clinical approaches and education as a treatment method?

(A) Limit setting

(B) Trauma-informed care.

(C) Psychoeducational.

(D) Conflict resolution.

(125) Every person has multiple layers to their personal life. As such, which social work practice aims to understand the complexities of those layers, including social lives, family lives, and community lives, and how they play into an individual's social, cultural, and psychological life?

(A) Social perspective.

(B) Ecological perspective.

(C) Strength perspective.

(D) Generalist perspective.

(126) Within which age group do individuals become adults, reach their physical and sexual maturity, seek to develop romantic relationships, seek pathways for career building, and begin making critical decisions regarding reproduction?

(A) Over the age of 80.

(B) Between the ages of 36 and 64.

(C) Between the ages of 18 and 35.

(D) Between the ages of 65 and 79.

(127) Which technique is taught to individuals for daily use to cope with life stressors and improve or maintain overall health and wellness?

(A) Stress management.

(B) Task-centered approach.

(C) Self-care and coping.

(D) Psychoeducational.

(128) What therapeutic technique focuses on writing a plan and setting small, specific goals that need to be met?

(A) Limit-setting technique.

(B) Partializing technique.

(C) Stress management technique.

(D) Task-centered technique.

(129) Penny has been making social contacts with an assortment of community organizations to add to the resources at the social service agency where she works. What Penny is doing is formally known as what?

(A) Assessing.

(B) Mentoring.

(C) Managing.

(D) Networking.

(130) Lori and Patrick have been married for 5 years and have 2 small children. Patrick is injured in an accident at work that leaves him permanently disabled. Lori and the children are greatly affected by Patrick's injury, as it causes him to need help with many aspects of his daily life, including the use of a wheelchair. What type of effect will Patrick's injury have on his family?

(A) Patrick's entire family will face challenges as they grow and adjust in order to accommodate the effects of such a disability or face fracturing the family unit.

(B) There will be no long-term effects on Patrick's family as a whole, as the disability and changes will only affect his life.

(C) Such a catastrophic incident will shake the family's foundation in ways that mean it may never recover.

(D) Patrick and his family will be able to go about their daily lives in much the same way but will need outside help to care for Patrick and meet his needs.

(131) What are the practical, ethical, and behavioral standards that a social worker follows?

(A) Ethical standards.

(B) Legal standards.

(C) Professional standards.

(D) Therapeutic standards.

(132) A coworker has started coming into work looking increasingly disheveled. They smell like alcohol, their work is beginning to suffer with files that are disorderly or missing information, and they have missed several client appointments. What is the most immediate concern that the site supervisor needs to address?

(A) Put the social worker on administrative leave while the situation is resolved.

(B) Bring the concerns to the attention of the seemingly impaired social worker.

(C) Have one or more social workers take over the individual's caseload to ensure that clients are being taken care of adequately.

(D) Tell the individual they must submit to the company's drug testing policy because there is suspected misconduct.

(133) In Erikson's psychosocial development theory, which stage occurs between the ages of 40 and 65 and is characterized by a more comprehensive grasp of caring for others and self-care, as well as successful achievement of milestones in sustaining personal relationships with others, building careers, having families of their own, and contributing to their communities?

(A) Generativity vs. Stagnation.

(B) Identity vs. Role Confusion.

(C) Autonomy vs. Shame.

(D) Ego Integrity vs. Despair.

(134) What is the technical term referring to a project plan with clear and measurable objectives in the 5 key practices of therapy?

(A) Initial disclosure.

(B) In-depth exploration.

(C) Commitment to action.

(D) Counseling intervention.

(135) Missy's husband, Eric, beat her to within inches of her life. Since waking up in the hospital, Missy has completely wiped the memories of the event from her mind. She refuses to press charges against her husband and returns home with him when she is released from the hospital despite her family's pleas not to do so. This form of psychological defense mechanism is known by which of the following formal terms?

(A) Regression.

(B) Projection.

(C) Repression.

(D) Sublimation.

(136) Which of the following is not an important principle to keep social workers, administrative staff, and support staff safe within a social services environment?

(A) Ensure an open and inviting atmosphere with no boundaries or limitations.

(B) Review referral client, new client, and existing client files for histories of violence or current violent offenses.

(C) Have an outlined and developed protocol in place to alert staff members in the event of an outburst or escalation within the facility that could quickly become violent or pose serious danger to the entire staff.

(D) Have an evacuation procedure in place should an occurrence of violence break out in a facility that allows as many staff members as possible to exit and follow a set protocol for police involvement.

(137) What is the psychological defense mechanism that is defined by an individual who pushes the incident aside to avoid an emotional and mental toll for which they are not prepared to cope?

(A) Repression.

(B) Displacement.

(C) Denial.

(D) Sublimation.

(138) What is the technical term for the final assessment, dismissal, or forwarding of care within the 5 key practices of therapy?

(A) Commitment to action.

(B) Evaluation, termination, or referral.

(C) In-depth exploration.

(D) Counseling intervention.

(139) Marcus is in his late 20s and experienced a traumatic brain injury due to a severe car accident last year. Now that Marcus has been released from rehab, he is meeting with the social worker to determine available services to allow him to live as independently as possible. What is the first thing the social worker may need to do to figure out Marcus's needs?

(A) Crisis assessment.

(B) Treatment assessment.

(C) Historical assessment.

(D) Needs assessment.

(140) Hannah and Debbie have been working together for the past 5 years. When a new employee, Walker, starts at the agency, Debbie and Hannah offer to help him through their facility's programs and services, explain the processes and forms to be completed for each client, and answer any questions. Looking out for a new employee this way is known as which of the following?

(A) Supervising.

(B) Enabling.

(C) Mentoring.

(D) Dictating.

(141) What psychological defense mechanism is characterized by removing memories that are associated with traumatic or painful events as a means of avoiding them entirely?

(A) Repression.

(B) Projection.

(C) Rationalization.

(D) Sublimation.

(142) Which form of therapy is characterized as goal-oriented, short-term therapy with a focus on behavioral and cognitive issues?

(A) Cognitive behavioral therapy.

(B) Psychodynamic therapy.

(C) Dialectical behavior therapy.

(D) Holistic therapy.

(143) David watches his 24-year-old daughter Alicia rock back and forth on the floor with a teddy bear in her arms. Several weeks earlier, David's daughter was sexually assaulted on her way home from the library, where she was studying for her college finals. Since that time, Alicia has escaped from the trauma of what happened by mentally retreating to her 4-year-old self. This form of psychological defense mechanism is known as which of the following?

(A) Repression.

(B) Projection.

(C) Regression.

(D) Displacement.

(144) If a social worker has an agitated client in their office and they feel it may become an explosive situation, which of the following tools would be most effective to resolve or mitigate the issue?

(A) Risk assessment.

(B) De-escalation techniques.

(C) Self-defense.

(D) Crisis intervention.

(145) Olivia has been working under a new manager for the last several weeks. The manager is entirely unqualified for the position, attempts to micromanage Olivia and her tasks at work, and has cost her several deadlines because of incompetence. After weeks of dealing with these work stressors, Olivia comes home and takes her frustrations out on her husband. The argument starts over a basket of unfolded laundry. Olivia is not actually upset about the laundry because she easily could have done it now that she is home. What psychological defense mechanism is utilized when an individual copes with their thoughts or feelings regarding a given situation by taking it out on a less-threatening person who poses a lower risk of reacting to the outburst than the person to whom those thoughts and feelings are actually aimed?

(A) Sublimation.

(B) Repression.

(C) Regression.

(D) Projection.

(146) The Anderson family go through a series of interviews regarding their home life, financial data, and personal information. The information is gathered to see what services may be available to them. When the assessment is complete, the Anderson family is informed that they qualify for housing vouchers, medical care assistance for their disabled daughter, and respite care. What type of assessment gathers such information?

(A) Eligibility criteria.

(B) Best practice.

(C) Ethical based practice.

(D) Just cause.

(147) Amelia has been living in her home for the past 35 years. Recently, her home went into foreclosure after the death of her husband. Amelia refuses to accept the situation, will not address the topic at all, and is going about her daily activities as though nothing is happening. What type of psychological defense mechanism is Amelia utilizing?

(A) Denial.

(B) Projection.

(C) Rationalization.

(D) Displacement.

(148) Conducting research in social work can be beneficial for the following reasons, except:

(A) To develop better and more effective intervention protocols.

(B) To determine the effectiveness of existing treatments and protocols.

(C) To track a client's progress.

(D) To understand an environment's external factors and how they influence the individual.

(149) Carmen goes to the gym 3 times a week. Every time she is there she spends at least 20 minutes taking her emotions and frustrations out on the gym's punching bag. That release she allows herself makes all the difference when dealing with work and life stressors. What is this type of psychological defense mechanism known as?

(A) Displacement.

(B) Repression.

(C) Projection.

(D) Rationalization.

(150) What form of therapy is characterized by a duration of a year or more and an emphasis on specific life events and their effect on an individual's thoughts and feelings?

(A) Holistic therapy.

(B) Psychodynamic therapy.

(C) Dialectical behavior therapy.

(D) Cognitive behavioral therapy.

(151) Which of the following is not a stressor that usually causes families to experience significant negative impacts on health, growth, and development?

(A) Having a new baby or adding a child.

(B) Experiencing a separation or divorce.

(C) Remodeling a home.

(D) Moving to a new home in another school district.

(152) The right to refuse or withhold services or treatment, the right to withdraw life-sustaining support, and a patient's free will to make those decisions for themself is especially important during which of the following stages?

(A) Labor and delivery.

(B) Surgery and recovery.

(C) Substance abuse and sobriety.

(D) Death and dying.

(153) Which of the following medications is commonly used as a mood stabilizer?

(A) Effexor.

(B) Lithium.

(C) Zoloft.

(D) Valium.

(154) Which drug is a common antipsychotic medication for patients?

(A) Xanax.

(B) Adderall.

(C) Haldol.

(D) Prozac.

(155) The temporary or indefinite removal of a child from their home is known by which of the following technical terms?

(A) Foster care placement.

(B) Familial placement.

(C) Permanent placement.

(D) Out-of-home placement.

(156) In Erikson's psychosocial development theory, which stage occurs in adults 65 and older and is commonly characterized as the achievement of wisdom through the reflection of a fulfilled life over time?

(A) Ego Integrity vs. Despair.

(B) Generativity vs. Stagnation.

(C) Intimacy vs. Isolation.

(D) Autonomy vs. Shame.

(157) Holly works as a lawyer in a high-end law firm downtown. Often, people find it surprising that she has a career in law due to the way she dresses. She has deep purple hair that she wears in a signature high ponytail. She prefers to wear black pinstriped pantsuits, with deep v-necklines, with her favorite 6-inch spiked heels. Holly is noticeably confident in her appearance and has taken pride in dressing this way since her late teens as she feels confident and most like herself. During which stage of Erikson's psychosocial development theory would Holly most likely have developed such a bold confidence and self-identity?

(A) Intimacy vs. Isolation.

(B) Initiative vs. Guilt.

(C) Identity vs. Confusion.

(D) Industry vs. Inferiority.

(158) What is the process of evaluating mental health in an assessment?

(A) Comprehensive assessment.

(B) Crisis evaluation.

(C) Intervention process.

(D) Mental status exam.

(159) Family caregivers struggle with the following except:

(A) Physical and emotional stress.

(B) Sufficient self-care and respite.

(C) Sleep deprivation.

(D) Financial strain.

(160) Legal and ethical violations within the professional field that are visible to others are known by which of the following terms?

(A) Body language.

(B) Nonverbal cues.

(C) Red flags.

(D) Signifying bonds.

(161) Erika was beaten nearly to death by her ex-husband. She spent a week in the ICU. After that, she was admitted to a psychological care unit for further evaluation and treatment. This happened because when Erika woke from her coma, she spoke, acted, and behaved like she was 6 years old again. When asked, she told the doctors she was in fact 6 and asked for her dad several times. What is this type of psychological defense mechanism known as?

(A) Regression.

(B) Sublimation.

(C) Displacement.

(D) Repression.

(162) According to Freud's psychosexual development theory, at what stage do individuals develop their attraction to peers in a sexual way?

(A) Anal stage.

(B) Oral stage.

(C) Phallic stage.

(D) Genital stage.

(163) What is the technical term for abusing a substance out of impulsivity?

(A) Negative reinforcement.

(B) Stimulus-response learning.

(C) Incentive salience.

(D) Inhibitory control dysfunction.

(164) When working in the field, a situation arises in which decisions need to be made, but the social worker feels that there is a conflict between their core beliefs and the decisions that need to be made for the client. Such a quandary is known as what?

(A) Ethical dilemma.

(B) Emotional dilemma.

(C) Ethical practice dilemma.

(D) Environmental dilemma.

(165) Annabelle arrived at work with a black eye. She tried to hide it with make-up, but when her coworker and friend Julie demanded to know what happened, Annabelle revealed that her husband hit her. Julie is appalled and insists that Annabelle call the police and have him arrested. Annabelle shut the idea down immediately, saying that the entire incident was her fault because she accidently broke his favorite beer mug. This scenario is an example of what psychological defense mechanism?

(A) Rationalization.

(B) Denial.

(C) Sublimination.

(D) Repression.

(166) Respect, collaboration, consultation, and referral toward your professional peers is a part of which of the following?

(A) Moral responsibility.

(B) Legal responsibility.

(C) Ethical responsibility.

(D) Spiritual responsibility.

(167) Travis has a high-stress job in personal security. To manage the various stressors of his job, he runs 6 miles each morning. This form of stress management is referred to as which type of psychological defense mechanism?

(A) Regression.

(B) Sublimation.

(C) Denial.

(D) Repression.

(168) What is the technical term for abusing a substance as a habit?

(A) Negative reinforcement.

(B) Stimulus-response learning.

(C) Positive reinforcement.

(D) Inhibitory control dysfunction.

(169) At what stage of Freud's psychosexual development theory do children grow and develop through sucking, such as breastfeeding?

(A) Oral stage.

(B) Phallic stage.

(C) Latency stage.

(D) Genital stage.

(170) What form of health care refers to properly coping with life stressors, finding a healthy way to express and expel anger and other feelings, and having the confidence to talk to others about emotions and stressors?

(A) Physical health.

(B) Mental health.

(C) Cognitive health.

(D) Spiritual health.

Test 4: Answers and Explanations

(1) (C) Networking.

Networking is a great way for social workers to get to know people and organizations within a community, develop professional relationships, access additional resources, and make other connections important to their field.

(2) (B) Intimacy vs. Isolation.

Because David experienced many relationships with misconnections, he now has trouble determining the legitimacy of his feelings and making a romantic commitment. According to Erikson's psychosocial development theory, David most likely experienced difficulties during the Intimacy vs. Isolation stage. Since he did not make strong connections or build healthy relationships, he is unsure of his abilities to continue to nurture his present relationship and is therefore uncertain about making a lifelong commitment.

(3) (A) Conflict management among professional peers.

Listening to coworkers, providing problem-solving solutions, being open to other ideas, showing empathy toward one another, and contributing to the collective are all ways to build professional peer relationships and resolve conflicts within the workplace.

(4) (D) 6.

There are 6 core values in the social work profession: service, social justice, dignity and worth of the person, importance of human relationships, integrity, and competence. These core values are key in social work morals, ethics, rules, laws, and job performance.

(5) (A) Phallic stage.

The phallic stage of Freud's psychosocial theory occurs when children are between the ages of 3 and 6. According to Freud's theory, this is when boys and girls develop stronger attachments to the parent of the opposite sex.

(6) (C) Phallic stage

The phallic stage is the third stage in Sigmund Freud's psychosexual development theory and occurs when children are 3 to 6 years old. During this stage, children often develop close attachments to the parent of the opposite sex and have pleasure centers that are focused on their genitals.

(7) (B) Recertification.

Social workers are required to keep a current social work license to continue their practice in the field. Social workers must complete additional education and training hours each year in order to recertify and keep their license current.

(8) (A) Community involvement.

Community involvement addresses common issues in socioeconomic environments, finds or develops resources, and becomes familiar with a community through professional socializing.

(9) (C) Psychological.

Psychological abuse is defined as the intentional use of words and nonphysical actions with the purpose of manipulating, hurting, or scaring a person through mental or emotional means. Psychological neglect may involve depriving a child of affection.

(10) (A) Latency stage.

The latency stage of Freud's psychosexual development theory occurs between the age of 6 and the time the child enters puberty. This stage is defined as a period when children repress their sexual interests to develop relationships with peers and friends and build their intellectual skills.

(11) (C) Integrity.

Integrity is the core value that indicates strong moral principles and honesty as an individual. Integrity is one of the 6 core values of social work.

(12) (D) Job coaching.

Job coaching is a service that helps individuals get technical training or job-specific education, creates possibilities for potential employment connections, and facilitates internships in various companies and organizations.

(13) (B) Evidence-based practice.

Evidence-based practice refers to the use of empirical evidence to frame intervention and treatment methods that help ensure effectiveness.

(14) (D) Latency stage.

According to Sigmund Freud's psychosexual development theory, children between the ages of 6 and the time they enter puberty commonly repress their sexual interests in lieu of developing their social relationships and expanding their intellectual skills and abilities.

(15) (D) Service.

In the field of social work, service is the action of helping, providing assistance to, and working for the benefit, improvement, and gain of others.

(16) (B) Advocacy.

Advocacy is defined as helping or acting in the best interest of other individuals or clients to assist with their needs.

(17) (C) Create a functional behavioral assessment.

The fourth step in intervention planning is to create a functional behavioral assessment to find reasons for the behavior and why it occurs.

(18) (A) Enabler.

Tyler would be considered the enabler among the 6 roles family members can play in cases of addiction and substance abuse. Tyler has taken responsibility to care for his younger siblings, makes sure things are done around the house, and even learned how to pay household bills as his mother feeds her addiction.

(19) (D) Dignity and worth of the person.

In the 6 core values of social work, dignity and worth of the person deems that each individual deserves to have a sense of pride and self-respect. Social workers must respect the intrinsic dignity and worth of the individual.

(20) (C) Classes.

In addition to counseling and therapy services, social workers also provide or coordinate resources for classes in healthy relationships, parenting, decision-making, and independent living. These classes generally facilitate and teach healthy relationship strategies, nurturing and healthy parenting techniques, strong decision-making skills, and techniques that assist in successful independent living.

(21) (A) Medication.

The most common action a doctor will take when treating a patient with a serious case of anxiety, depression, bipolar disorder, or sleep disorder that cannot be managed alone is to recommend a medication to assist the individual in coping with the issue.

(22) (B) Infant stage – birth to 2 years.

Infancy, or the infant stage, is defined as the first 2 years of life. Adelaide's bond with her son is an incredibly important part of this life stage.

(23) (C) Right to obtain medical records.

The right to obtain medical records is a client and patient right that is inherently theirs and protected under the Health Insurance Portability and Accountability Act (HIPAA). This right allows them to get copies of their medical records and view medical information at their provider's office.

(24) (A) Treatment and services.

Twelve-step programs, addiction recovery programs, sobriety support groups, and sober living are all covered under treatment and services. Social workers can connect clients to these resources. Such programs help those with substance abuse issues get clean, stay clean, and move forward with the support needed to live a healthy life of sobriety.

(25) (D) Dialectical behavior therapy.

This therapy is a form of cognitive behavioral therapy. It helps build skills and change behavior patterns to help the individual handle their emotional health, cope with stress in a healthy way, improve their relationships with others, and live a life of healthy mindfulness.

(26) (A) Anal stage.

According to Sigmund Freud's psychosexual development theory, children between the ages of 1 and 3 have pleasure centers that focus on the anus and derive pleasure from their ability to eliminate waste. They gain control of their body's ability to do so through potty training.

(27) (B) "Parker, you seem more upset than usual today. Can you tell me what you're feeling or what has upset you?"

Phrasing the question in this way allows Henry to acknowledge that his client, Parker, is feeling upset. Then, Henry proceeds to give his client an opening to talk about those feelings by asking him what he is feeling or what has caused his reaction. By doing this, Henry is opening the floor for a conversation.

(28) (C) Behaviors the individual would like to improve and the time frame needed.

Behaviors to improve and the time frame in which to do it are a part of intervention planning. They are not a part of a discharge plan as those goals have already been met and those behaviors addressed to reach the point of being discharged from the treatment or service.

(29) (D) Fields of practice.

Gena, Edna, and Patrick are all social workers who operate in different settings known as fields of practice. Fields of practice indicate areas in which social workers are needed and employed. Such settings include but are not limited to professional, mental health, health care, school social work, gerontology, global social work, child and family service social work, and criminal justice social work.

(30) (C) Elder stage.

Maybell is over 80 years old. She stays as active as she can but has help from a home health aide when she needs it. She does some things for herself, but they are becoming harder to do as the days go by and it takes more out of her to do them. This steady decline is indicative of elder stage.

(31) (A) To confront clients who are being inconsistent or uncooperative and call them out on their behaviors.

As a social worker, you will encounter a wide variety of personalities, behaviors, and issues in the clients you work with. At times, there will be clients who either directly or indirectly cause conflict in their treatment or progress. When this occurs, social workers need to be comfortable and assertive enough to draw attention to the inconsistencies that their clients are generating and call them out when they make choices or take actions that are not in the best interests of achieving their goals.

(32) (D) Follow-up care.

Follow-up care is when a social worker occasionally checks in on discharged clients for a set amount of time to assess their situation, physical and mental well-being, and ensure that they are not experiencing any relapses. The social worker also assesses any needs to be readdressed or new issues that have arisen.

(33) (B) Holistic therapy.

This therapy differs from behavioral therapies as it highlights nature and not behavior. The key point of this form of therapy is to focus on the person as a whole. This form of therapy can be a good choice for those with anxiety, depression, and low self-esteem, among other things.

(34) (A) Sensorimotor stage.

The sensorimotor stage of Jean Piaget's cognitive development theory is focused on infants and toddlers from birth through to 2 years of age when they use their senses and actions to experience the world. During this stage of development, infants and toddlers develop the concept of object permanence.

(35) (D) Functional assessments.

Functional assessments measure an individual's ability to take care of themself. Such assessments are conducted to determine whether a person is capable of living independently, whether they need in-home assistance, or whether they require placement in a facility to ensure their care needs are met.

(36) (C) The individual's ability to live independently.

An individual's ability to live independently does not factor into their placement in a facility because they will not be living in their own home. The reason for being sent to the facility, how long they will be staying in the facility, and their ability to care for themself will all factor into the placement, type of facility, and required assistance to meet their needs while there.

(37) (B) Counseling intervention.

Counseling intervention is the fourth step in the 5 key stages of the practice of therapy. It focuses on addressing serious issues in an individual.

(38) (D) 13 to 17 years old.

Between the ages of 13 and 17 is the adolescent development stage. During this stage, individuals develop a personal identity, go through puberty, have growth spurts, develop their mind, and become abstract thinkers.

(39) (B) Take frequent breaks and ensure healthy emotional and mental health respites.

Taking frequent breaks and ensuring respites are solutions to burnout and promote longevity in the social work profession. These tasks do nothing for time management, though they are beneficial to the overall health and wellness of a social worker.

(40) (A) Active listening and feedback.

Active listening is the process in which a social worker sits down with a client and allows them to disclose their thoughts and feelings in a way that is supported, expresses understanding, and allows the client to feel heard. Once the client has expressed themself and feels validated, the social worker can offer feedback regarding the things that the client has said.

(41) (C) Generalist practice.

Generalist practice refers to the use of the assessment and intervention practice of the problem-solving approach to engage, assess, plan, implement, evaluate, and terminate treatment and services.

(42) (A) Concrete operational stage.

According to Jean Piaget's cognitive development theory, the concrete operational stage occurs between the ages of 7 and 11. During this time, children learn to think in a logical way in terms of concrete events.

(43) (C) Posting security guards at major entrances.

While such an action can cause a false sense of security, or even be helpful in an actual safety crisis, studies have shown that posting security guards causes clients and staff to feel as though their environment is not safe, increases anxiety, and exacerbates stressful situations.

(44) (B) Creating a sense of accomplishment and encouragement.

When a social worker and client set goals that the client can easily reach, this creates a sense of accomplishment when the client reaches that goal. This not only encourages them to set the next goal but also reinforces the fact that it is just as attainable as the first.

(45) (A) Global assessment of functioning.

The global assessment of functioning is a scale used to assess an individual's likeliness to cause self-harm, harm others, be able to care for themselves, and be able to function while coping with their individual issues. This scale rates individuals from 0 to a 100 to determine their likeliness or unlikeliness for each question involved.

(46) (B) Middle-aged adult.

During middle age, an individual's problem-solving skills have become fine-tuned. With that achievement, they also begin to notice changes in their bodies that are related to getting older.

(47) (D) Direct supervisor.

Typically in an organization, a social worker is the entry-level position. Their direct supervisor is the first person they will report to. Direct supervisors, in turn, generally report to department managers or facility supervisors depending on the size of their facility and the structure of their hierarchy. Finally, the person who oversees the operations of the facility itself will report to the highest levels of management.

(48) (C) Motivate.

Setting a timer can be an incredible motivator for children. It can determine the time frames in which something occurs, indicate the end of an activity, indicate the beginning of something else, or indicate to a child that they have reached their goal. Children often respond well to motivators such as this.

(49) (B) In-depth exploration.

In-depth exploration is the second stage of the 5 stages of practicing therapy. In-depth exploration refers to a detailed and thorough examination or study.

(50) (A) Preoperational stage.

During the preoperational stage of Jean Piaget's cognitive development theory, children between the ages of 2 and 6 learn about the world through playing pretend, developing their language and communication skills, and developing a sense of self through egocentrism. This is all achieved through the development and association of words and images that represent things within their world.

(51) (D) Advocate.

Social workers are responsible to advocate for clients when they are unable to speak for themselves, need support in order to do so, or are too young to self-advocate.

(52) (A) Advocacy group.

Nina could most likely benefit by joining an advocacy group composed of other individuals who have spouses or family members who are alcoholics or suffer from substance abuse.

(53) (B) Indirect practice.

Erin engages in indirect practice. These social work practices are not face-to-face. Such practices include but are not limited to administrative, supervisory, research, policy development, community development, and consultation roles.

(54) (C) Anal stage.

The anal stage of Freud's psychosexual theory of development occurs when children are between 1 and 3 years of age. This stage of his theory states that children derive pleasure by having a desire to control their bodily elimination through potty training.

(55) (C) Take unfinished work home with you at the end of your shift in order to work in a comfortable setting and not be in your office after hours.

This is not a healthy approach to reducing burnout. In fact, taking work home with you at the end of the day increases the likelihood of burnout because that does not give you time to decompress.

(56) (B) Crisis intervention therapy.

In this moment Peter will experience the best results and the quickest help through crisis intervention therapy. Considering his state, a therapist may even recommend a temporary stay at an inpatient facility while Peter balances his system and resolves his depressive state enough to ensure that he is no longer a danger to himself.

(57) (C) Teach the new alternative behavior.

The sixth and final step of intervention planning is to teach a new way to cope with the root cause, replacing the old behavior with a new one.

(58) (A) Young children.

Young children between the ages of 4 and 6 gain independence through potty training and achieving self-help skills, improve their gross motor skills, use their imaginations to grow and learn through play, explore the world around them, and develop peer group relationships.

(59) (B) Keep social workers on call 24 hours a day, 7 days a week. This includes not rotating the schedule on a regular basis or having specific social workers who handle on-call cases only.

By insisting that social workers are on call 24/7, not ensuring that the social workers who manage on-call cases are rotated on a regular basis, and not having designated social workers who manage on-call cases only, organizations can cause burnout and high turnover rates within their systems. However, when the company uses specific social workers to manage only on-call cases or regularly rotates social workers who handle on-call cases, burnout rates can be reduced.

(60) (B) Trauma-informed care.

Trauma-informed care is designed to put the power back into the victim's hands. The idea is for Quinn to feel safe in the hospital and in control of the choices that are being made, as well as to collaborate with care staff as to what is happening and how it will happen. This builds trust between Quinn and those involved in her care and empowers Quinn by putting the choices and control back in her hands.

(61) (C) Organizational support.

Organizational support are the policies, practices, and systems associated with adequately meeting individual needs within the cultural consideration of intervention planning.

(62) (D) Formal operational stage.

The formal operational stage of Jean Piaget's cognitive development theory is described as the stage in which thinking can be done in a hypothetical way and abstract thought is used to interpret and process information to determine a hypothesis. This stage starts at age 12 and continues through adulthood. During this time, individuals develop abstract logic and develop mature moral reasoning if they have successfully completed the other 3 stages and work through the fourth stage in the same healthy manner.

(63) (A) Mission statement.

A mission statement is typically a written formal presentation of the values that are important to an organization and the goals it aims to achieve. Mission statements are often placed in locations where patrons can see and review them, copies are given to new employees and clients, and the public can access them freely through a forum such as a website or social media page.

(64) (C) The family life cycle.

The family life cycle theory explains how family development revolves around the patterns of change that occur in a family over time.

(65) (B) Implied consent.

While Eva did not say yes or otherwise give her doctor verbal permission to insert a feeding tube and start the high calorie nutrition, she did use nonverbal communication by nodding her head when the doctor requested to start the procedure. Consent given in this manner is nonverbal, but it is still considered consent because it is implied by Eva's body language.

(66) (A) 7 to 12 years.

Between the ages of 7 and 12, children typically slow their growth rate. This will resume when the child starts puberty. Children developmentally begin to better correlate cause and effect, improve reading and math skills, and are often very eager to learn. This is also the time in a child's life when they generally seek to be engaged, feel like they are useful, and want to contribute. They are at an age where safety, awareness of their surroundings, and conflict resolution are all important points.

(67) (A) System relationships.

System relationships are defined as those relationships that are developed between a professional, such as a social worker, and their clients or patients. The "system" refers to the social work system in which social work professionals and clients interact.

(68) (D) Negative reinforcement.

Negative reinforcement is the technical term for using a substance to avoid pain. Pain can be physical, mental, or emotional.

(69) (C) Awareness and knowledge.

Awareness and knowledge in reference to cultural consideration and its place in intervention planning involve being aware of yourself, the limits of your knowledge, and any biases you may have.

(70) (B) Stage 2: The abusive act.

It is during stage 2 of abusive relationship development that actual abuse takes place.

(71) (B) Knowing professional competency levels and limitations.

Knowing professional competency levels and limitations is not a part of professional development. It is simply an awareness of a professional's level of understanding within their field of practice, acknowledgement of the limits to that knowledge base, and knowing when to ask for help from individuals with more extensive knowledge outside that individual's professional competency level.

(72) (A) Positive reinforcement.

Positive reinforcement is the abuse of a substance as a means of finding pleasure or enjoyment.

(73) (B) Informed consent.

Cortney informing Tessa up front about all of the criteria to enter the treatment program, and Tessa understanding all the information being given to her then choosing to enter the program with consent, represents informed consent. Informed consent is defined as informing an individual or client of any and all information they need in order to make a decision based on the complete knowledge available to them.

(74) (A) Development.

Cognitive, emotional, physical, and sexual development play key roles in interacting throughout the lifespan.

(75) (C) Record-keeping.

Accountability, transparency, accessibility, protection, compliance, and information retention are all key principles of social work record-keeping.

(76) (D) Incentive salience.

Incentive salience is the abuse of a substance to satisfy a craving.

(77) (A) Collect data to measure the behavior.

The second step in intervention planning is to measure behavior based on collected data.

(78) (C) Rational choice.

Rational choice is the theory that an individual will use rational thought to make decisions that allow them to line up their personal objectives with the outcomes that their decisions will impact. They ultimately make choices that serve their own best interests.

(79) (D) 6 years.

Typically, social workers are required to maintain and retain records for adult clients for 6 years. When a client exits services, their records should be kept by the organization until 6 years after their discharge. If a client has been in care for more than 6 years but is still in care, records should be maintained and retained until 6 years after the client is finally discharged from services.

(80) (C) Trauma.

The first and most important step in helping a trauma victim is to give them back control of the situation.

(81) (B) Just cause.

Yolanda has just cause or a fair reason for imposing disciplinary actions on the employee due to multiple warnings and repeated negative workplace behaviors. Just cause is defined as an action or decision regarding an individual made on the behalf of another individual when there is legal justification for such grounds based on poor decision-making, rule-breaking, or poor behaviors.

(82) (A) Person-in-environment theory.

The person-in-environment theory concludes that individuals are influenced heavily by the environments in which they are raised. These environments include their homes, communities, economic environment, and the cultural environment that influences them.

(83) (D) Six years from the time they reach the age of majority in their state or province.

Most states and provinces require that records regarding a minor child be kept for a minimum of 6 years after the child has reached the age of majority in their given location.

(84) (A) Sublimation.

Sublimation is a psychological defense mechanism in which individuals develop healthy outlets for emotional and mental stressors. Tonya's use of kickboxing and running to expel negative emotions and thoughts related to her job and her use of yoga to decompress and reset before returning to work are healthy coping mechanisms for dealing with regular stressors in her life.

(85) (B) A healthy parent-and-child relationship.

The social worker would most likely take into consideration the affectionate and loving relationship between mother and child, the nurturing way that the mother corrects her child in an encouraging and helpful manner, and the overall homey feel of their house, and find that there is a healthy parent-and-child relationship between the pair.

(86) (D) Birth to 3 years.

Birth to 3 years of age is considered a critical time in a child's development. Science shows that children of this age group have a higher brain development than any other time in their lives, as the child's brain is like a sponge and absorbs everything that they are exposed to. During this time, ensuring that a child properly bonds with their mother or primary caregiver is a vital part of this growth and development. It sets the foundation for all future growth and development. Ensuring that children in this age group regularly see their pediatricians for well-child visits, eat a balanced diet, have good skin and scalp care routines, and sleep in a healthy manner is also important for their health and development.

(87) (C) Sharing information within your own organization.

Sharing information within your own organization is not a principle in breaching confidentiality. Not everyone who is employed by an organization has the privilege of accessing clients' personal and private information. Only specifically authorized personnel who are related to your client's case have the right to that information without just cause.

(88) (B) Rationalization.

Rationalization is the psychological defense mechanism in which an individual attempts to use rational thinking to explain away or excuse negative or unacceptable behavior rather than cope with what has occurred and face the fallout from those actions.

(89) (C) Malfeasance

The illegal activities that Mayor Rothburn is conducting are known as malfeasance. Malfeasance are behaviors committed by a professional or a publicly appointed person that are ethically and morally wrong as well as illegal.

(90) (A) 4 to 6 years.

From 4 to 6 years of age, children's growth spurts slow down and they grow at a slower rate overall. During this stage, children develop better gross motor skills, some fine motor skills, self-help skills like getting themselves dressed, and begin or finish potty training. Much of their learning is through friends and peers in play groups, at school, or in daycare. During this time, praise, reward systems, and clear boundaries are important to a child's development and independence. It is also key that children are encouraged to develop healthy hygiene habits, like washing properly and brushing their teeth, along with good sleeping and eating habits.

(91) (B) Norepinephrine-dopamine reuptake inhibitor.

Norepinephrine-dopamine reuptake inhibitors are a newer prescription medications. They are antidepressants that work differently than more commonly prescribed medications of this type. They typically do not have side effects associated with antidepressant use.

(92) (C) Governance.

Governance is the framework that manages a system or organization and may also issue rules, procedures, and guidelines.

(93) (A) Clinical summary.

A clinical summary comes at the end of a social work intervention assessment. The summary covers the final findings of the assessment and any recommendations that are being made for the client.

(94) (B) Generativity vs. Stagnation.

Generativity vs. Stagnation is the 7th step in Erikson's psychosocial development theory. During this time, maintaining a healthy balance of caring for others and self-care is a priority. Such growth is typically achieved in later adulthood when an individual has learned to sustain personal relationships and raised their children. At this point, individuals have learned to care for themselves and others and have also learned to balance the related challenges. Lilith works, takes care of her mother, and takes care of herself. She ensures that she sets aside time for herself and commits to caring for her mother.

(95) (A) Time management.

Time management is defined as being able to use your time in a productive and efficient manner. This especially applies to time management related to an individual's work responsibilities.

(96) (D) Case managers.

Case managers are typically responsible for securing and ensuring resources and managing available financial support.

(97) (C) Malpractice.

The underhanded behavior that Bert conducted regarding his clients is known as malpractice. Malpractice is any action that is wrong, negligent, or harmful and violates the professional standard of care or professional ethics.

(98) (A) Semimonthly assessments.

Semimonthly assessments mean that the social worker conducts their assessments twice a month.

(99) (A) Organized.

Social workers need to stay organized to stay on top of their caseload. As such, making daily and weekly to-do lists, setting and sticking to a schedule, addressing referrals and important requests as soon as they are received, setting and meeting daily goals, and having a set day for paperwork are a few key ways to ensure you are organized and have a sense of self-accomplishment from completing manageable daily goals.

(100) (C) Social work group.

Social work group is the setting in which the functioning of the entire group is improved through coping with group or community issues.

(101) (D) Background and current functioning.

The background and current functioning part of a social work assessment includes family composition, education, employment, vocational skills, religious and spiritual involvement, military service involvement, physical abilities, physical and mental health issues, social and recreational activities, basic necessities, and environmental factors.

(102) (C) 13 to 17 years.

Between 13 and 17 years of age, adolescents experience significant growth spurts and puberty-based changes. Their reproductive systems become fully developed as well. Teens develop their sense of self, personalities, value systems, and personal identities. Personal relationships with peers and romantic relationships are influential during this time. Teenagers become abstract thinkers, begin testing and challenging authority, and seek certain levels of privacy and respect.

(103) (B) Develop self-care and coping mechanisms.

Social workers should ensure that they are practicing self-care and have healthy coping mechanisms to deal with the daily stress, caseloads, emotional and psychological strains, and professional boundaries related to their job.

(104) (B) Transgenerational family therapy.

Transgenerational therapy uses past issues or difficulties as a means of foreshadowing future conflicts. This approach proves valuable because solutions to past problems may be utilized to solve problems in the future. Using past problems can also assist in dismissing solutions that have been proven to be ineffective in the family dynamic.

(105) (D) Mentor.

Zoe will be a mentor to the new hire. A mentorship is the relationship in which a more experienced or knowledgeable individual guides a new or less experienced individual through their professional position by sharing knowledge and experience that they have gained.

(106) (A) Atypical development.

Atypical development in reference to a child means that they are not developing in the expected way compared to the majority of children their age.

(107) (C) For-profit.

A for-profit organization is any organization that earns a profit through the products or services it offers.

(108) (A) Narrative family therapy.

Narrative family therapy refers to the idea that each person has their own individual story to tell throughout their life. These stories help identify and shape that person. Narrative family therapy helps separate the person or people from the problem they are encountering and allows them to rely on their own skills and abilities to objectively see the problem rather than feeling like their story shapes how they should be dealing with that problem or finding its solution.

(109) (B) Sources of data.

Sources of data are described as conducted interviews, observations, consults, records from the agency the social worker belongs to or other involved agencies, client involvement, who was present during interviews (such as colleagues, supervisors, outside consultants), and the length of time to gather information.

(110) (D) Infant reactive attachment disorder.

Infant reactive attachment disorder is an infant or early childhood disorder that occurs when infants fail to seek comfort from their mother or primary caregiver or when care and comfort is withheld. Such occurrences result in infants and young children who do not like or want physical contact, do not cry or otherwise seek out comfort, avoid making eye contact, and are hypervigilant.

(111) (D) Board of directors.

A board of directors is an organized group that has legally defined responsibilities to a corporation, organization, or system to run that organization according to bylaws.

(112) (B) Systemic family therapy.

Systemic family therapy uses a belief system as the focus of the therapy process. Utilizing a family's sociocultural beliefs and perceptions to see the roles within the family dynamic is key to this form of therapy. It is important to take things in cultural context in order to change behavioral patterns and promote solutions that are sustainable and helpful to the whole family. This form of therapy is broken down into 5 key parts, which include deconstruction of the problem, identification of patterns within the family, exploration of beliefs and understanding the explanations of those beliefs, dissection of emotions and attachments within the family construct, and contextual factors. This form of therapy is based on the notion that the characteristics of a family and the relationships between those elements play key roles in how the family construct behaves and operates.

(113) (A) Referral.

Andre's primary care doctor arranged a referral for Andre to see the psychologist. A referral is defined as a request that is made on the behalf of an individual regarding a service, treatment, or consultation that the professional feels should be provided by another professional or service.

(114) (A) Basic human needs.

Anton first ensures that his clients have access to and utilize their basic human needs. Ensuring this helps eliminate imminent risks.

(115) (D) Advisory board.

An advisory board is an informal group that gathers and reviews information to advise on a given topic or multiple topics.

(116) (C) Psychoeducational.

A psychoeducational group is a group that is led by a professional. The professional will use education and psychosocial aspects to address issues and provide support.

(117) (D) Needs assessment.

A needs assessments is the process of pinpointing the needs of an individual, couple, family, group, or community by assessing the available resources and systemic faults or failures. This finds the needs that are not being met, challenges being faced, and required resources. A plan to help is then built around those findings.

(118) (B) Genital stage.

The genital stage of Freud's psychosexual theory of development occurs at puberty and continues throughout the lifespan. This stage is the point at which an individual develops sexual attraction.

(119) (C) Professional development.

Professional development is the improvement and expansion of professional competencies, knowledge, skills, and effective techniques as they pertain to the career field.

(120) (D) Educational groups.

An educational group is taught by a professional who has been educated and certified to teach and use a proven set of techniques or methods.

(121) (B) Strength perspective.

Strength perspective is a social work approach that focuses on the helpful resources a client already has, such as environment, community, social circles, and family, as the core of the recovery process rather than focusing on the individual's problems. The idea here is to lift the individual up by the strengths in their life as a means of coping with their issues.

(122) (A) Human development.

Bandura's, Bowlby's, Erikson's, Freud's, and Piaget's theories all connect to human development, healthy contributing factors, and the consequences of not having basic needs met during critical points in development.

(123) (B) Confidentiality.

Client confidentiality is a legal and ethical binding that social workers have to their clients with a few exceptions, such as the client being an imminent danger to themself or others.

(124) (C) Psychoeducational.

A psychoeducational approach uses a balance of education and clinical influences to deal with an underlying emotional trauma. This approach is most often used with children. It can lower the chances of an individual experiencing an emotional relapse associated with the trauma. Also, it is more likely that the individual will stick to their treatment plan. This approach improves quality of life, assists with improving social understanding, and engages the individual in their rehabilitation and treatment in an active and positive way.

(125) (D) Generalist perspective.

The generalist perspective is defined as an understanding of human functions and how they work together in individual system networks. This perspective is a popular social work tool used to better understand the innerworkings of an individual and what influences they are affected by.

(126) (C) Between the ages of 18 and 35.

Between the ages of 18 and 35, individuals officially become adults and reach their physical and sexual maturity levels. Individuals also develop finely tuned problem-solving skills, seek interpersonal and intimate relationships, achieve and build career pathways, and make decisions regarding reproduction and starting a family. During this time, learning effective communication, being honest, and respecting the values of others are all key. Maintaining a healthy lifestyle, having regular checkups, and remembering self-care are all important parts of staying healthy at this stage in the young adult life.

(127) (A) Stress management.

There are multiple ways of coping with stress. Stress management tools can be utilized daily in order to cope with stress and maintain well-being over time.

(128) (B) Partializing technique.

Partializing technique refers to creating goals and taking a planned approach using small steps or actions in order to ultimately achieve the desired outcome. Social workers and clients work together to assess the client's ability to make these decisions, evaluate their capabilities in reaching these achievements, and set attainable goals.

(129) (D) Networking.

Penny is networking with the organizations in her community. Networking is defined as the process of making contacts and establishing relationships with those contacts within a community to foster and grow a network of resources.

(130) (A) Patrick's entire family will face challenges as they grow and adjust in order to accommodate the effects of such a disability or face fracturing the family unit.

When an individual experiences a life-changing injury, it affects that person's entire network, including family, friends, work peers, and the community of people around them.

(131) (C) Professional standards.

Professional standards are the combined practices, ethics, and behaviors that a social worker meets through accountability, confidentiality, fiduciary duties, objectivity, and transparency.

(132) (C) Have one or more social workers take over the individual's caseload in order to ensure that the clients are being taken care of adequately.

The first responsibility of the social work supervisor is to ensure that the clients are properly taken care of. Shifting the caseload ensures that someone is taking care of the clients' needs while the rest of the situation is addressed with the social worker who appears to be impaired. Once the clients' needs have been met, the supervisor can bring the concerns that have been raised to the attention of the impaired social worker and begin following the procedures that the organization has in place regarding such behaviors and how to properly handle them based on that company's rules and bylaws.

(133) (A) Generativity vs. Stagnation.

The 7th stage of Erikson's psychosocial development theory is the Generativity vs. Stagnation stage. During this stage, individuals develop a sense of care, including self-care and care for others. They have also reached milestones of sustaining interpersonal relationships and contributing to their communities.

(134) (C) Commitment to action.

Commitment to action is the third stage of the 5 key practices of therapy and is defined as an outlined plan with clear and measurable objectives, a set time frame, and goals to be met along the way.

(135) (C) Repression.

Repression is the psychological defense mechanism in which an individual essentially removes the memories of a traumatic event or situation as if it had never occurred in the first place. Repression usually occurs because the individual is not ready or is unwilling to deal with the emotional, psychological, and sometimes physical implications of such an incident.

(136) (A) Ensure an open and inviting atmosphere with no boundaries or limitations.

While you want to set clients at ease, make them feel welcome, and create an environment in which they feel comfortable when meeting, assessing, and providing services, it is also particularly important to set boundaries, enforce rules, and have protocols in place to handle a situation in the event that it escalates. This will help prevent harm to those working with the client and those working in the same building or facility.

(137) (C) Denial.

Denial is characterized by an individual's desire to avoid dealing with the emotional impact that an event, circumstance, or stressor is causing them. Rather than coping with the emotions in a healthy way, the individual pushes them aside to avoid the emotional toll that may occur if they allow themself to experience those emotions at that time. Denial should be addressed or it can spiral out of control and affect a person's overall mental health.

(138) (B) Evaluation, termination, or referral.

Evaluation, termination, or referral are the fifth and final stage of the 5 key practices of therapy. This is when the therapist does a concluding assessment, finds that the client has met their treatment goals, and discharges them from treatment or refers them to another professional or program for further or more extensive care, services, or treatment.

(139) (D) Needs assessment.

Once Marcus and the social worker have met, the social worker will most likely assess Marcus's needs and then determine what he is capable of doing on his own for comparison and to figure out the gaps. They can then provide the best options for services to fit his needs.

(140) (C) Mentoring.

Hannah and Debbie will mentor the new employee by using the information they have gained from their 5 years of experience. They will help him learn the ropes of the job and help him get to know other employees.

(141) (A) Repression

Repression is defined as the body's way of dealing with extremely emotional traumas or memories by expelling those memories from the mind entirely. This is done as a means of protecting the body and the mind from the damage that feeling those emotions will cause.

(142) (A) Cognitive behavioral therapy.

This form of therapy is generally designed to take place for a short period of time. It is a goal-oriented therapy that focuses on cognitive and behavioral links.

(143) (C) Regression.

Regression is defined as the psychological defense mechanism in which an individual escapes the trauma of an experience by mentally going back in time to when they felt safe. In this scenario, David's daughter Alicia regressed to her 4-year-old self to avoid dealing with the trauma of a sexual assault.

(144) (B) De-escalation techniques.

De-escalation techniques are specifically designed and taught to address a hostile or explosive situation and help the individual reach a more reasonable and safer state. De-escalation techniques often include acknowledging the individual's feelings, expressing concern for their best interests and how such behaviors are unhealthy for them, and working to get them to reciprocate and resolve the situation.

(145) (D) Projection.

Projection is defined as a psychological defense mechanism when an individual may take their frustrations out on a person or thing. Olivia's scenario is an example of projection. By taking out her anger on her husband, Olivia understands that he will most likely forgive her and they will be able to make up. Olivia perceives that expressing her feelings to her new manager would most likely result in negative outcomes and is therefore a far greater risk than taking those frustrations out on her husband.

(146) (A) Eligibility criteria.

Eligibility criteria is a set of qualifications that need to be met for an individual, couple, family, group, or community to receive or use services or benefits that may be available to them.

(147) (A) Denial.

Amelia is utilizing the psychological defense mechanism of denial to avoid dealing with the incredibly emotional and upsetting circumstances of her home's foreclosure.

(148) (C) To track a client's progress.

Tracking a current client's progress in their intervention plan is not usually a benefit of conducting research in social work, especially since all clients' progress is documented throughout their treatment and services. Documenting a client's progress for research purposes would be specifically beneficial to social work only if clients receiving a specific treatment type or using a specific method to reach goals are being studied to determine the effectiveness of that particular program.

(149) (A) Displacement.

Displacement is the psychological defense mechanism that is characterized by an individual taking out their emotions, such as frustration or anger, on a person or thing that is nonthreatening as a means of getting those feelings out. Carmen's use of a punching bag as an outlet is considered a healthy coping mechanism.

(150) (B) Psychodynamic therapy.

This form of therapy puts a focus on specific life events that have occurred in addition to past or present relationships. It explores how those things affect our feelings, thoughts, actions, and relationships in the present. This form of therapy takes upward of a year or more to complete.

(151) (C) Remodeling a home.

While remodeling a home can be a stressful situation for a family, it does not have significant long-term detriments to the healthy growth and development of family members. Stress related to remodeling is short-lived and usually resolves with no residual effects.

(152) (D) Death and dying.

When an individual has reached the end of their life, regardless of length, it is especially important that they feel in control of their end-of-life care. Such decisions include being able to refuse treatments, have treatments withheld, and withdraw life-sustaining support. These are all important aspects of allowing their body to succumb to death naturally rather than synthetically extending their life in ways that could cause more harm, pain, and suffering.

(153) (B) Lithium.

Lithium is a mood stabilizer. It works by strengthening and reinforcing nerve connections in the brain to better regulate mood, cognition, and behavior.

(154) (C) Haldol.

Haldol is an antipsychotic drug that decreases activity and excitement in the brain. It controls movement and verbal tics, and is used to treat severe behavioral issues, especially in children.

(155) (D) Out-of-home placement.

Out-of-home placement is when a child is removed from their home for a variety of reasons and placed in the care of others either for a short period of time or indefinitely, depending on the situation. For example, out-of-home placement may occur if a single mother is severely injured in a car accident and there is no one to take care of the child while she recovers in the hospital, or when there are problems in the home and the child is placed elsewhere until they are resolved.

(156) (A) Ego Identity vs. Despair.

The eighth and final stage of Erik Erikson's psychosocial development theory is the Ego Identity vs. Despair stage. In this stage, an individual reflects on the life they have lived and finds a sense of wisdom through their experiences and contributions. They should gain an overall sense of happiness when looking back at their life.

(157) (C) Identity vs. Confusion.

According to Erikson's development theory, Holly would most likely have developed her self-identity and confidence during the Identity vs. Confusion stage. This stage occurs when an individual is in their teen years. When this stage is reached successfully, the individual will typically develop a single identity by testing roles, exercising their freedoms, and receiving positive reinforcement and encouragement as they are developing.

(158) (D) Mental status exam.

Mental status exams are a component of the assessment process. These assessments gauge an individual's mental health, substance use, and disorders. This information is used to create a treatment plan.

(159) (B) Sufficient self-care and respite.

Family caregivers struggle with many things such as stress, financial difficulties, sleep deprivation, isolation, and depression. Getting sufficient self-care and respite is not something that caregivers typically prioritize. Responsibilities of caring for a family member fall on that individual, and they often lack resources, are unaware of the resources are available, or are afraid to ask for help in order to manage their self-care and respite needs. Ironically, family caregivers often experience feelings of selfishness when they feel overwhelmed or in need of a break.

(160) (C) Red flags.

Red flags are defined as actions taken by professionals that violate the ethical and legal binds within their professional field and create unhealthy bonds between professionals and clients. While they may not always be noticeable at first, red flags are typically small signs that can be noticed by professional peers, supervising or management staff, or friends and family of the professional and client involved. These may indicate the relationship no longer abides by professional boundaries and crosses professional ethics lines.

(161) (A) Regression.

Regression is a psychological defense mechanism that is characterized by an individual's mental escape from a trauma, event, or serious emotional experience by mentally going back to a time before the experience.

(162) (D) Genital stage.

According to Freud, the genital stage occurs from puberty and beyond. He surmised that if the first 4 developmental stages are all reached in a successful and healthy manner, then this is the time in an individual's life when they reach sexual maturity and develop attractions to the opposite sex.

(163) (D) Inhibitory control dysfunction.

Inhibitory control dysfunction is the abuse of a substance out of impulsive behavior.

(164) (C) Ethical practice dilemma.

An ethical practice dilemma refers to an issue or multiple issues that arise in the field of social work in which decisions must be made, but in which there is a conflict in core values as they apply to that decision.

(165) (A) Rationalization.

Rationalization is a psychological defense mechanism that is characterized by the use of rational thought to justify or explain attitudes or behaviors with logical reasoning, regardless of how appropriate or inappropriate those behaviors may be.

(166) (C) Ethical responsibility.

Ethical responsibility refers to the codes and standards that apply to social workers, their professional peers, and professional practices. Being ethically responsible to your professional peers refers to your professional competency, aversion to discrimination, and private conduct. You must ensure that you are honest, do not commit fraud, do not act in deceptive ways, do not misrepresent yourself or others, and are accountable and knowledgeable regarding your responsibilities in a professional capacity.

(167) (B) Sublimation.

Sublimation is a psychological defense mechanism that is characterized by taking all the negative feelings you are having and channeling them into safe and constructive activities.

(168) (B) Stimulus-response learning.

Stimulus-response learning is the abuse of a substance as a habit that the individual has developed.

(169) (A) Oral stage.

The oral stage of Sigmund Freud's psychosexual development theory is defined by an infant's pleasure center being focused on mouthing things and primarily characterized by an infant's drive to suck on and place things in their mouth. At birth, this response is what helps newborns root for their mother's breast in search of food—a basic human need.

(170) (B) Mental health.

Mental health refers to caring for your mental and emotional health and daily stressors.

Made in United States
North Haven, CT
10 February 2024

48597812R20222